P9-CDG-818

Lending Library
Call (713) 529-1912

SHERMAN AND THE BURNING OF COLUMBIA

Sherman and the Burning of Columbia

By
MARION BRUNSON LUCAS

Foreword by BELL I. WILEY

TEXAS A&M UNIVERSITY PRESS
College Station and London

Copyright © 1976 by Marion Brunson Lucas
All rights reserved

Library of Congress Cataloging in Publication Data

Lucas, Marion Brunson, 1935–
    Sherman and the burning of Columbia.

    Bibliography: p.
    Includes index.
    1. Columbia, S. C., Burning of, 1865. 2. Sherman,
William Tecumseh, 1820–1891. I. Title.
E477.75.L82   973.7'38   76-17979
ISBN 0-89096-018-6

Manufactured in the United States of America
FIRST EDITION

to
Italene
Amy, Susan, Scott

Contents

Foreword   11

Acknowledgments   15

Chapter   1. Prologue   19

            2. The Evacuation of Columbia   51

            3. The Capture of Columbia   72

            4. The Burning of Columbia   83

            5. The Extent of the Devastation   119

            6. Who Burned Columbia?   129

            7. Conclusions   163

Appendix A. *Inventory of Ordnance Stores Captured in
            Columbia, S.C., February 17, 1865*   169

Appendix B. *Soldiers Directory of Public Officers in Columbia*   173

Bibliography   175

Index   183

List of Illustrations

Map. Central South Carolina   32

Map. Columbia and Vicinity   48

following page 96

After the Fire: Richardson Street North from the State House

Map. Columbia: Major Features

Map. Columbia: Buildings Burned

Map. Columbia: 1860 Dwellings

After the Fire: Ursuline Convent

Foreword

THE burning of Columbia, South Carolina, in February, 1865, has been a subject of considerable controversy since the day it occurred. Confederates and their descendants blamed Sherman and his soldiers for starting the holocaust and letting it rage with little or no effort to bring it under control. Some residents of Columbia at the time of the fire asserted that they saw drunken Union soldiers roaming the streets without restraint, setting fire to house after house with torches made of cotton soaked in turpentine. Sherman vigorously denied that he and the men he commanded were responsible for burning the South Carolina capital. He placed major blame on Confederate General Wade Hampton.

There can be no doubt that many of Sherman's soldiers entered South Carolina determined to make the state suffer for initiating secession. Sherman wrote Halleck shortly before invading the state that "the whole army is crazy to be turned loose in Carolina" and "burning with an insatiable desire to wreak vengeance upon South Carolina," but there was probably more of rhetoric than of serious intent in many of the denunciations and threats hurled by the Federals at their foes.

Marion B. Lucas, professor of history at Western Kentucky University, enters this century-old controversy with scholarly calm and detachment. His major concern as he searched out and studied all known material bearing on the subject was to find out what happened and why, and to let the blame fall on those who deserved it regardless of whether they were Northerners or Southerners. The results of his efforts are eminently satisfying. He brings order out of contradiction and confusion by carefully weighing the evidence and presenting the results of his study in a simple, straightforward, and interesting manner. His account is remarkably dispassionate, and to me it is convincing.

The study, which is much more comprehensive than the title indicates, begins with a brief description of wartime Columbia. In succeeding chapters Lucas tells of the evacuation of the city, its occupation by Sherman's forces, the conflagration of February 17–18, and the extent of destruction. He closes his admirable account with an assessment of responsibility.

Professor Lucas concludes that the burning of the city resulted from a series of fires, beginning with cotton ignited by Southerners as they were leaving Columbia. The fire smoldered in the huge piles of cotton bales that had accumulated in "Cotton Town" on Richardson Street, thus converting that portion of the city into a firetrap. City firemen, with the help of the vanguard of Federal invaders, tried hard to bring the initial conflagration under control, but a brisk and persistent wind rekindled the flames, and new fires were started by resident hoodlums released from prison, by blacks celebrating their new-found freedom, and by poorly disciplined Union soldiers. Many of the incendiaries were intoxicated on liquor dispensed by well-meaning citizens of the city or seized in raids on grogshops and distilleries. Burning cotton and shingles borne through the air by the wind spread the flames rapidly until about three o'clock in the morning of February 18, when a belated roundup of drunks by the Federal provost marshal and the abatement of the wind enabled firemen, soldiers, and local civilians to get the situation under control.

By a careful analysis of a study made by William Gilmore Simms soon after the war, Professor Lucas shows that instead of nearly all of the city being devastated by fire, as some claimed then and later, only 458 buildings, or about one-third of the total, were destroyed.

The author exonerates Sherman of the charge of burning the city, and he deems it impossible to attribute sole blame for the conflagration to any individual or group. He faults Confederates for not removing the cotton that had accumulated in warehouses and streets before the arrival of the invaders or for not declaring the town an open city. He censures O. O. Howard, the general to whom Sherman entrusted control of the occupied city, for tardiness in rounding up the drunks who roamed the streets until after midnight of February 17. He concludes that the burning of Columbia was "an accident of war," resulting from a mixture of influences and circumstances, including remissness on the part of both Confederates and Federals. The principal demons in the drama were cotton, whiskey, and wind.

BELL I. WILEY

Acknowledgments

THOUGH only one author's name appears on the title page, I, like many others, have been greatly aided by interested colleagues, librarians, and friends. E. L. Inabinet, Director of the South Caroliniana Library of the University of South Carolina, and his expert staff could not have been more helpful. Mrs. Clara Mae Jacobs of the Manuscripts Division, who seemed to be aware of the contents of virtually every manuscript in the depository, was especially kind to this researcher, and to her I am deeply indebted. Since her retirement Allen H. Stokes has continued in her tradition. My thanks also go to Mrs. Preston Darby for her assistance on numerous occasions. The staffs of the Southern Historical Collection of the University of North Carolina, the Manuscript Department, William R. Perkins Library of Duke University, and the National Archives were also generous in their assistance.

Four members of the History Department at Western Kentucky University, Francis H. Thompson, Richard L. Troutman, Lowell H. Harrison, and Jack W. Thacker, read the entire manuscript and made helpful suggestions despite their busy schedules. A special thanks goes to Dr. Thacker, who, during the years this manuscript was in the making, has been a keen critic and a constant encouragement. He read the manuscript at every stage of its development, and his suggestions were always perceptive. Two colleagues from other disciplines, Franklin Conley and Ronald A. Veenker, were generous enough to read portions of the manuscript from the point of view of nonspecialists, and their advice enabled me to avoid several pitfalls. Western Kentucky University assisted me in completing this book, once by a grant from the Faculty Research Committee and later through a reduction in teaching load. For this help I am grateful.

The expertise of Franklin Conley, Norman Tomazic, Tom Foster, James E. Sanders, George D. Roberts, Delbert C. Towell, Wandel L. Dye, and S. Reza Ahsan has been invaluable in the production of the maps.

Several former teachers and colleagues have expressed interest in this project over the years and have helped sustain my interest in the project. They include Robert D. Ochs, George C. Rogers, Daniel W. Hollis, the late William A. Foran, Gustavus G. Williamson, Jr., and J. Crawford Crowe.

I wish to express my appreciation to two graduate students, George Randolph Bowling and Nelda K. Wyatt, for aid in checking footnotes, and to two undergraduate students, Debbie Chase for typing and Bill Mounce for photographing maps.

Most of the typing for this manuscript was done by my wife, Italene Glascock Lucas. She has typed draft after draft without complaint, and for her untiring effort I am deeply appreciative. I hardly know how to tell her that I have begun a new project.

M. B. Lucas

April 1, 1976

SHERMAN AND THE BURNING OF COLUMBIA

1

Prologue

THE location of Columbia, South Carolina's capital, was chosen in 1786 to resolve a conflict for control of the state between the rich, powerful planters of the Low Country and the more numerous Piedmont farmers of the Up Country. The political compromise was to locate the capital equidistant between the sections on the sand hills overlooking the confluence of the Saluda and Broad rivers where the Congaree is formed. The town was impressively planned, with wide streets carefully laid out at right angles and enclosed within four double boulevards. The streets were soon lined with beautiful magnolia, oak, and mimosa trees and, with the passing of years, tastefully decorated homes, many with lovely formal gardens of roses, azaleas, camellias, and wisteria.

In 1801 South Carolina College was chartered, and with its opening four years later Columbia became the educational center for the state. The fall college term and the convening of the legislature in December brought to Columbia a social and cultural prestige second only to that of its tidewater rival, Charleston. Such distinguished college professors as Francis Lieber and Joseph Le-Conte mingled and dined with outstanding state leaders like the staunch old Up-Country unionist Benjamin F. Perry and the Low-Country aristocrat Henry W. DeSaussure.[1]

[1] Frank Freidel, *Francis Lieber, Nineteenth-Century Liberal*, pp. 127–128; Rosser H. Taylor, *Ante-Bellum South Carolina: A Social and Cultural History*, p. 31; William W. Freehling, *Prelude to Civil War: The Nullification Controversy in South Carolina, 1816–1836*, p. 20.

From its beginning, Columbia grew slowly, and by 1860 its population of 8,052—more than 3,500 of whom were Negroes—was a distant second to that of the Palmetto State's largest city, Charleston.[2] But Columbia did grow, and in 1854 the deteriorating sixty-four-year-old wooden building that had served as the state-house for South Carolina was moved to the northeast corner of Assembly and Senate streets to make room for a magnificent new granite structure at the head of Richardson Street. Work on the new capitol was still in progress when the Civil War broke out in 1861, and its unfinished state, like that of the federal Capitol in Washington, seemed to illustrate the incompleteness of the Union.[3]

Columbia had a vigorous business community in 1860. There were four hotels, two located near the capitol building and frequented by state legislators, one in the business district and convenient for cotton buyers, and another in the center of a large residential section. There were ten churches and fourteen schools, two of which were public. Columbia's two breweries supplied fourteen saloons, where politics and cotton were no doubt the chief topics of conversation. Law was one of the most highly respected professions in the South, and Columbia was amply supplied with thirteen lawyers, who, along with their planter friends, virtually dominated every aspect of society and government.[4]

The business portions of the city were confined almost entirely to the east and west sides of Richardson Street, with numerous residences interspersed between the offices and stores. The town hall–market, the center of business activity, was located on the

2 U.S. Department of Commerce, Bureau of the Census, *Ninth Census of the United States: 1870. Population*, I, 258, 260.

3 George A. Buchanan, "Government: Municipal, State and Federal," in *Columbia, Capital City of South Carolina, 1786–1936*, ed. Helen Kohn Hennig, pp. 60–63; Constance McLaughlin Green, *Washington: Village and Capital, 1800–1876*, p. 238. The names of several of Columbia's streets were changed after the Civil War. Richardson officially became Main, Upper Boundary became Elmwood, Lumber was changed to Calhoun, Plain to Hampton, Gates to Park, Medium to College, and Winn to Gregg. See A. S. Salley, "Origin and Early Developments," in *Columbia, Capital City*, ed. Hennig, p. 9.

4 J. F. Williams, *Old and New Columbia*, pp. 85–86; Margaret Babcock Meriwether, "Literature and the Theater," in *Columbia, Capital City*, ed. Hennig, p. 193; *The Columbia Directory, Containing the Names, Business and Residence of the Inhabitants*, pp. 45, 47–48, 56.

northwest corner of Richardson and Washington streets. It was a large building with a clock tower, open arcades on the first floor for the market, and a side stairway to the second-floor city offices.

The growing of cotton on plantations worked by slave labor was a vital part of the Southern economic philosophy, and Columbia, located in the heart of an old cotton-producing section, was a marketing center. From Upper Boundary Street northward two blocks along Richardson Street was an area known as "Cotton Town." There were located the offices and huge warehouses of the cotton brokers who purchased much of the midland crop in addition to the cotton floated downriver to the fall-line city. As a result of the overproduction that had plagued the South for years, the removal of cotton from the international trade after secession, and continued cultivation during the Civil War, these warehouses and numerous basements and outbuildings in the city were packed with cotton from 1861 until the burning of Columbia in 1865.[5]

Fire protection was of paramount interest to antebellum towns because of the numerous wooden structures with common walls, especially in the business districts. In its pioneer days the South Carolina capital had been plagued by devastating fires, but during the antebellum years, largely as a result of increased protection, the potentially dangerous fires had been contained.[6] To guard against the constant threat of fire, Columbia in 1860 boasted four strategically placed fire companies manned by volunteers. Columbia's waterworks provided the town's firemen with a supply ample for every emergency. Constructed in the 1830's and greatly improved and expanded in the 1850's, the municipal water system had by the 1860's become a source of pride for the capital city.[7] However, during the Civil War, when the amount of cotton stored in Columbia mounted rapidly, the danger of fire increased. In Jan-

[5] Williams, *Old and New Columbia*, pp. 43–44; Clifford Dowdey, *The Land They Fought For: The Story of the South as the Confederacy, 1832–1865*, p. 81; deposition of Richard O'Neale, April 23, 1873, No. 236, David Jacobs *vs.* United States, *Mixed Commission on British and American Claims. Appendix: Testimony*, XXIII, 8.

[6] Williams, *Old and New Columbia*, pp. 85–86; *Columbia Directory*, p. 55; Buchanan, "Government," p. 75.

[7] Buchanan, "Government," p. 75; Lillian Adele Kibler, *Benjamin F. Perry, South Carolina Unionist*, p. 226.

uary, 1864, thirteen months before Major General William T.
Sherman approached the city, an immense fire was discovered at a
cotton warehouse on Lady Street. The fire departments, soldiers,
and citizens responded to the peal of the fire alarm and concentrated their efforts on saving surrounding buildings, but the cloud
of "firey particles" floating over the city led scores of families to
conclude that all was lost and to move their belongings into the
streets. After many hours of hard work, however, the flames were
controlled, but a second fire broke out later in the day at another
cotton warehouse. Before the day ended, 3,500 bales of cotton, 800
of which were sea island, were consumed, resulting in a loss of
$3,000,000 in cotton and $400,000 in other property.[8] In July,
1864, a second destructive fire erupted at another warehouse near
Cotton Town, and 935 bales were destroyed. The editor of the
Tri-Weekly South Carolinian, in evaluating the problems the city
faced from such fires, stated that only "the deep calm of a July
afternoon" prevented the entire town from going up in flames.[9]

Local citizens were also proud of the capital's railroads. Columbia was an important rail center, providing connections with
the Up Country, other fall-line towns, and Charleston. The South
Carolina Railroad terminal, which also served the Greenville and
Columbia line, was located on Gervais Street about halfway between the State House and the Congaree River. The Charlotte and
South Carolina depot was in the eastern part of town about one
mile away, but the actual connections between the two stations
followed a circuitous route on the south side of town.[10]

---

[8] *Columbia Tri-Weekly South Carolinian*, Jan. 21, 22, 1864. In attempting
to analyze the cause of the fire, the editor commented: "The fire is supposed by
many to be the work of an incendiary, but it is equally probable that it may
have originated from the cinders of a passing locomotive, and been smouldering
for hours before it was discovered." The assessment continued: "It is a well-
known fact, however, that cotton is the most difficult of all substances to control
when once attacked by the insidious element, and a week or two may elapse
before this will be subdued."

[9] Ibid., Aug. 2, 1864. In January, 1865, the firemen in Columbia organized
into a military company and began preparing "to take their places at the post
of danger, when the hour arrives that calls them to the defence of Columbia"
(*Columbia Daily South Carolinian*, Jan. 12, 1865).

[10] Williams, *Old and New Columbia*, p. 46; *Columbia Directory*, p. 54.
The employees of Columbia's railroads began organizing into militia companies

During the fall and winter months Columbia was crowded with visitors who attended the legislature, the courts, or the festivities at South Carolina College. In the antebellum period, commencements at the college were held on the first Monday in December and included a magnificent procession of governmental and academic officials. The climax of the oratory and the politicizing was the commencement ball, which was attended by many of South Carolina's leading citizens.[11] The grandest event of the year for Columbia came when the South Carolina General Assembly met. The politicians made their annual trek to take part in the government of the state and to participate in the dinners, parties, and other social gatherings. During legislative sessions the streets of the capital teemed with activity, and the small sand-hill seat of government took on a gay atmosphere.

When the legislature met on November 5, 1860, to choose presidential electors, the prevailing topic of discussion was secession. By that time the "fire-eaters," whose propaganda had been very effective, were being pushed forward by their constituents. One week after convening, when it became apparent that Abraham Lincoln had been elected, the legislators, following the Calhoun State Rights formula, unanimously decided to call a convention of the people to consider secession. The hastily summoned convention met on December 17, 1860, at the Baptist Church in Columbia and quickly declared its intention to secede. Fear of a smallpox epidemic, however, caused the convention to adjourn to Charleston, where, on December 20, South Carolina departed the Federal Union. News of the passage of the Ordinance of Secession was the signal for celebration in Columbia. There followed several excited days of cannon firing, bell ringing, and bonfire demonstrations. South Carolinians were united as never before, with displays of Southern patriotism on every hand.[12]

With the firing on Fort Sumter in 1861, the South began the process of converting much of its energy to conducting the war,

---

to defend the city in June, 1864. *Columbia Tri-Weekly South Carolinian*, June 21, 1864.

[11] Kibler, *Benjamin F. Perry*, p. 226; Mary Reynolds Forbes, "Society," in *Columbia, Capital City*, ed. Hennig, p. 245.

[12] Williams, *Old and New Columbia*, p. 97.

and as it went through a metamorphosis, the Palmetto State capital could not escape transformation. In the four years that followed, an extensive military establishment evolved in Columbia, thus making the city a prime target. The State Arsenal, with its fine parade ground, was located on Laurel Street at the site of the present governor's mansion; adjacent and to the south was the Arsenal Academy, a state military preparatory school. Because all males between eighteen and forty-five were required to participate in militia training, there were a number of military organizations in Columbia in 1861. Leading citizens, to fulfill their responsibility, organized volunteer companies such as the Governor's Guards, the Richland Rifles, the Carolina Blues, the Columbia Artillery, and the Congaree Cavalry. Sometimes special groups created companies, as was the case of the Irishmen who formed the Emmett Guard. Those unable to gain membership in one of these organizations—men usually of the lower classes—were placed in unnamed militia companies.[13]

Shortly after the commencement of fighting, a war mobilization camp was established in the city at the fairgrounds on the north side of Upper Boundary Street, but with the passage of time a more permanent camp was set up at Killian, about nine miles north of the capital. The hospital established by the Confederate government to care for these troops was transferred in 1862 to the more adequate facilities of the South Carolina College buildings, which were left vacant when the entire student body volunteered for the army. Three buildings, including the chapel, were used for the hospital.[14] Throughout the war troops constantly passed through Columbia, some on their way to front lines, others on furlough, and still others, the wounded, on their way home. To aid these "worn and wounded soldiers," the women of Columbia established two volunteer missions, Wayside Hospital and Ladies' Hospital, near the railroad terminals. Closely connected with the hospitals was Columbia's Wayside Home, where the ladies of the city provided transient soldiers with a "comfortable

13 Ibid., pp. 44–45, 94.
14 Ibid., p. 102; Daniel Walker Hollis, *University of South Carolina: South Carolina College*, pp. 212, 222–225; Edwin L. Green, "Higher Education," in *Columbia, Capital City*, ed. Hennig, p. 89.

supper and a cheerful welcome."[15] Though Columbians were spared involvement in front-line fighting for almost four years, those ladies who cared for these "smashed-up objects of misery" witnessed some of the worst horrors of the war.[16] Working in conjunction with these medical missions was the Hospital Aid Association of the Reverend Robert W. Barnwell, a professor at South Carolina College. This organization, with its headquarters in Virginia, raised thousands of dollars and tons of supplies on behalf of Confederate soldiers.[17]

Probably the most effective eleemosynary agency was the Central Association for the Relief of Soldiers of South Carolina. Dr. Maximilian LaBorde, also a professor at South Carolina College, organized the Central Association in 1862 in an attempt to coordinate relief efforts for soldiers on a statewide basis. As a result of LaBorde's indefatigable efforts, the legislature was persuaded to contribute large sums of money, to which were added the cash and supplies donated by citizens. With the cooperation and support of the railroads, LaBorde sent cars throughout South Carolina to collect supplies which each Wednesday were shipped to Richmond, where the Central Association maintained a Wayside Home for Palmetto State soldiers. Other activities of the Central Association included maintenance of the Wayside Home in Atlanta, organization of an ambulance corps, and provision of supplies to South Carolina prisoners of war.[18]

[15] Isabella D. Martin and Myrta Lockett Avery, eds., *A Diary from Dixie as Written by Mary Boykin Chesnut*, pp. 205–206n; *Columbia Tri-Weekly South Carolinian*, May 28, 1864.

[16] Ben Ames Williams, ed., *A Diary from Dixie by Mary Boykin Chesnut*, pp. 430–431; A. T. Smythe, M. B. Poppenheim, and Thomas Taylor, eds., *South Carolina Women in the Confederacy*, I, 98. The *Columbia Tri-Weekly South Carolinian*, March 12, 1864, stated that in the first two years 32,165 soldiers registered at Wayside Hospital and $19,349 was spent in aiding them. The number of wounded using these facilities increased steadily, especially after the commencement of the Wilderness Campaign. See *Columbia Tri-Weekly South Carolinian*, May 28–July 2, 1864.

[17] Charles Edward Cauthen, "Confederacy and Reconstruction," in *Columbia, Capital City*, ed. Hennig, p. 32; Smythe, Poppenheim, and Taylor, *South Carolina Women*, I, 21, 103, 104.

[18] *Columbia Daily South Carolinian*, Oct. 19, Dec. 7, 1864; *Columbia Tri-Weekly South Carolinian*, Jan. 28, 1864; *Columbia Daily Southern Guardian*, March 16, 1863.

One of the largest efforts of Columbians to raise money and supplies for Confederate soldiers, and certainly the most interesting, was the Great Bazaar, which was staged in January, 1865. In mid-1864 a number of prominent women began preparation for the bazaar, and in the fall an appeal went out to citizens of the South to send goods produced in the Confederacy, as well as cash donations, as a great display of support for the Southern cause. The South Carolina legislature placed the State House at the disposal of the sponsors, and the railroads responded with free transportation for goods shipped to Columbia. Beginning on Tuesday, January 17, 1865, only one month before the burning of Columbia, the house and senate chambers were filled with booths from every Southern state. The ladies of Columbia, however, were forced to provide exhibits for several states that had virtually ceased to be a part of the Confederacy because of Federal occupation. The gaily decorated displays, all of which were donated, were filled with ribbons, lace, fine cloth from Europe, homemade quilts, culinary delights of every description, and handicrafts. Some of these goods were raffled, others auctioned, and still others sold. Backers of the Great Bazaar were pleased with the amounts of supplies and cash raised,[19] but in the final analysis, lagging support and the declining military situation forced an early closing of the exhibits. Indeed, there was a haunting fear in the minds of some that Sherman would reap the profits instead of the ill-supplied Confederate soldiers for whom they were intended.[20]

In 1863 Joseph LeConte, the outstanding professor of chemistry and geology at South Carolina College, was able to employ his scientific knowledge for the Confederacy when he was appointed head of a large-scale government operation for manufacturing medicines located at the fairgrounds. From this establishment, one of the few domestic sources for the supply of medicine in the entire Confederacy, the army received needed alcohol, nitrate of silver, chloroform, and other chemicals. Dr. J. Julian Chisolm, military

---

[19] *Columbia Tri-Weekly South Carolinian*, Dec. 25, 1864; *Columbia Daily South Carolinian*, Nov. 25, 1864, Jan. 19, 1865; Smythe, Poppenheim, and Taylor, *South Carolina Women*, I, 217–218, 243–247.

[20] Williams, *Diary from Dixie by Mary Boykin Chesnut*, pp. 472–473, 475; Earl Schenck Miers, ed., *When the World Ended: The Diary of Emma LeConte*, pp. 13, 15.

surgeon and medical purveyor for Columbia, was closely assocated with Dr. LeConte in this endeavor. Late in the war the activities of LeConte and Chisolm were augmented by the development of a government distillery in Columbia, which produced between two hundred and five hundred gallons of whiskey and alcohol each day. During 1864 LeConte, given the rank of major, absorbed additional duties as chemist for the Niter and Mining Bureau, for which he used the laboratory at South Carolina College. Though there was some effort to develop niter beds on the outskirts of Columbia, the supply was never sufficient, and LeConte was forced on occasion to travel throughout South Carolina, Georgia, Alabama, and Tennessee in search of saltpeter.[21]

A mill for manufacturing gunpowder for the Confederacy was located slightly north of the Congaree River bridge between the river and the Columbia Canal, which ran parallel to the Broad and Congaree rivers and which was leased by its owners to the Confederate government soon after the war began. There, charcoal was made from the willow trees brought downriver and then crushed into a fine powder which was mixed with saltpeter and sulfur to produce gunpowder.[22] A short distance south of the bridge, the Confederate government operated a small armory, and a large storehouse for military weapons was located near the river southeast of the present penitentiary.[23]

One of Columbia's most important war industries was the Palmetto Iron Works, located on the corner of Lincoln and Laurel streets. This plant manufactured explosive shells, solid shot, minie bullets, and several types of cannon. Nearby, on Arsenal Hill,

[21] Clement Eaton, *A History of the Southern Confederacy*, pp. 98–99; H. H. Cunningham, *Doctors in Gray: The Confederate Medical Service*, pp. 146–148; Joseph LeConte, *The Autobiography of Joseph LeConte*, ed. William Dallam Armes, p. 184; Cauthen, "Confederacy and Reconstruction," p. 35; Hollis, *University of South Carolina*, p. 228; *War of the Rebellion: A Compilation of the Official Records of the Union and Confederate Armies*, Ser. 4, III, 1074 (hereafter cited as *OR*).

[22] Cauthen, "Confederacy and Reconstruction," p. 35; Williams, *Old and New Columbia*, pp. 109–110. There evidently were a number of small mills along the riverbank in Columbia engaged in producing powder. The assistant inspector general of the XV Corps, Lieutenant Colonel L. E. Yorke, reported destroying twenty-five powder mills. See *OR*, Ser. 1, XLVII, pt. 2: 502–503.

[23] Williams, *Old and New Columbia*, p. 110.

overlooking Sidney Park in the northwestern part of town, Shields Foundry produced war material; a rifle factory was also built in the city during the war. Another war industry, a sword factory, was located on Richardson Street at Upper Boundary. There, the firm of Kraft, Goldsmith, Kraft and Company forged sabers and swords from scraps of iron and steel gleaned throughout the South. The firm also produced a host of other items such as sword guards, spurs, buckles, bits, bugles, and ornaments for military clothing. From wood the factory made scabbards and saber handles. Bayonets for infantry weapons were manufactured at a factory on Washington Street between Gates and Lincoln streets.[24]

Several firms in Columbia manufactured clothing for the Confederate government. A shoe factory on Richardson Street maintained a large work force, and a uniform factory was located on Taylor Street. The uniforms were cut out in the factory and taken into the homes of ladies in the community for completion. Buttons for the uniforms were produced at a factory on Richardson Street. One of the largest war industries in Columbia at the time of its destruction was the army sock factory operated by John Judge and Company and located at the southeast corner of Richardson and Lumber streets. The material for the socks was knitted into long tubing and cut off at the appropriate length. The tubing was then distributed among the ladies of the city, who finished the socks by drawing the toes together, making heels, and trimming the tops. Judge's enterprise employed twenty-five persons in manufacturing knitting needles and seventy-five in the mill itself, while five hundred or more ladies toiled in their homes. A small cotton mill was established by the government near Sidney Park to produce yarn for the sock factory. Until July 1, 1864, when it was destroyed by an accidental fire, a factory on Richardson Street produced tarpaulins and oilcloth for the Confederate government.[25]

24 Ibid., pp. 107–108, 110; Frank E. Vandiver, *Ploughshares into Swords: Josiah Gorgas and Confederate Ordnance*, p. 241; *Columbia Tri-Weekly South Carolinian*, May 10, 1864. Williams estimated that "thousands" of swords were produced by the factory, a figure which is substantiated by the 3,095 sabers captured by the Union army in Columbia (see Appendix A).

25 Williams, *Old and New Columbia*, pp. 107–110; Cauthen, "Confederacy and Reconstruction," p. 36; Quartermaster Department to John Judge,

Perhaps Columbia's largest Confederate enterprise was the Saluda Factory, located on the west side of the Saluda River about one mile north of the Congaree River bridge. In the early years of the war it had been enlarged, equipped with machinery to manufacture woolen cloth, and sold to the government. The Saluda Factory employed a force of about one thousand workers by 1862.[26] During 1863 South Carolina Quartermaster General James Jones managed to purchase machinery in England for manufacturing cotton cards, and after much difficulty and disappointment he found a machinist to put the equipment together. Early in 1864 the card factory, located on the State House grounds, began operation. It consisted of three buildings, one of which contained nine machines and another of which housed a steam engine that powered the entire establishment. Nearly one hundred cards were produced each day by a crew consisting primarily of women and young white and black lads. In an attempt to hold down inflation, the state sold the cards at one-fifth the current price.[27]

In 1862 the Confederate secretary of the treasury, Christopher G. Memminger, a native South Carolinian, moved the Confederate printing presses to Columbia, and thereafter most of the notes and bonds were lithographed in the state capital. Many of Columbia's finest young ladies were employed in the Treasury Note Bureau signing the ever increasing number of notes. In the end, the Confederate treasury issued over $1.5 billion in paper currency, three times the number of Federal greenbacks printed.[28] In addition to these war-related industries, the Confederate and state governments maintained a host of ordnance, commissary, conscription, and other offices along Richardson and adjacent streets from which the war effort in South Carolina was directed.[29]

Columbia, then, was obviously of great strategic worth to the

---

Jan. 5, 1863, John Judge Papers, Southern Historical Collection, University of North Carolina, Chapel Hill; *Columbia Tri-Weekly South Carolinian*, July 2, 1864.

[26] Cauthen, "Confederacy and Reconstruction," pp. 35–36.

[27] *Columbia Tri-Weekly South Carolinian*, Aug. 18, 1864.

[28] Eaton, *History of the Southern Confederacy*, p. 238.

[29] *Columbia Daily South Carolinian*, Oct. 9, 1864. A complete list of the twenty-eight officials and their locations can be found in Appendix B.

South. Its military installations, its railroads, and the fact that it was to a great extent the last breadbasket of the Confederacy made the city far more important than Charleston. From a military standpoint the South Carolina capital was Sherman's next logical objective once Savannah had been taken and his army resupplied.

On September 2, 1864, the victorious army of General Sherman marched into Atlanta, Georgia, dealing the Southern cause a severe blow. Politically, Sherman's success greatly boosted Union morale and assured the reelection of Abraham Lincoln in November; militarily, it led to the scattering of Confederate forces under General John Bell Hood and to Hood's eventual defeat in the Battle of Nashville in mid-December, 1864. After two and one-half months in Atlanta, Sherman reduced his army to the barest minimum, cut contact with his supply base in Chattanooga, Tennessee, and began his famous march to the sea.[30] With unusual success Sherman's forces devastated an area perhaps 60 miles wide from Atlanta to Savannah, a region which provided food and other supplies for the Army of Northern Virginia. The Union army wrecked railroads, bridges, manufacturing establishments, and anything else useful to the Confederacy. In slightly more than thirty days, having marched 220 miles, Sherman captured the Georgia port of Savannah, completing the division of the Confederacy.[31]

With Savannah safely in Federal hands, Sherman wrote his commanding general, U. S. Grant, presenting the final phase of his most daring strategy of the war:

> I feel no doubt whatever as to our future plans; I have thought them over so long and well that they appear as clear as daylight. I left Augusta untouched on purpose, because now the enemy will be in doubt as to my objective point after crossing the Savannah River, whether it be Augusta or Charleston, and will

[30] William Tecumseh Sherman, *Memoirs of General William T. Sherman*, II, 107–110, 171–172; J. G. Randall and David Donald, *The Civil War and Reconstruction*, pp. 425–426; James Ford Rhodes, *History of the United States from the Compromise of 1850 to the Final Restoration of Home Rule at the South in 1877*, V, 16–17.

[31] B. H. Liddell Hart, *Strategy, the Indirect Approach*, p. 151; Sherman, *Memoirs*, II, 177ff.

naturally divide his forces. I will then move either on Branchville or on Columbia, on any curved line that gives me the best supplies, breaking up in my course as much railroad as possible; then, ignoring Charleston and Augusta both, occupy Columbia. . . .[32]

In early January Sherman received Grant's approval of his plans, and preparations were soon under way for the invasion of the birthplace of secession.[33] Very few changes from the organization of his troops during the march to the sea were made. The right wing, the Army of the Tennessee, commanded by Major General O. O. Howard, consisted of the XV Corps of Major General John A. Logan and the XVII Corps of Major General Francis P. Blair, Jr. Major General Henry W. Slocum commanded the left wing, the Army of Georgia, which was composed of the XIV Corps under Major General Jefferson C. Davis and the XX Corps under Brigadier General Alpheus S. Williams. Each corps consisted of about thirteen thousand men, to which must be added the four thousand men of Brigadier General Hugh J. Kilpatrick's cavalry and some two thousand artillerymen, with sixty-eight cannon, making a total of fifty-eight thousand men.[34] In an effort to achieve the greatest mobility and speed Sherman ordered that his army be stripped bare of baggage. All tents and camp furnishings, including those of the officers, were left behind.

To keep the defenders of South Carolina unsure of his destination, the Northern general employed the new military tactics he had developed so successfully during the march to the sea. His army was divided into two prongs, one apparently heading for Charleston and the other deceptively aimed at Augusta, thus baffling the defenders of the Palmetto State about his military objective. Torn between their desire to protect Charleston and Augusta—"on the horns of a dilemma," as Sherman phrased it—the Confederate generals divided their forces, with the consequence

[32] *OR*, Ser. 1, XLIV, 797.

[33] B. H. Liddell Hart, *Sherman: Soldier, Realist, American*, p. 359; Rhodes, *History of the United States*, V, 85.

[34] *OR*, Ser. 1, XLVII, pt. 1: 42, 177; Clement A. Evans, ed., *Confederate Military History*, V, 361; John G. Barrett, *Sherman's March through the Carolinas*, pp. 31–32. Only the right wing, consisting of approximately 27,762 infantrymen of the XV and XVII corps, entered Columbia.

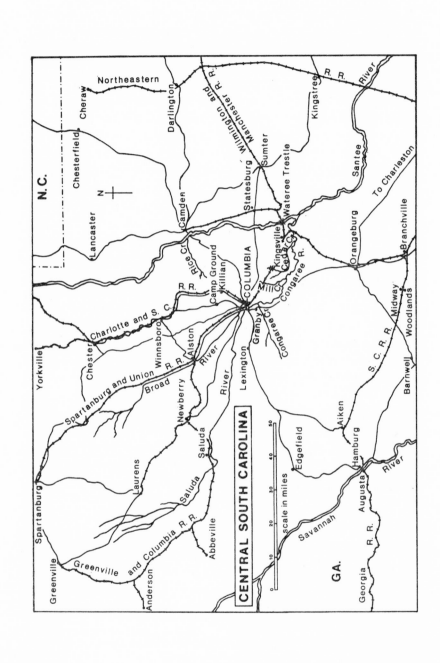

CENTRAL SOUTH CAROLINA

that they were unable to defend any area of the state successfully. Without supply lines, living off the land whenever necessary, and with mobility that seemed impossible even to General Robert E. Lee, Sherman moved at will in South Carolina, often finding his opposition melting away. Repeatedly, the Confederate soldiers gave up strong positions before a major assault was made, thus leaving the countryside almost completely open before the Union army.[35]

The belief that General Sherman would burn Columbia was prevalent in the South Carolina capital long before his army actually invaded the state. On November 17, 1864, two days after Sherman began his march to the sea, Mrs. Mary Boykin Chesnut, that astute observer of the Southern scene who was then in Columbia, wrote forebodingly in her diary: "Although Sherman took Atlanta, he does not mean to stay there. . . . Fire and the sword are for us here; that is the word."[36] Eight days later, as Mrs. Chesnut sat depressed, contemplating the future, she envisioned that "Sherman's bugles" would soon be blasting in the distance, and she realized that "a brigade or so of troopless, dismantled Generals" was all South Carolina had to oppose the Union army. "The deep waters are closing over us," Mrs. Chesnut wrote on December 19 after hearing the latest dismal news of the war from one of Columbia's leading citizens, Dr. D. H. Trezevant, "and we in this house are like the outsiders at the time of the Flood." All the while, she lamented, the South Carolina Legislature did little to prepare the state's defense, but rather spent their time debating the encroachments of the Confederate government on state rights. She summed up the situation as "desolation, mismanagement, despair."[37]

A few days after Sherman entered Savannah, Emma LeConte, Professor LeConte's precocious daughter, expressed the same fear in her diary:

> They are preparing to hurl destruction upon the State they hate most of all, and Sherman the brute avows his intention of con-

[35] Liddell Hart, *Strategy*, pp. 151–152; T. Harry Williams, *P. G. T. Beauregard, Napoleon in Gray*, pp. 248–252.

[36] Martin and Avery, *Diary from Dixie*, p. 333. Mrs. Chesnut was not aware that Sherman had already left Atlanta when she wrote these lines.

[37] Williams, *Diary from Dixie by Mary Boykin Chesnut*, pp. 453, 465.

verting South Carolina into a wilderness. Not one house, he says, shall be left standing, and his licentious troops—whites and negroes—shall be turned loose to ravage and violate. . . . But is this a time to talk of submission? Now when the Yankees have deepened and widened the breach by a thousand new atrocities? A sea rolls between them and us—a sea of blood. Smoking houses, outraged women, murdered fathers, brothers and husbands forbid such a union. Reunion! Great Heavens! How we hate them with the whole strength and depth of our souls![38]

Constantly before her fertile young mind was a vision of Columbia "sacked and laid in ashes." She anticipated that no mercy would be shown her beloved state, and that undoubtedly South Carolina College, where she resided with her parents, would be burned along with the other public buildings. "Everyone seems to feel," she lamented, "that Columbia is doomed."[39]

Before Sherman's invasion of South Carolina began, Mrs. Rachel Susan Cheves, a former resident of Columbia who received a pass through the Federal lines, arrived from Savannah, bringing with her a prophecy of impending destruction. Upon learning that many of her friends intended to remain in Columbia through the anticipated Union occupation, she advised them to flee for their lives. A Federal officer whom she had known before the conflict had ominously warned her that upon leaving Savannah she should not go to Columbia: "It is the cradle of Secession and must be punished." This story and others like it were readily accepted in the capital.[40]

Once the Union army entered South Carolina, refugees from Georgia and the Low Country flooded into Columbia with accounts of brutality, sufferings, violence, and burnings.[41] The influx of

[38] Miers, *When the World Ended*, p. 4. There were no Negro soldiers with Sherman.

[39] Ibid., pp. 8, 13, 15. The use of the college laboratory by the Confederate government made it subject to destruction by Sherman.

[40] Cheves to John LeConte [March ?, 1866], Rachel Susan Cheves Papers, Manuscript Division, Duke University Library, Durham, N.C.; Harriott Horry Ravenel, "Burning of Columbia," March 12, 1898, manuscript article from letter of March, 1865, Harriott Horry Ravenel Papers, South Caroliniana Library, University of South Carolina, Columbia; Smythe, Poppenheim, and Taylor, *South Carolina Women*, I, 321.

[41] *Columbia Phoenix*, March 21, 1865.

these cold, hungry refugees, caught in the final savagery of an already brutal conflict, created in Columbia a sense of desperation readily apparent in the sharply increased crime rate. By the end of 1864 the exigencies of war had ended the lighting of the streets, thus making them unsafe for travel at night; robbery, and even murder, was an ever increasing danger after sundown.[42] In late November the home of one of Columbia's most distinguished war heroes, Major General Wade Hampton, was entered by thieves who scribbled antiwar phrases on the walls before departing with everything of value.[43]

In spite of Sherman's obvious threat to Columbia, both the civilian and the military authorities in the city were tardy in realizing the danger and even slower in acting. Beginning in late November, as Sherman was moving across Georgia with his left wing threatening Augusta, the *Tri-Weekly South Carolinian* assessed the local situation as "grave," and urged that the capital city be fortified for any eventuality. When several days passed without activity, the editor attempted to prod city leadership out of its lethargy: "Are our authorities dumb, dreaming or horrified? If not, what means our inaction? . . . Are we to wait until the last moment, and then hear the frantic appeals for help that will ring out far and near? A fearful responsibility rests somewhere."[44]

When proper authorities did not respond, the first step in preparation for the defense of Columbia came in December, 1864, when local citizens, worried about the openness of South Carolina to invasion, met to initiate action. In a petition drawn up and forwarded to Confederate Secretary of War James A. Seddon, they asked that a corps of the Army of Northern Virginia be sent to aid South Carolina, pointing out that the destruction of the state's railroads and supplies would grievously injure the Southern cause.[45]

---

[42] Cauthen, "Confederacy and Reconstruction," pp. 30–31.

[43] John L. Manning to wife, Dec. 11, 1864, Williams-Chesnut-Manning Papers, South Caroliniana Library, University of South Carolina, Columbia; Williams, *Diary from Dixie by Mary Boykin Chesnut*, p. 455.

[44] *Columbia Tri-Weekly South Carolinian*, Nov. 23, 27, 1864.

[45] *OR*, Ser. 1, XLIV, 1011–1012. Out of respect for the signatories, Seddon sent the petition to President Jefferson Davis on January 5, 1865. Davis returned the petition to Seddon on February 7 with instructions to consult Gen-

It was not until January 9, 1865, long after the seriousness of the predicament should have been recognized, that Mayor Thomas Jefferson Goodwyn called a town meeting to evaluate the situation. Concluding that the enemy would shortly move on Columbia, the citizens resolved to suspend "as far as practicable" all business activities in order to concentrate on preparations for defense. To implement their program a committee of five was created in each of Columbia's four wards to recruit white and black labor and to solicit equipment and money for building fortifications.[46] The call went out to Columbians to respond with anything that would "turn dirt," but the response was not gratifying. After ten days of effort Mayor Goodwyn was forced to report that Columbians had answered the call with "few hands and fewer tools." The *Daily South Carolinian* concluded that Columbians had "reached that lethargic state in which men prefer to suffer anything rather than act."[47]

At the same time that the citizens were petitioning the Confederate government for aid, the newly elected governor of South Carolina, Andrew Gordon Magrath, an outspoken critic of President Jefferson Davis, also attempted to bring pressure to bear on Richmond. On Christmas Day, 1864, he wrote Davis, requesting that troops from Virginia be transferred to South Carolina to fortify Branchville, a vital rail junction seventy miles south of Columbia and midway between Augusta and Charleston. The borders of the Palmetto State, Magrath correctly pointed out, were Richmond's second line of defense.[48]

In the weeks that followed, Magrath constantly renewed his requests to President Davis, and on each occasion he carefully tied the fate of Virginia to that of South Carolina, especially emphasizing the importance of Charleston, one of the few port cities still in Confederate hands. Charleston and Richmond were vital to

---

eral Robert E. Lee. On February 9 the petition was sent to Lee, who on February 11 returned it to Seddon, stating that he could spare no more troops.

[46] *Charleston Daily Courier*, Jan. 11, 1865.

[47] *Columbia Daily South Carolinian*, Jan. 12, 19, 1865.

[48] Magrath to Davis, Dec. 25, 1864, Andrew Gordon Magrath Papers, South Caroliniana Library, University of South Carolina, Columbia; Charles Edward Cauthen, *South Carolina Goes to War, 1861–1865*, pp. 222–223.

each other, inseparable in the defense of the Confederacy, Magrath argued, and if one fell, the other would inevitably follow.[49] As 1864 ended he enlisted the support of Robert W. Barnwell, a distinguished Columbian then in Richmond, to appeal personally to Davis for troops,[50] but results were not forthcoming, and by January, 1865, when he learned that the Confederate government did not believe Charleston could be held, Magrath bitterly resigned himself to the inevitable.[51]

Having failed to secure military aid from the Confederate government, but still hoping for a miracle, Magrath reluctantly turned for assistance on January 11 to Georgia's enigmatic Governor Joseph E. Brown, though the shallowness of the Carolinian's call for common cause against Sherman was all too apparent. Magrath must have thought that Brown, a Palmetto State native, would perhaps overlook South Carolina's refusal to allow its militia to cross into Georgia during Sherman's advance on Atlanta, but the memory of South Carolina's particularism was too fresh in the minds of Georgians, and Brown's response could not have been a surprise. He would join with Magrath in a "strong protest" against the policies of President Davis, Brown wrote, but as for military help, he had none.[52]

The coup de grace to Magrath's efforts to procure military aid came in a letter from General Lee. Magrath's letters to Davis had eventually been forwarded to Lee, who was appointed general-in-chief of all Confederate armies on January 23, 1865. On January 27 the general informed Magrath of the impossibility of sending troops to South Carolina. Lee emphasized that should he leave Virginia, Lieutenant General U. S. Grant would follow, and "you

[49] Magrath to Davis, Dec. 25, 1864; telegram, Davis to Magrath, Dec. 30, 1864; telegrams, Magrath to Davis, Jan. 21, 22, 1865, Magrath Papers. What Magrath failed to see was that the fate of Charleston hung on the defense of central South Carolina. If Sherman could get behind Charleston, the city would have to be evacuated.

[50] Magrath to Barnwell, Dec. 30, 1864, Magrath Papers. Barnwell was a former president of South Carolina College, United States senator, and delegate to the Montgomery convention.

[51] Magrath to William J. Hardee, Jan. 11, 1865, Magrath Papers.

[52] Magrath to Brown, Jan. 11, 1865; Brown to Magrath, Jan. 16, 1865, Magrath Papers.

can judge whether the condition of affairs would be benefited by a concentration of two large Federal armies in S.C. . . ." Lee then enumerated the troops in South Carolina, who totaled about thirty-three thousand, and stated that they should be able to hold the state.[53] Nevertheless, realizing that the will of South Carolinians needed to be bolstered, Lee released a token force of two thousand troops, consisting of Major General M. C. Butler's division of Wade Hampton's cavalry, for the defense of their native state. Though Lee, with his back to the wall before Richmond and Petersburg, obviously needed every commander he had, he permitted Hampton, who had served brilliantly with Major General J. E. B. Stuart, to accompany Butler's cavalry.[54]

As Hampton entrained for South Carolina on January 22, 1865, it was not without reservations. He had often proclaimed his determination to fight for the Confederacy until ultimate victory was achieved, but he immediately recognized that the situation could become awkward in South Carolina. With no command of his own, he was to assist in mounting Butler's division, but if a suitable command were presented, Hampton had Lee's permission to accept it until called back to Virginia. The unhappy prospect was that he might be placed under Major General Joseph Wheeler, who outranked him and commanded the Confederate cavalry in South Carolina. To the proud, aristocratic Hampton, the thought of having to serve under a man eighteen years his junior was so distasteful that he planned to request a transfer to the infantry if the situation actually arose.[55]

[53] Lee to Magrath, Jan. 27, 1865, Magrath Papers. Lee, in his polite but firm manner, chided the governor, saying that if he had had sufficient troops they would have been sent to South Carolina automatically.

[54] Barrett, *Sherman's March through the Carolinas*, p. 65; Evans, *Confederate Military History*, V, 359; OR, Ser. 1, XLVI, pt. 2: 1113.

[55] Barrett, *Sherman's March through the Carolinas*, pp. 65–66; deposition of Wade Hampton, April 23, 1873, No. 236, *Mixed Commission*, XXIII, 2. Hampton described his feelings to William Porcher Miles in the following manner: "I am not particular what that command consists of as I am willing to fight anywhere in defence of our State. But I confess that I do not fancy the possibility of my being thrown under the command of Genl. Wheeler, who long my junior in the service, now ranks me" (Hampton to Miles, Jan. 21, 1865, William Porcher Miles Papers, Southern Historical Collection, University of North Carolina, Chapel Hill).

When Butler and Hampton arrived in Columbia in late January, 1865, they were met by an enthusiastic crowd, many of whom believed that the long-delayed preparations for the defense of Columbia had at last begun. Some even believed that other troops would follow, making the city safe from attack,[56] but others, including Governor Magrath, were more realistic. They knew "the end had come."[57] Recognizing that his efforts for outside help had come to nought, and unable to raise sufficient forces within the state, Magrath's only recourse by the time the invasion of South Carolina began was to issue a proclamation calling for a scorched-earth policy which, if carried out, would have made barren the path in front of Sherman:

> Remove your property from the reach of the enemy; carry what you can to a place of safety; then quickly rally and return to the field. What you can not carry, destroy. Indulge no sickly hope that you will be spared by submission; terror will but whet his revenge. Think not that your property will be respected, and afterward recovered. No such feeling prompts him. You leave it but to support and sustain him; you save it but to help him on his course. Destroy what you can not remove. He will make your return to your homes over a charred and blackened road; prepare you the same way for him as he advances.[58]

Although Magrath had been aware since mid-January that there was little hope for a successful defense of South Carolina should the enemy decide to invade, there was no official hint of impending disaster to city officials and the inhabitants of Columbia. As late as February 14, only three days before the Union army marched into Columbia, Mayor Goodwyn officially announced that on the basis of statements from the highest military authority, he could assure the inhabitants that Columbia was safe.[59] Indeed, Columbians who were in a position to know were

---

[56] Barrett, *Sherman's March through the Carolinas*, p. 66; Smythe, Poppenheim, and Taylor, *South Carolina Women*, I, 273.

[57] Williams, *Diary from Dixie by Mary Boykin Chesnut*, p. 472.

[58] *The Governor of the State, to the People of South Carolina*, undated printed proclamation in miscellaneous manuscript and printed materials folder entitled "Legislative System, Messages, 1860–1865," South Carolina Archives, Columbia.

[59] "Jno. W. G." to sister, March 1, 1865, William T. Sherman Papers, Manuscript Division, Library of Congress, Washington, D.C.

led to believe that the city would be held. Joseph LeConte was assured by Hampton that should evacuation become necessary the professor would be informed in sufficient time to remove Niter and Mining Bureau equipment. Even these assurances, however, did not allay LeConte's doubts as stories of reinforcements did not materialize and days of inaction passed:

> First we hear of them at Branchville, then at Orangeburg, then approaching Columbia by the Orangeburg road. Still the authorities—Beauregard, Hampton, etc—*seem* confident that they cannot take Columbia & will not attempt it. It is true the force here is a mere handfull [*sic*], some 5000–6000, but Hardee's Corps is expected from Charleston which alas! must now be evacuated by our forces, and Stuart's [Stewart's] & Cheatham's divisions of Hood's army are expected from Augusta, and, and, somebody else from somewhere else. Ah! Expected! how often have we been cheated by 'great expectations.'[60]

On February 10 LeConte's faltering confidence received a severe jolt when orders arrived from Richmond to dismantle and ship the chemical laboratory equipment to the Confederate capital.[61] The directive caught LeConte's associate, Dr. St. Julien Ravenel, completely by surprise; it was the first indication he had received from anyone just how tenuous the situation was.[62] Innumerable rumors were spreading throughout the city, and on February 14 LeConte was informed, falsely as it proved, that the force marching on Columbia numbered only three hundred men. Knowing that the Confederate forces were sufficient to repulse such a raid, LeConte was once again reassured that the town was safe.[63] Then on February 15 LeConte learned that the city's first line of defense had been carried the previous day and that the second line was being hard pressed. "How can the place stand?" he asked

[60] Joseph LeConte, "A Journal of Three Months Personal Experience During the Last Days of the Confederacy," Feb. 8–15, 1865, Joseph LeConte Collection, South Caroliniana Library, University of South Carolina, Columbia; *Columbia Phoenix*, March 21, 1865. LeConte's "Journal," written after his return home, has been published under the title *'Ware Sherman, A Journal of Three Months' Personal Experience in the Last Days of the Confederacy*.

[61] LeConte, "Journal," Feb. 8–15, 1865.

[62] Ravenel, "Burning of Columbia," Harriott Horry Ravenel Papers.

[63] Miers, *When the World Ended*, p. 30.

himself, yet ". . . the authorities talk confidently." Late that evening, as he walked home from the Charlotte railroad station, where he had checked to see if his laboratory equipment had been evacuated, he saw a large Confederate wagon train, about one-half mile long, slowly moving toward the depot. "For the first time," LeConte wrote in his journal, "my hopes utterly gave way. '*Columbia is doomed!*' "[64]

The frustration of the governor and citizens in the defense of South Carolina was only surpassed by that of the Confederate government. From the beginning of Sherman's march from Atlanta, the Confederate defense had never consisted of more than rear-guard cavalry skirmishes and a scorched-earth policy; the same held true in South Carolina.[65] By the time Sherman's intentions to move into South Carolina were known, the best President Davis could do was to transfer a few generals to the Palmetto State in the hope of infusing some life into his depleted, worn forces. General P. G. T. Beauregard, who had left Charleston for Montgomery, Alabama, one month before to command the recently created Military Division of the West, returned to lead the forces defending South Carolina. His instructions were to take part of the Army of Tennessee with him. On January 19, 1865, when Lee released M. C. Butler he also reactivated Major General D. H. Hill, who had been shelved after Chickamauga because of differences with Davis. Hill was placed in command of Confederate forces at Augusta, Georgia.[66]

---

[64] LeConte, "Journal," Feb. 8–15, 1865.

[65] *OR*, Ser. 1, XLIV, 859, 975–976.

[66] Evans, *Confederate Military History*, V, 359; Williams, *P. G. T. Beauregard*, pp. 241, 249–250; Nathaniel Cheairs Hughes, Jr., *General William J. Hardee: Old Reliable*, p. 276. The command situation in South Carolina was thoroughly confused throughout January and February, 1865. Beauregard was ordered to return to South Carolina in mid-January, but the order placing Beauregard in overall command in South Carolina was not issued until February 16. Wade Hampton arrived in South Carolina on January 28 and on February 7 was placed in charge of Butler's cavalry division, a brigade of which was led by another well-known South Carolinian, Major General P. M. B. Young. On February 11 Hampton, having "no troops yet to operate," was placed in command of the forces in Columbia and its vicinity. On February 16 Hampton, relieving Wheeler, was given command of all the cavalry operating in South Carolina. See Hughes, *General William J. Hardee*, p. 274; *OR*, Ser. 1, XLVII,

Beauregard arrived in Augusta on February 1 and during the next two days held his first council of war. At the conference, only fifteen days before the Northern army reached Columbia, Beauregard; Lieutenant General William J. Hardee, commander of the Department of South Carolina, Georgia, and Florida; and Major General G. W. Smith, commander of the Georgia militia, enumerated their forces and appraised their situation. Hardee reported 13,700 effectives, 3,000 of whom were state militia, in addition to Butler's cavalry of 1,500, many of whom were not fully equipped, and Wheeler's 6,700 cavalrymen, who were under Hardee's command. Smith and Brigadier General William M. Browne had 1,200 Georgia militiamen and 250 reserves. Beauregard had with him from the Army of Tennessee Lieutenant General Stephen D. Lee's "corps" of 4,000, but Major General B. F. Cheatham's "corps" of 3,000 and Major General A. P. Stewart's "corps" of 3,000 along with 800 artillerymen were scattered from Mississippi to Georgia and were not expected to arrive before February 10 or 11.[67] The number of troops available to defend South Carolina, the generals concluded, was 33,450. This figure was somewhat misleading, however, because Governor Brown shortly forbade the Georgia militia to cross into South Carolina, and much of the remnant of the Army of Tennessee never did arrive.[68]

Beauregard and his staff, unable to interpret Sherman's intentions—the Confederate commander had learned nothing from opposing Sherman in Georgia—had to face the critical question of where to concentrate their troops—Augusta, Branchville, or Charleston? They finally decided to defend all three approaches to South Carolina, the worst military decision they could have made since it necessitated the division of their already outnumbered

---

pt. 2: 1112, 1157, 1204; deposition of Hampton, *Mixed Commission*, XXIII, 2–3, 32; John P. Dyer, *"Fightin' Joe" Wheeler*, pp. 219–220.

[67] *OR*, Ser. 1, XLVII, pt. 2: 1078, 1083–1085; deposition of Hampton, *Mixed Commission*, XXIII, 5; Thomas Lawrence Connelly, *Autumn of Glory: The Army of Tennessee, 1862–1865*, p. 514; Williams, *P. G. T. Beauregard*, pp. 249–250.

[68] Hughes, *General William J. Hardee*, pp. 275–276, 278; Connelly, *Autumn of Glory*, p. 514.

forces. The plan called for Hardee's troops to defend the lower part of the state, falling back upon Charleston if overpowered. Should it become clear that Sherman's target was Charleston, Hardee was to evacuate that city and retreat toward Columbia.[69] Evidence indicates that Beauregard never expected to hold Charleston, since on December 27, 1864, before he left for Montgomery, he had ordered Hardee to make preparations "silently and cautiously" for the evacuation of the city.[70] Wheeler, who was being reinforced by Stephen D. Lee, was to divide his forces, with the main body to defend Branchville and, if necessary, fall back toward Columbia. Lee's cavalry was to cover Augusta and retreat toward that Georgia city, which was being defended by Hill. If it became apparent that Sherman was not going to attack Augusta, Lee's and Hill's troops were to be sent to Columbia.[71]

The policy adopted at the conference was in reality little more than a delaying action, and Beauregard must have recognized it from the beginning. The fact was that Beauregard did not intend to fight at Charleston or Augusta, and though it appears that he was attempting to concentrate in Columbia, there was no possibility that such a plan could be accomplished. Sherman's swift movement took away the advantage of interior lines, putting the Union army closer to Columbia than Beauregard's scattered forces were. Thus, the Southern commander's plans were negated before they could be implemented. Consequently, when Beauregard decided on February 14 to evacuate Charleston, he found that the garrison was flanked on the west and would have to retreat northwesterly toward Chester, South Carolina, rather than to Columbia as originally planned.[72] The effect of Beauregard's strategy, then, was to

[69] *OR*, Ser. 1, XLVII, pt. 2: 1084–1085; Williams, *P. G. T. Beauregard*, pp. 245–248.

[70] *OR*, Ser. 1, XLIV, 994. Hardee's command stretched inland to Augusta. Hughes, *General William J. Hardee*, p. 274.

[71] *OR*, Ser. 1, XLVII, pt. 2: 1084–1085, 1132; Liddell Hart, *Sherman*, p. 363.

[72] *OR*, Ser. 1, XLVII, pt. 2: 1132–1133, 1179–1180; Williams, *P. G. T. Beauregard*, p. 250. Chester, fifty miles north of Columbia, was a more unrealistic destination than the capital since Sherman was nearer Columbia than Hardee was.

preclude the adequate defense of Charleston or Augusta and ultimately to seal the fate of Columbia.

Though the plan of Beauregard and his subordinates lacked
imagination, the Southern commander was not without an alternative. He must have realized that Sherman would repeat the
tactics he had used in Georgia—a fact which was shortly apparent
—and that his best opportunity lay in concentrating his forces in
order to strike a severe blow against one wing of Sherman's army.
Beauregard's most propitious move would have been to attack
Sherman's left wing, which was headed in the direction of Augusta, a plan which would have been easiest since the Confederate
commander and his reinforcements were moving into South Carolina from the west. It seems safe to say that an assault on the left
wing would have stopped the drive toward Charleston, possibly
even forcing the right wing to turn toward Augusta. Since Charleston was not going to be defended, and an inland penetration behind the city would have forced its evacuation anyway, the attack
on Sherman's left flank seemed to be Beauregard's best option.

Further, the troop situation was not as hopeless as it appeared.
While it is true that Confederate forces were outnumbered more
than two to one, arms, ammunition, food, and other supplies were
available in abundance in Columbia. The weather also favored the
Southern commander. Sherman's march was harassed by constant
rains, which swelled the numerous swamps, flooded the creeks and
rivers, and made what few roads existed virtually impassable. It
was not unusual for Union soldiers to be forced to wade through
water up to their waists and to corduroy miles of roads with trees
and fence rails. In addition, the Confederates maintained railroad
communications between Columbia and Augusta until February 7
and between the capital and Charleston until February 15, which
would have allowed for rapid troop movement. With the Union
army divided by forty miles of swamps and muddy roads, it appears that a concentration of Southern forces could have been
accomplished. In the great days in Virginia in 1862, Southern
soldiers, when daringly led, had performed brilliantly under even
worse circumstances. The eminent British military historian, B. H.
Liddell Hart, summed up Southern possibilities in the following
manner: "In a country which afforded so many and strong natural

barriers a force of 33,000 should have been able to resist one of barely double its strength."[73]

The missing ingredient within the Confederate camp, however, was a belief in the possibility of success. The defeatism of Beauregard's leadership was abundantly clear when he reported to President Davis the decision reached at the council of war: "During the pending negotiations for peace, it was thought of the highest importance to hold Charleston and Augusta, as long as it was humanly possible."[74] Obviously, Beauregard never intended to put up a tenacious fight in Branchville, Charleston, Augusta, Columbia, or points north.

As late as February 6, 1865, Beauregard, still in Augusta, wrote the commanding officer at Columbia, Lieutenant Colonel Robert S. Means, that he was unsure of Sherman's intentions, but he urged that defensive preparations be made should the enemy decide to attack Columbia and Charleston simultaneously.[75] In response to these orders, some breastworks were constructed at Congaree Creek, a few miles below the capital, to intercept the enemy at that point.[76] Upon Beauregard's arrival at Columbia on February 10,[77] he learned that Hampton had no command and so placed him in charge of the troops in the vicinity of the capital.[78] Beaure-

[73] Liddell Hart, *Sherman*, pp. 360–364; *OR*, Ser. 1, XLVII, pt. 2: 1179–1180; Sherman, *Memoirs*, II, 273–274; Julian Wisner Hinkley, *A Narrative of Service with the Third Wisconsin Infantry*, p. 168.

[74] *OR*, Ser. 1, XLVII, pt. 2: 1085. Beauregard's reference was to the Hampton Roads Peace Conference, February 3, 1865, during which President Lincoln and Secretary of State William H. Seward met with Confederate agents R. M. T. Hunter, Alexander H. Stephens, and James A. Campbell. The conference broke up on the rocks of restoration of the Union and abolition.

[75] Ibid., pp. 1073, 1107.

[76] Deposition of Hampton, *Mixed Commission*, XXIII, 6.

[77] Williams, *P. G. T. Beauregard*, p. 250.

[78] *OR*, Ser. 1, XLVII, pt. 2: 1157. Apparently Hampton was not actively engaged in command of Butler's cavalry before February 10 and did not consider that the position he held during Beauregard's absence was one of official responsibility. When asked what his duties were relative to the forces in Columbia before he was ordered by President Davis to assume command of the cavalry in South Carolina on February 16, 1865, Hampton told the Mixed Commission, "I had no connection at all with them" (deposition of Hampton, *Mixed Commission*, XXIII, 35). In an undated diary entry between January 17 and February 10, 1865, Mrs. Chesnut seemed to confirm Hampton's assessment of his activities in Columbia: "Last night, General Hampton came in. I

gard also found several dispatches from Hardee, who was obviously nervous about the military situation and unsure when he should evacuate Charleston. Though physically ill and severely pressed for time, Beauregard left for the port city on February 13 to personally evaluate the situation.[79] While he was away, Hampton began building breastworks between the South Carolina Railroad depot and the Congaree River. Two or three thousand bales of cotton were used to construct these defenses.[80]

Beauregard returned to Columbia on February 15, and that night, in a despondent communique, he apprised General Robert E. Lee of the situation. He was "now positive" that Sherman's destination was Charlotte, North Carolina, Beauregard wrote, but he was unsure of the disposition of the insufficient troops at his disposal. He inquired if he should continue retreating in front of the enemy toward North Carolina or move westward into Georgia.[81] The implication was clear that Columbia would not be held, and the only problem remaining was the extrication of the Confederate army.

Later that night Beauregard ordered his troops on the western side of the Congaree River to hold their positions as long as "practicable" without endangering their capture and then to protect the bridge long enough to save their equipment. Upon being forced to retreat across the river, orders were issued to destroy the end sections of the bridge, thus preserving the main span. To cover this retreat, Beauregard ordered that guns be mounted to enfilade the approaches to the bridge. Two of the cannon were manned by Arsenal Academy cadets. Additional gun emplacements were constructed between the river and the town to prevent Union batteries from getting close enough to shell Columbia. During the early hours of the morning of February 16, the last Confederate troops retreating across the Congaree River bridge burned it against

---

am sure he would do something to save us, if he were put in supreme command here. As it is, he takes no interest, for he has no power" (Williams, *Diary from Dixie by Mary Boykin Chesnut,* p. 475).

[79] *OR,* Ser. 1, XLVII, pt. 2: 1158, 1167.

[80] Deposition of Pompey Adams, Dec. 13, 1872, No. 103, Wood and Heyworth *vs.* United States, *Mixed Commission,* XIV, 314.

[81] *OR,* Ser. 1, XLVII, pt. 2: 1193; Williams, *P. G. T. Beauregard,* p. 251.

Beauregard's express orders.[82] Shortly thereafter, the Saluda River bridge was destroyed by fire.[83] Later that same day Beauregard ordered Wheeler to prepare the Broad River bridge for destruction should it become necessary to burn it. Beauregard outlined the situation to Lee on the afternoon of February 16: "The present military situation is thus: Our forces, about 20,000 effective infantry and artillery, more or less demoralized, occupy a circumference of about 240 miles from Charleston to Augusta. The enemy, well organized and disciplined, and flushed with success, numbering nearly double our force, is concentrated upon one point (Columbia) of that circumference. Unless I can concentrate rapidly here, or in my rear, all available troops, the result cannot be long doubtful."[84]

By the night of February 15, only fifteen days after the invasion of South Carolina had begun in earnest, the Union army was within about four miles of Columbia. That night the so-called Battle of Columbia began, and there occurred the first of a number of unfortunate confrontations. Major General Charles R. Woods's First Division, XV Corps, quite carelessly camped in some open fields opposite Columbia within range of the Confederate artillery east of the Congaree River. Their exact position was betrayed after dark by their campfires, and they were bombarded all night, resulting in at least one death, several wounded, and a cold, uncomfortable night for the remainder.[85]

The next morning, February 16, the Union skirmish line car-

[82] *OR*, Ser. 1, XLVII, pt. 2: 1197–1198; deposition of Hampton, *Mixed Commission*, XXIII, 6, 18, 29; J. P. Thomas to R. J. Davant, Dec. 6, 1865, James L. Orr Papers, South Carolina Archives, Columbia; John Peyre Thomas, *The History of the South Carolina Military Academy, with Appendixes*, pp. 195–196. Although he was unaware that the defenders were Arsenal cadets, Major General William B. Hazen, looking across the river from the Union position, observed "mere boys" feverishly digging these gun emplacements. W. B. Hazen, *A Narrative of Military Service*, p. 348.

[83] Edwin J. Scott, *Random Recollections of a Long Life, 1806 to 1876*, p. 175.

[84] *OR*, Ser. 1, XLVII, pt. 1: 1048; pt. 2: 1207.

[85] Sherman, *Memoirs*, II, 277, 279; *Story of the Fifty-Fifth Regiment Illinois Volunteer Infantry in the Civil War, 1861–1865*, pp. 407–408; Oliver Otis Howard, *Autobiography of Oliver Otis Howard, Major General, United States Army*, II, 118–119.

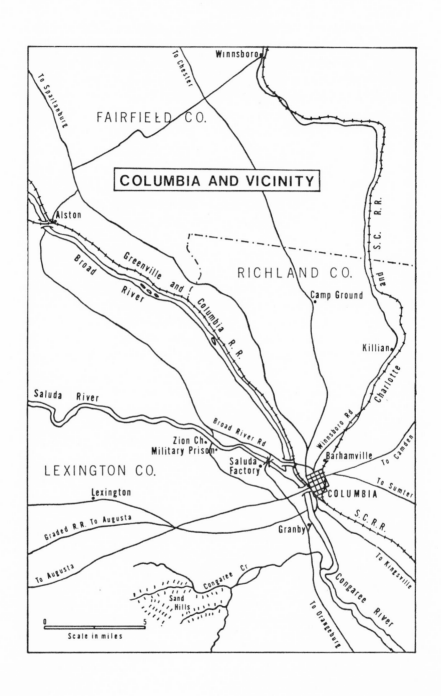

ried the Confederate defenses around the Congaree River bridge about daylight, but found the bridge burned. Confederate sharpshooters, just a few hundred yards across the Congaree, opened fire on the approaching Union troops and proved to be "exceedingly" annoying. A regiment of sharpshooters and two guns from Captain Francis DeGress's battery were quickly placed in action and succeeded in silencing the Confederate cannon and sharpshooters. Another section of the battery, from a hill about a mile from the State House, began harassing Columbia by shelling the South Carolina Railroad station, where it appeared that supplies were still being evacuated. Troop concentrations and other strategic points were also shelled intermittently; there was no indication at that time that Columbia would be surrendered.[86] Indeed, Sherman and many of his troops were of the opinion that the town would not be taken without a fight.[87]

On February 16 Sherman issued Special Field Order No. 26, giving instructions for the occupation of Columbia: "General Howard will cross the Saluda and Broad rivers as near their mouths as possible, occupy Columbia, destroy the public buildings, railroad property, manufacturing and machine shops, but will spare libraries and asylums and private dwellings."[88] The terms of this order had probably been discussed by Sherman and Howard before they reached Columbia, and the actual document had more than likely been dictated sometime on the fifteenth. It was a routine order for Sherman; indeed, it was virtually the same order that was issued upon the occupation of Savannah. Later, however, doubt arose in Sherman's mind regarding the order. The cannonading of his troops in their sleep on the night of the fifteenth had especially nettled him. He considered the cannon fire a deliberately malicious act, contrary to "civilized warfare," and con-

[86] *OR*, Ser. 1, XLVII, pt. 1: 197–198, 227, 271, 379; LIII, 1053.

[87] David P. Conyngham, *Sherman's March Through the South, with Sketches and Incidents of the Campaign*, p. 325; E. J. Sherlock, *Memorabilia of the Marches and Battles in which the One Hundredth Regiment of Indiana Infantry Volunteers Took an Active Part: War of the Rebellion, 1861–5*, p. 195; *Story of the Fifty-Fifth Illinois*, p. 407.

[88] *OR*, Ser. 1, XLVII, pt. 2: 444.

templated the destruction of Columbia in retaliation. After reflection and discussion of his thoughts with Howard, however, Sherman decided to let the original order stand.[89]

[89] Deposition of William T. Sherman, Dec. 11, 1872, No. 103, No. 292, Cowlam Graveley *vs.* United States, *Mixed Commission*, XIV, 95–97.

2

The Evacuation of Columbia

IT was not until refugees from the surrounding counties began to pour into the capital and the sound of cannon was heard in the distance that the authorities began the evacuation of Columbia, less than a week before the city fell. The Confederate leaders, thoroughly confused by Sherman's tactics and speed, were so imbued by an air of defeatism that they were unable to function adequately on either the military or civilian levels.[1] As a result, the evacuation of badly needed military supplies was a disaster, and nothing was done to prepare the citizens for occupation by the enemy.

Oddly enough, it was the Confederate authorities in Richmond, Virginia, who, on February 10, 1865, even though they had no first-hand information of the military situation, took the first step in the evacuation of Confederate property from Columbia. On that date Joseph LeConte received orders to dismantle the chemical laboratory in Columbia and ship it to Richmond. Professor LeConte worked diligently from the tenth until the thirteenth packing his equipment in boxes. Early Tuesday morning, February 14, the boxes were transported to the railway depot for

---

[1] *Richmond Whig*, March 7, 1865. The article was written in Charlotte on February 22 by F. G. DeFountaine, editor of the *Columbia Daily South Carolinian*. See also Joseph LeConte, "A Journal of Three Months Personal Experience During the Last Days of the Confederacy," Feb. 8–15, 1865, Joseph LeConte Collection, South Caroliniana Library, University of South Carolina, Columbia; *War of the Rebellion: A Compilation of the Official Records of the Union and Confederate Armies*, Ser. 2, VIII, 210, 213 (hereafter cited as *OR*); *Columbia Phoenix*, March 21, 1865.

evacuation, and upon his arrival there LeConte found the station "jammed to suffocation" with people trying to flee Columbia. The docks were filled to capacity with government and private freight, and since there appeared to be no established priorities, a contest developed for every available inch of space. LeConte spent the entire day of the fourteenth in an unsuccessful attempt to secure freight cars to evacuate the laboratory equipment. Early the next morning he returned to renew his efforts, and during the day, after "much entreaty and considerable threatening," LeConte was able to get his cargo loaded. That evening, about six o'clock, Le-Conte returned to the depot to ascertain if his equipment had actually left Columbia and learned that it had, but he found the terminal still crowded with panic-stricken refugees pleading to be taken aboard the trains.[2]

Everyone wanted a car, and the president of the Charlotte and South Carolina Railroad, Colonel William Johnson, and his assistants faced the impossible task of attempting to coordinate transportation. The major problem was that the South Carolina and Greenville tracks were under the immediate threat of being cut by Sherman's left wing a few miles northwest of Columbia, leaving only the Charlotte line open. This situation necessitated the movement of all rolling stock at the South Carolina depot to the Charlotte station. Unfortunately, the circuitous, time-consuming route between the terminals was inadequate for the emergency, creating a bottleneck; as a result, much irreplaceable equipment was lost. Amazingly, in the fight for space, the government managed to evacuate a number of young ladies employed with the Treasury Department as note signers in two special trains consisting of five cars each. The girls were able to leave Columbia with "all their baggage [and] supplies," their only losses being their hoop skirts, which could not be crowded into the cars.[3]

As the enemy drew ever nearer to Columbia, hundreds of

[2] LeConte, "Journal," Feb. 8–15, 1865.

[3] *Richmond Whig*, March 7, 1865; *Richmond Dispatch*, Feb. 23, 1865, quoted in the *New York Herald*, Feb. 26, 1865. Mrs. Wade Hampton left the city on one of these trains. See James Conner et al., eds., *South Carolina Women in the Confederacy*, II, 182.

anxious citizens sought to save their valuables by leaving the city through any means available. Among them was Joseph LeConte, who hurriedly decided on February 14 to pack anything moveable and leave town. The pandemonium at his house on the South Carolina College campus could almost be compared to that at the railroad stations, with clothing thrown over furniture and trunks in the middle of the floor. In an atmosphere of tension and misery, the LeContes packed up everything that could be moved—linen, blankets, clothing, silver, jewelry, and even wine.[4] About 6:00 A.M. on Thursday, February 16, Joseph LeConte; his brother John LeConte and John's son Johnny; Major Allen J. Green, the Columbia post commander; and twenty-two Negroes, sixteen of whom were Niter Bureau employees, left Columbia heading northwestward in a caravan of two wagons, two carts, and one buggy. On these vehicles they carried all their worldly possessions in addition to the Niter Bureau property, all of which was eventually lost.[5]

In these last-minute efforts of the government and inhabitants to get property out of town, citizens and officials alike began to panic. The situation was described to Emma LeConte by her father: "The streets in town are lined with panic-stricken crowds, trying to escape. All is confusion and turmoil."[6] By Wednesday, February 15, Columbia had become the scene of so much confusion and disorder that the authorities were forced to declare martial law. That night, as the retreating Confederates streamed into town, there were several reports of robberies, violence, and riotous con-

---

[4] Earl Schenck Miers, ed., *When the World Ended: The Diary of Emma LeConte*, pp. 30–31; LeConte, "Journal," Feb. 8–15, 16, 1865. LeConte was warned by a mysterious "Mr. Davis," who appears to have been a Confederate secret agent. Davis visited the LeConte home on several occasions during the evacuation with warnings of the city's impending capture.

[5] LeConte, "Journal," Feb. 8–15, 16, 1865. While attempting to escape Columbia, LeConte's wagons were overtaken by Union soldiers of Sherman's left wing, who sequestered all food and destroyed the wagons and other property, including the Niter Bureau equipment. Upon returning home, LeConte learned that no soldiers had entered his home and, since the fire did not reach the college campus, that all his property had been saved. LeConte, "Journal," Feb. 18–24, 1865.

[6] Miers, *When the World Ended*, p. 30.

duct on their part. Some of the stores on Richardson Street were broken into and their contents taken.[7] A letter to the *Richmond Whig*, written from Charlotte on February 22, described the pillage of Columbia on February 16:

> A party of Wheeler's cavalry, accompanied by their officers, dashed into town, tied their horses, and as systematically as if they had been bred to the business, proceeded to break into the stores along Main [Richardson] street and rob them of their contents. A detachment of detailed men fired on one party and drove them out. Captain Hamilton, the Provost Marshal, with another officer, drew swords and pistols on another party, and succeeded in clearing several establishments; but the valiant raiders still swarmed like locusts, and to-day, a hundred miles away from Columbia, you may see men smoking the cigars and wearing on their saddles the elegant cloths stolen from the merchants of that city. . . .
>
> Under these circumstances you may well imagine that our people would rather see the Yankees or old Satan himself than a party of the aforesaid Wheeler's cavalry.[8]

When Wade Hampton attempted to stop some of this looting, one of the cavalrymen drew his weapon and threatened the general. Without condoning their actions, Hampton rationalized their conduct by stating that the men were stragglers who were cut off from their brigades and under the influence of alcohol they had acquired in Columbia. Colonel E. E. Portlock, a Confederate officer who saw the Hampton incident, wrote of the disorder in Columbia: "It is beyond question that many disgraceful acts were committed during the evacuation of Columbia, but there were other troops than Wheeler's corps there and all doubtless participated."[9] As the

---

[7] *Columbia Phoenix*, March 21, 1865; Edwin J. Scott, *Random Recollections of a Long Life, 1806 to 1876*, p. 175.

[8] *Richmond Whig*, March 7, 1865. William Gilmore Simms described the atmosphere in Columbia as "riotous conduct" and "highway robberies," and though "some few stores were broken open and robbed," he thought "it was indeed wonderful that, with so many soldiers in town, with so much confusion among the people, there should have been so little disorder" (*Columbia Phoenix*, March 21, 1865). This criticism of Wheeler was not an isolated event. See John P. Dyer, *"Fightin' Joe" Wheeler*, pp. 213–215.

[9] Henry S. Nourse, "The Burning of Columbia, S.C., February 17, 1865," in *Operations on the Atlantic Coast 1861–1865; Virginia 1862, 1864; Vicksburg*, IX, 430; B. H. Liddell Hart, *Sherman: Soldier, Realist, American*, p. 366.

contents of the stores were scattered in the streets, goods sometimes came into the possession of respectable citizens. Emma Le-Conte reported that a visitor to her home who had been on Richardson Street when the stores were broken into brought her "a present of a box of fancy feathers and one or two other little things he had picked up."[10]

One of the few successes the Confederate authorities had in the evacuation of Columbia was the removal of Union prisoners. Early in the war a decision had been reached to establish a prison for Union soldiers in Columbia, but when plans for the compound did not materialize, the authorities were forced to use the local county jail. By September, 1863, there were three hundred men packed into two floors of a building seventy feet long and fifty feet wide with a small adjoining prison yard. Included in this number were twenty-seven Confederate deserters and several civil prisoners. The conditions were such that many of the prisoners were forced to live in the prison yard. The extremely crowded conditions, the lack of a sufficient number of guards, and the presence of Confederate, state, and county authorities with conflicting authority to control different classifications of prisoners led to much confusion and numerous escape attempts, some of which were successful. There were constant complaints from local prison officials about the inadequacies of the facilities, but the Confederate government was never in a position to provide better quarters.[11]

With the demise of the exchange cartel in mid-1863, the burden on Confederate prisons increased, and the number of prisoners in Columbia grew dramatically in late 1864 when a large number of captured Union officers were shipped to the South Carolina capital. The site chosen for a prison to house them was on

Hampton denied that there was any misconduct, stating that he "never saw or heard anything of stragglers in the streets of Columbia" except on one occasion when he confronted some of Wheeler's men, who were looting a public building. When asked to desist, "they made some remonstrance," Hampton continued, but "I would say for them that I think they had been drinking" (deposition of Wade Hampton, April 23, 1873, No. 236, David Jacobs *vs.* United States, *Mixed Commission on British and American Claims. Appendix: Testimony*, XXIII, 45).

[10] Miers, *When the World Ended*, p. 36; *Columbia Phoenix*, April 1, 1865.
[11] *OR*, Ser. 2, VI, 296; VII, 611–612.

the west side of the Saluda River several miles northwest of the city. Brigadier General John H. Winder, commissary general of the Confederate prisons, described the area as "nothing but an open field" and "entirely unfit" for habitation. The compound was guarded by about 350 "very raw recruits" commanded by Lieutenant Colonel R. Stark Means of the "Invalid Corps."

During their internment at the new prison, no meat was issued to the prisoners, their major food supply being "sorghum and corn-meal."[12] For shelter the prisoners at Camp Sorghum, as it came to be known, dug holes in the mud and covered them with twigs, leaves, and branches from the abundant pine trees in the area. Others, more fortunate, were able to build small pine shanties.[13] Escapes from Camp Sorghum were so numerous that Columbians kept up a steady stream of complaints to the newspapers and to Governor M. L. Bonham, who was nearing the end of his term. To solve the problem of the poor living conditions and the large number of escapes, Governor Bonham agreed to move the prisoners to the South Carolina Insane Asylum until a permanent site could be constructed fourteen miles north of the city on the Columbia-Charlotte railroad. By the time this decision was reached on December 6, 1864, a total of 373 prisoners had made good their escape.[14] The transfer of the prisoners to the male section of the asylum was accomplished in mid-December.[15]

Through newspapers and compassionate citizens, the Union prisoners learned of many of Sherman's accomplishments, and in late January word that his troops were crossing the Savannah River raised hopes of liberation.[16] These expectations, however, were soon dashed when on February 12, only five days before Sherman reached Columbia, Beaureguard was ordered to transport

[12] Ibid., VII, 894, 1046, 1196–1197; *Columbia Daily South Carolinian*, Oct. 19, 1864.

[13] Samuel Hawkins Marshall Byers, "The Burning of Columbia," *Lippincott's Magazine* 29 (March, 1882): 256.

[14] *OR*, Ser. 2, VII, 1062, 1179–1180, 1184, 1196, 1220. Governor Bonham and other local leaders were adamantly opposed to locating a new prison near Columbia.

[15] Byers, "Burning of Columbia," p. 256; Gilbert E. Sabre, *Nineteen Months a Prisoner of War*, pp. 165–166.

[16] Sabre, *Prisoner of War*, p. 168; Byers, "Burning of Columbia," p. 256.

the eighteen hundred Union prisoners to Charlotte.[17] The next day six hundred prisoners were moved out. That night there was a frantic search by many of those remaining for a hiding place to escape evacuation. Some buried themselves beneath sand, twigs, and leaves, while others removed boards and hid in the ceilings and eaves of the buildings. The next day, February 14, after the remaining prisoners had been removed, Confederate details probed the asylum grounds to ferret out those attempting to escape. Some were discovered and sent to Charlotte; others remained undetected. When the Union army entered Columbia on February 17, 1865, it was greeted by more than thirty former Union prisoners who had managed to evade Confederate authorities.[18]

While the Confederate authorities were successful in removing the Union prisoners, their evacuation of ordnance and commissary stores was a fiasco. During the first week in February, Captain C. C. McPhail, the head of the Confederate armory, became apprehensive about the defense of Columbia and on his own initiative began building boxes for the evacuation of his machinery and stores. Then, late on the evening of February 11, he learned unofficially of an order from the post commander for the removal of stores as a precautionary measure. Believing that the order would be officially issued shortly, Captain McPhail commenced packing his equipment and supplies in the prepared boxes.

On Sunday morning, February 12, McPhail requested thirty freight cars to evacuate the armory equipment, but he was informed by the post commander that the order was for "preparations" only and should not be construed to mean the suspension of operations. Convinced that the danger was imminent, Captain McPhail continued to pack his equipment, completing the task on Monday night, February 13. Meanwhile, he attempted to secure wagons to take the boxes to the depot and freight cars for their evacuation. McPhail constantly reminded Captain Thomas R.

[17] *OR*, Ser. 2, VIII, 210, 213. There is some confusion about exactly how many Union prisoners were in Columbia. The figures given by the Confederate authorities range from twelve hundred to eighteen hundred.

[18] Byers, "Burning of Columbia," pp. 257–258; Sabre, *Prisoner of War*, pp. 269–271. It required between ten and twelve cars to move the prisoners. *Richmond Whig*, March 7, 1865.

Sharp, the quartermaster of transportation, of the importance of saving the armory; his exhortations, however, went unheeded. Sharp, besieged for transportation from every side, had been ordered by Beauregard on the fifteenth to give first preference to medical and ordnance stores,[19] but in reality there appeared to be little coordination of any sort.

Desperately, McPhail sought out Hampton—Beauregard was in Charleston—and begged him to give a direct order for the evacuation of the armory equipment, or at least the removal of the irreplaceable stock machines. Hampton wrote out an order for the stock machines to be transferred to the depot, but the transportation department, maintaining that other goods had preference, would not honor it. With Hampton's orders in hand, Captain McPhail turned to the streets, where he was able to impress enough wagons to haul his stock machines to the South Carolina Railroad depot. There the machines sat until the night of the fifteenth, when, after McPhail had poured out his "most urgent and importunate solicitations," Beauregard provided four freight cars. McPhail managed to load some of the machines that night, but the next morning, February 16, the Union army appeared opposite Columbia and began shelling the railroad terminal. The shelling forced McPhail to send the freight cars to the Charlotte station, where they were to wait for the remaining machines, which were to follow by wagon. Before the boxes in the depot could be loaded onto wagons, however, the bombardment became "too hot" to allow men or wagons in the area, and as a result one or two pieces of machinery were lost.

In establishing his priorities, McPhail had concentrated on the armory's stock machines, but he was later forced to confess to the ordnance chief in Richmond, General Josiah Gorgas, that the delay by local authorities would have made it impossible to remove his equipment even if transportation had existed. By the night of the fifteenth the enemy artillery directly opposite the armory on the west side of the Congaree River "completely covered" the buildings, preventing anything from being saved after that date. "I am deeply mortified and chagrined to report," he

[19] *OR*, Ser. 1, LIII, 1051–1052. Beauregard gave the "preparations" order on or about February 10. See *OR*, Ser. 1, XLVII, pt. 2: 1208.

wrote, "that my entire establishment was lost." With the exception of the stock machines, McPhail continued, "I did not save an article of any kind."[20]

The evacuation of the other Confederate stores in Columbia was equally mishandled. On February 11 General Gorgas in Richmond telegraphed Major N. R. Chambliss in Charleston to give instructions for the evacuation of that city and to order him then to proceed to Columbia, where he was to assume command of the removal of supplies. Chambliss received the order on the twelfth, but because of the indirect rail route necessitated by the advance of the enemy he did not arrive in Columbia until the night of the fourteenth. To his dismay he found the "long trains" at the station filled not with government supplies but with the private property of fleeing citizens, all of whom had vouchers. Chambliss, making no attempt to appropriate those trains to remove government property, decided to wait until the next morning to begin the evacuation. The next day, the fifteenth, as it became apparent that nothing had been done to evacuate supplies, Chambliss went to see the chief quartermaster, Major Roland Rhett. Together they proceeded to the office of Major John T. Trezevant, ordnance officer and head of the arsenal, where a priority list for the removal of vital supplies was drawn up. With this list Chambliss and Rhett went to Beauregard's headquarters, where Colonel John M. Otey, chief of staff, wrote out an order to Captain Sharp, transportation quartermaster, to provide wagons and freight cars for the evacuation of the supplies. By the time these arrangements had been worked out, however, Major Trezevant's "store" had come under fire from the enemy, making it impossible to load the supplies. The two men then parted, with Rhett promising to acquire wagons and have them at the warehouse after dark when it was presumed

[20] Ibid., LIII, 1052–1053; John Peyre Thomas, *The History of the South Carolina Military Academy, with Appendixes*, p. 196. A Confederate straggler in Columbia on February 16–17, 1865, believed that the Union artillery was concentrating on military objectives: "[We] found a dozen or more cavalry men on the same mission as ours, which was to take in the city, lest that part where the enemy were shelling. They seemed to have been put onto the whereabouts of ammunition storage and they kept up a continuous thump at that point from their artillery . . ." (William Andrew Fletcher, *Rebel Private, Front and Rear*, pp. 172–173).

that the supplies could be loaded, though Chambliss was not without misgivings.[21]

During the remainder of the day Chambliss, believing that nightfall might be too late, continued his efforts to procure wagons to move the supplies. Offers of five hundred dollars to passing wagons were ineffective, with the response always the same: the wagon was being used by "some officer" to remove "valuable government supplies." After dark Chambliss went to the railroad station and waited in vain for the arrival of Trezevant's stores. Realizing that the military situation was rapidly deteriorating, and witnessing the "panic" at the railroad station, Chambliss decided to walk to Trezevant's warehouse to ascertain the delay. He found the building deserted.

About midnight Chambliss returned to the depot, still hoping to commandeer freight cars. When the arsenal mechanics, who were being withdrawn with their machines, arrived, Chambliss discovered a freight car filled with Treasury Department employees and their luggage, whom he "turned out by force." Chambliss and the mechanics then loaded some ammunition that was already at the terminal into the car, and by "dint of threats" managed to get it attached to a train leaving Columbia.[22]

The loss of Confederate ordnance and commissary stores in Columbia was extensive. On February 15 Major Trezevant had estimated that it would require twenty freight cars to evacuate the 300,000 pounds of supplies at the Columbia arsenal, which consisted of fifty boxes of machinery, five hundred boxes of valuable stores, and two hundred pigs of lead. In addition, there were in Columbia seventy carloads of equipment that had been shipped from the Charleston arsenal. Of the ninety carloads of government supplies, the Confederate officials managed to evacuate 105,000 rounds of small ammunition, some "cash receipts," and a few official papers, which meant that the Charleston and Columbia arsenals were, as Major Chambliss phrased it, "squandered"

---

[21] *OR*, Ser. 1, LIII, 1049–1050. Chambliss's report stated that Otey ordered Sharp "to furnish the transportation *if possible*, which Major Rhett said he would see that he did . . ." (italics added). Chambliss was not involved in the evacuation of the armory.

[22] Ibid., p. 1050.

in the evacuation of Columbia.[23] In attempting to explain what one member of his staff called the worst "confusion and mismanagement" he had ever seen,[24] Beauregard was forced to confess a "lack of energy" on the part of the authorities.[25] General Josiah Gorgas, chief of Confederate ordnance, termed the loss of machinery and stores as perhaps the greatest of the war. An investigation by Gorgas's office was still unfinished when the war ended.[26]

The State of South Carolina also possessed a large military establishment in Columbia, and its failure to evacuate its war supplies rivaled the inefficiency of the Confederate government. As in the case of the Confederate authorities, there was apparently no planning from beginning to end. South Carolina Commissary General Richard Caldwell maintained a state commissary department warehouse on Richardson Street near Upper Boundary. From these supplies Caldwell provided food for several state regiments which were operating in central South Carolina and for Major John Niernsee's laborers, who were engaged in strengthening the defenses in and around the capital. Caldwell was busy making plans to feed an additional five thousand militiamen "expected" to come to the defense of Columbia when he was informed by the state auditor on February 15 that Governor Magrath had ordered the removal of important state papers from the capital. Since other departments were preparing to leave, the auditor wondered if Caldwell wanted transportation to evacuate commissary supplies. Taken aback by this turn of events, but anxious not to lose his entire stock, Caldwell asked for and received a requisition for ten freight cars. Though he had not yet received official orders regarding evacuation, Caldwell spent the remainder of the day attempting to secure the ten cars promised. Late in the afternoon he was able to procure two freight cars, having been told that all others were

[23] Ibid., pp. 1049–1051. Chambliss thought it possible that "some few supplies" from Charleston may not have reached Columbia and thereby may have escaped destruction.

[24] "Jno. W. G." to sister, March 1, 1865, William T. Sherman Papers, Manuscript Division, Library of Congress, Washington, D.C.; John G. Barrett, *Sherman's March through the Carolinas*, p. 67.

[25] *OR*, Ser. 1, XLVII, pt. 2: 1208.

[26] Ibid., LIII, 1049–1050; Frank E. Vandiver, *Ploughshares into Swords: Josiah Gorgas and Confederate Ordnance*, pp. 260–261.

in "Confederate service." They were loaded during the night, but for want of an engine the cars remained at the terminal until the morning of the seventeenth. The goods arrived safely in Chester on the eighteenth under the charge of Captain J. R. Chrietzberg, who decided on the night of the twentieth to take the freight on to Charlotte, North Carolina. A few miles south of Rock Hill, South Carolina, the locomotive was forced to detach the cars to go in search of water. Upon returning for the abandoned train, the engine rammed the unlighted freight cars, so severely damaging the first car, which was laden with South Carolina commissary property, that it had to be left behind.[27]

At Charlotte Captain Chrietzberg managed to acquire an engine and freight car to retrieve the stores, but when he reached the abandoned car he found that the supplies had been appropriated by a detachment of the Confederate army. Dejected, Chrietzberg returned to Charlotte, where he learned to his further dismay that most of the supplies in the Charlotte rail yard would probably be burned because of the approach of the enemy. Rather than see the commissary department's goods go up in smoke, he offered them to the Confederate authorities, who accepted only the bacon. The remainder of the goods were sold to the Charlotte merchant house of Stenhouse and Macaulay. Caldwell had evacuated only two carloads of supplies, which were then promptly lost.

South Carolina Quartermaster General John T. Sloan appears to have been slightly more successful in evacuating state property. On February 12 the card-making machines, cards, and other materials from the state-owned factory were packed and shipped to Charlotte by way of Winnsboro, South Carolina. In Charlotte the factory superintendent, F. F. C. H. DuBose, after determining that he would be unable to protect the machines from vandalism and inclement weather, sold them to the firm of Stenhouse and Macaulay.[28] To remove additional property, Sloan secured nineteen

[27] South Carolina, *Report of the Special Joint Committee, in Regard to Certain Public Property on Hand at the Evacuation of Columbia, and the Surrender of Gen. Johnston's Army*, pp. 16–22. It is not clear whether there were no flares available or whether this collision was a case of neglect. Caldwell's report indicated that he never received orders to evacuate Columbia.

[28] Ibid., pp. 17, 22–24. The reference could be to the factory behind the State House or possibly the one near Sidney Park.

horses and mules to haul supplies to the railroad. But on the night of February 14, before he could make use of them, Governor Magrath ordered that they be given temporarily to Captain B. F. Evans for placing cannon for the defense of Columbia. Sloan never saw the teams again. After that, Sloan was unable to acquire any transportation for the removal of quartermaster stores. He spent the fifteenth and sixteenth aiding the state auditor in transferring the archives and records of South Carolina to the Charlotte terminal. Fortunately, the state archives were evacuated safely and eventually were returned to Columbia.

The state ordnance officer, W. G. Eason, was able to evacuate only seventy-five thousand rounds of small-arms cartridges, which he distributed to the army in Charlotte. He blamed the failure to withdraw more material on the dearth of transportation.[29]

The loss of state supplies in the evacuation of Columbia was so appalling that it later sparked an investigation by South Carolina authorities. In 1866 the legislature created by Andrew Johnson appointed a special joint committee to ascertain the facts surrounding the withdrawal. The commissary, quartermaster, and ordnance officers were asked to describe their activities during the evacuation and to enumerate state property they had on hand at the surrender of General Joseph E. Johnston. Commissary General Richard Caldwell reported that the only property in his possession was the burned-out commissary building. The committee was informed by Quartermaster General Sloan that he had state funds consisting of $4.75 in specie, $551.40 in paper money, and a worthless promissory note for $34,890.00. The ordnance officer, W. G. Eason, reported no state property in his possession. The conclusions of the special joint committee were forthright: "From all the information obtained, it appears to admit of no doubt but that Columbia was evacuated in great haste and confusion, without any settled plan, or controlling head, to direct the conduct of affairs. Each officer of the State Government appears to have acted upon his own responsibility in determining when to leave the city, whither to go and how to get transportation. Each functionary appears likewise, to have been left pretty much to himself in deciding

[29] Ibid., pp. 15, 24–25.

what property to remove, and how to dispose of it after removal."[30] Without calling his name, the joint committee of the legislature placed the blame for the chaos and loss of state property in the evacuation of Columbia on South Carolina's chief executive, Governor Andrew Gordon Magrath. Though he must share much responsibility for the disaster, the criticism is not entirely fair. Neither Magrath nor the people of South Carolina were properly informed of the situation by Confederate military authorities. Beauregard and Hampton, who appears to have been little help to his superior in liaison with the governor, did not expect to stop Sherman, but failed to apprise state and local authorities of that fact. For their failure to communicate with Magrath, both Beauregard and Hampton must share the responsibility for the immense losses.

One of the most crucial problems that had to be dealt with by the authorities in Columbia's evacuation was the disposition of the cotton stored there. The Confederacy had quite early seen the value of cotton as a source of collateral, and soon that commodity was being stored in numerous Southern towns. By 1864 Columbia, conveniently remote from the battle fronts and propitiously located near railroads and rivers, had cotton stored in every available warehouse, basement, and vacant building.[31] Confederate policy, however, was that as the Union army advanced into the South, the stored cotton was to be burned; with Sherman in central South Carolina the authorities knew what had to be done. Consequently, on February 14 Beauregard, through General Hampton, ordered the post commander to move both Confederate and privately owned cotton outside the city to be burned.[32] Unfortunately, the

30 Ibid., pp. 3, 5, 15–16.

31 J. G. Randall and David Donald, *The Civil War and Reconstruction*, p. 259; Anthony Toomer Porter, *The History of a Work of Faith and Love in Charleston, South Carolina, Which Grew Out of the Calamities of the Late Civil War, and a Record of God's Wonderful Providence*, pp. 110–111.

32 Deposition of Hampton, *Mixed Commission*, XXIII, 14–15, 30–32; undated copy, Allen J. Green to [D. H. Trezevant?], in "Notes on the Burning of Columbia," miscellaneous manuscripts and copies of letters, Daniel Heyward Trezevant Papers, South Caroliniana Library, University of South Carolina, Columbia; *The Burning of Columbia. I. A Letter of Gen. Wade Hampton, June 24, 1873, With Appendix. II. Report of Committee of Citizens, Ex-Chancellor J. P. Carroll, Chairman, May 1866*, pp. 4–5 (hereafter cited as *Burning of Co-*

lack of transportation made it impossible for Major Green to carry out this order, so he decided to roll the bales into the streets, with the idea of burning the cotton there. The next day, February 15, the order to burn the cotton was published in the Columbia newspapers.[33] During the fifteenth and sixteenth most of the cotton was moved into the streets.

While it is not possible to pinpoint the location of all the cotton, some sites and amounts can be confirmed. The most conspicuous piles of cotton, as well as the most controversial, were those on Richardson Street. Beginning at Richland Street a large number of bales stretched down Richardson to Laurel Street, where, at the intersection in front of City Hotel, there were about 200 bales. Another pile of cotton was stacked at the corner of Blanding Street on Richardson, and about two blocks south between Plain and Washington streets there were 100 bales. Near the capitol square there were several concentrations of cotton. A little over a block to the north there were perhaps 150 bales on Richardson between Lady and Washington streets. Near the old statehouse there was yet another stack estimated at 50 bales. The remaining cotton on Richardson was the vast amount in the warehouses in Cotton Town which had not actually been moved into the streets.[34]

Off Richardson Street cotton had been piled in several other areas. There was an unknown quantity of cotton on Blanding

lumbia, Letter and Report). It has been suggested by James Ford Rhodes, *History of the United States from the Compromise of 1850 to the Final Restoration of Home Rule at the South in 1877*, V, 382, that the Confederate government burned one million bales of cotton during the first year of the war to keep them from falling into Northern hands. This policy continued throughout the war. When Hardee did not burn the cotton stored in Savannah, he received a letter from General Samuel Cooper on February 5, 1865, demanding an explanation. *OR*, Ser. 1, XLVII, pt. 2: 1105.

[33] *Burning of Columbia, Letter and Report*, p. 4.

[34] Deposition of Charlotte Goldstien, May 12, 1873, No. 236, *Mixed Commission*, XXIII, 12; deposition of John McKenzie, April 29, 1872, No. 37, Joseph J. Browne *vs.* United States, *Mixed Commission*, III, 28–29; deposition of Milo H. Berry, March 16, 1872, No. 37, *Mixed Commission*, III, 20; deposition of William Glaze, March 18, 1872, No. 37, *Mixed Commission*, III, 24; deposition of Junius Chapman, Dec. 12, 1872, No. 103, Wood and Heyworth *vs.* United States, *Mixed Commission*, XIV, 326–327; deposition of John McKenzie, April 9, 1872, No. 103, *Mixed Commission*, XIV, 11; James Guignard Gibbes, *Who Burnt Columbia?*, p. 7.

Street near Sidney Park, and about one hundred bales were lined up on Senate Street. Cotton was also placed on Sumter Street on the two blocks between Gervais and Washington streets, and another cluster stood near the Methodist Female College at the corner of Plain and Pickens streets. Finally, a large amount of cotton was placed on Gervais Street west of the capitol building, not far from a tremendous concentration of two thousand to three thousand bales on Pottersfield next to the South Carolina Railroad yards. The remainder of the cotton removed from storage was placed on the back streets of Columbia, and after the conflagration between eight hundred and twelve hundred bales were found unburned.[35]

At about eight o'clock on the night of February 16 Wade Hampton learned that he had been promoted to Lieutenant General and placed in command of the cavalry operating in South Carolina. Shortly thereafter, when he met with Beauregard to discuss Columbia's evacuation, Hampton urged that the cotton not be burned because it would endanger the city. Beauregard was apparently of a similar opinion but, for reasons never explained, delayed a final decision until the next morning.[36] Early on the seventeenth, upon assuming his command, Hampton once again discussed with Beauregard the problems involved in firing the cotton placed in the streets. The South Carolinian reiterated his position that the cotton should not be burned because the stiff wind blowing out of the northwest would spread the flames and destroy the en-

[35] Deposition of Edward Reed, Dec. 12, 1872, No. 103, *Mixed Commission*, XIV, 312; deposition of Gabriel Cooper, Dec. 18, 1872, No. 103, *Mixed Commission*, XIV, 320; deposition of James G. Gibbes, May 1, 1872, No. 103, *Mixed Commission*, XIV, 27; deposition of Edward Kyer, May 1, 1872, No. 103, *Mixed Commission*, XIV, 24; deposition of Manuel B. Jones, Dec. 12, 1872, No. 103, *Mixed Commission*, XIV, 308; deposition of Pompey Adams, Dec. 13, 1872, No. 103, *Mixed Commission*, XIV, 314; deposition of Charles R. Woods, Dec. 16, 1872, No. 103, No. 292, Cowlam Graveley *vs.* United States, *Mixed Commission*, XIV, 197; deposition of O. Z. Bates, April 8, 1872, No. 103, *Mixed Commission*, XIV, 6; deposition of McKenzie, April 29, 1872, *Mixed Commission*, III, 26; A. E. Wood, "Burning of Columbia, S.C.," *North American Review* 146 (April, 1888): 402; *OR*, Ser. 1, XLVII, pt. 1: 243. The college was not an official Methodist institution. *Columbia Daily South Carolinian*, May 4, 13, 1864.

[36] Deposition of Hampton, *Mixed Commission*, XXIII, 2–3, 32; A. R. Chisolm, "Beauregard's and Hampton's Orders on Evacuating Columbia—Letter from Colonel A. R. Chisolm," *Southern Historical Society Papers* 7 (May, 1879): 249.

tire town. Hampton argued further that Sherman obviously could not take the cotton with him and perhaps it might be spared the Federal torch. Beauregard concurred. Hampton's order not to burn the cotton, issued at approximately seven o'clock in the morning, was the first he gave on February 17 after assuming command.[37] It should be noted that the order could not be issued through the post commander, Major Allen J. Green, under whose authority it was originally published, since he had fled the city the previous morning. The matter was further complicated by the fact that the order could not be published in the newspapers, and with the confusion that existed in Columbia it was going to be exceedingly difficult—if not impossible—to see that every soldier became aware of the new order. Finally, Hampton did not post guards over the cotton during the evacuation either on the night of the sixteenth or the morning of the seventeenth.

The evacuation of Columbia was further complicated by a superabundance of alcoholic beverages. Many refugees taking flight to Columbia counted whiskey and wine among their essentials and took it with them. In addition, Charleston merchants early in the war had begun a policy of shipping large quantities of whiskey to the capital to prevent its destruction in the bombardment of the port city. To this amount must be added the extensive stocks of the Columbia merchants. David Jacobs, for example, had over four hundred gallons of whiskey and sixty cases of brandy in his store. Other stores possessed rich supplies of rye and corn whiskey, claret, madeira, and brandy, and when the Confederate authorities left Columbia they abandoned a large amount of whiskey at the medical purveyor's office. Finally, there were many

---

[37] T. J. Goodwyn to Colin Campbell Murchison, June 8, 1866, Thomas Jefferson Goodwyn Letter, South Caroliniana Library, University of South Carolina, Columbia; Rawlins Lowndes to Hampton, Aug. 15, 1866, copy, Trezevant Papers; Rawlins Lowndes to J. P. Carroll, copy, Trezevant Papers; Daniel Heyward Trezevant, *The Burning of Columbia, S.C.: A Review of Northern Assertions and Southern Facts*, p. 15. Mark Mayo Boatner III, *The Civil War Dictionary*, pp. 819–820, provides valuable tables and analyses for the computation of "time" for the Civil War period. In speaking of the order not to burn the cotton, Hampton said: "On the morning of the 17th; it was the first order I issued when I was assigned command . . ." (deposition of Hampton, *Mixed Commission*, XXIII, 32).

private collections in whiskey cellars throughout Columbia.[38] Mayor Goodwyn realized the potential danger of the whiskey and urged Beauregard and Hampton to destroy it, or at least remove it from Columbia. Both generals, however, were of the opinion that they had no authority in the matter, the whiskey being private property.[39] It was an unfortunate decision.

During the night of February 16–17, as the Confederate army withdrew, there was a complete breakdown in discipline. Straggling soldiers and town rabble created the "wildest terror" as they plundered warehouses and stripped depots.[40] In the midst of the chaos several fires broke out. "The city was illuminated with burning cotton," a Confederate officer wrote, describing the situation at three o'clock on the morning of February 17. Just how extensive these fires were is difficult to estimate, but at least two separate blazes can be located. One pile of cotton was seen burning that night on Blanding Street between Richardson and Sidney Park, and another fire was observed in the more than two thousand bales used for breastworks near the South Carolina Railroad depot.[41] The cause of these fires, or others that might have existed, has been difficult to ascertain, but there are several possibilities. One plausible explanation is that Union gunfire ignited them, which could easily have happened since some explosive shells were fired. Another answer might have been that Confederate soldiers, aware of the orders to burn the cotton upon evacuation, fired it. The Confederate army was pulling out of Columbia all during the night of February 16–17, and the order prohibiting the burning of cotton

[38] Barrett, *Sherman's March through the Carolinas*, p. 72; *Columbia Phoenix*, March 25, 1865; *Yorkville Enquirer*, March 9, 1865; Mrs. W. K. Bachman to Kate Bachman, March 27, 1865, copy, W. K. Bachman Papers, South Caroliniana Library, University of South Carolina, Columbia; Robert Wilson Gibbes to Washington Alston Gibbes, March 14, 1865, Robert Wilson Gibbes Papers, South Caroliniana Library, University of South Carolina, Columbia.

[39] Deposition of William T. Sherman, March 30, 1872, No. 37, *Mixed Commission*, III, 6; Rachel Sherman Thorndike, ed., *The Sherman Letters: Correspondence between General and Senator Sherman from 1837 to 1891*, p. 269; Barrett, *Sherman's March through the Carolinas*, pp. 72–73. In the evacuation of Richmond, Virginia, the city officials destroyed as much liquor as possible on their own initiative. *Columbia Phoenix*, May 3, 1865.

[40] *OR*, Ser. 1, LIII, 1050.

[41] Ibid.; deposition of Adams, *Mixed Commission*, XIV, 314; deposition of Peter Glass, Dec. 18, 1872, No. 103, *Mixed Commission*, XIV, 319.

was not issued until 7:00 A.M. on the seventeenth, only three and one-half hours before the Union troops entered. In the confusion of the evacuation and the orders regarding whether or not the cotton was to be ignited, the chances for error were great, and while the issue is one of the most controversial of the entire episode, the conclusion is inescapable that cotton was burning on the morning of February 17, 1865.[42]

About 6:00 A.M. on the seventeenth, Columbia was jolted awake by an enormous explosion at the South Carolina Railroad depot. Apparently, a pillager had inadvertently ignited some powder stored there and the warehouse was destroyed along with an undetermined number of plunderers. With the coming of daylight, law and order continued to deteriorate. Before the state commissary could be thrown open to the people, a "rough mob" broke into the building and appropriated a large quantity of rice, bacon, salt, and other supplies. Many of the goods were cast into the street, and Wheeler's cavalry carried off goods as they rode out of town. In the last-minute scramble for booty, much was wasted. "The negroes all went uptown to see what they could get in the general pillage, for all the shops had been opened and provisions were scattered in all directions," Emma LeConte wrote in her diary. "Henry says that in some parts of Main [Richardson] Street corn and flour and sugar cover the ground." Those supplies that were not taken by Confederate soldiers or townspeople were later appropriated by the Union quartermaster.[43]

The immediate events leading to the surrender of Columbia were quite confused. On the night of the sixteenth Beauregard informed Mayor Goodwyn that he hoped to have all Confederate

42 T. J. Goodwyn to Colin Campbell Murchison, June 8, 1866, Goodwyn Letter; Rhodes, *History of the United States*, V, 91; affidavit of J. C. Abney, March 26, 1928, in U.S. Congress, Senate, *Destruction of Property in Columbia, S.C., by Sherman's Army. Speech of Hon. Cole. L. Blease, a Senator from the State of South Carolina, Delivered in the Senate May 15, 1930*, 71st Cong., 2d sess., 1930, Senate Doc. No. 149 (Serial 9220), p. 37; deposition of Sherman, March 30, 1872, *Mixed Commission*, III, 8; Gibbes, *Who Burnt Columbia?*, p. 7. Goodwyn recalled later that someone, probably Hampton, "advised" him to place a guard over the cotton, but he apparently took no action.

43 *Columbia Phoenix*, March 21, 1865; Fletcher, *Rebel Private*, p. 174; South Carolina, *Report of the Special Joint Committee*, p. 19; *OR*, Ser. 1, XLVII, pt. 2: 476; Miers, *When the World Ended*, p. 40.

troops out of town before daylight, thus allowing the civilian officials to surrender the capital on the morning of the seventeenth, but no specific time or procedure was given. Without instructions, and anxious to avoid any unnecessary trouble, the mayor and two aldermen, J. H. Wells and John McKenzie, agreed to cross the Congaree early on the seventeeth and surrender the town before the Union army actually entered. The explosion of the depot early on the seventeenth, however, caught Mayor Goodwyn by surprise, and he rushed to the town hall with the intention of hoisting a white flag. Before he could do that, however, General Hampton, also awakened by the explosion, arrived upon the scene and ordered Goodwyn not to raise a flag of surrender until ordered to do so.[44] Hampton then left the mayor and rode off in a northwesterly direction to inspect the position of Major General Carter L. Stevenson, who was defending the eastern bank of the Congaree. Finding the Union army already on the eastern side of the river and Stevenson's position untenable, Hampton ordered him to retreat toward Winnsboro with Wheeler covering his withdrawal. Hampton next sent word to Butler at Granby, five miles south of Columbia, to withdraw northward through the eastern part of town, destroying the Charlotte and South Carolina Railroad station as he passed through, and then to link up with Stevenson on the Winnsboro Road.[45]

Having set the final retreat in motion, Hampton returned to the town hall and instructed Mayor Goodwyn to hoist a white flag. The mayor and aldermen John Stork, Orlando Z. Bates, and John McKenzie were given instructions where to find the advancing Union forces, and between 8:00 and 9:00 A.M. they rode out in a carriage to surrender Columbia.[46]

[44] Goodwyn to Colin Campbell Murchison, June 8, 1866, Goodwyn Letter; deposition of McKenzie, April 9, 1872, *Mixed Commission*, XIV, 8; deposition of Hampton, *Mixed Commission*, XXIII, 9–11; *Columbia Phoenix*, March 21, 1865. E. J. Scott stated that Hampton threatened "to shoot any one who offered to raise the white flag" before he directed it be raised. Scott, *Random Recollections*, pp. 175–176.

[45] Deposition of Hampton, *Mixed Commission*, XXIII, 9–10. Butler's withdrawal route placed him on the Winnsboro Road at approximately the same time the Union army entered by that route.

[46] Goodwyn to Colin Campbell Murchison, June 8, 1866, Goodwyn Letter; *Burning of Columbia, Letter and Report*, p. 7.

The burning of the Charlotte terminal by Butler between ten and eleven o'clock was one of the last acts of the evacuating Confederates. With the smoke of the burning railroad station on the horizon, the remnants of the forces defending Columbia, about five thousand strong, left the city.[47]

[47] Deposition of Hampton, *Mixed Commission*, XXIII, 5, 34.

3

The Capture of Columbia

ON February 16, 1865, the two prongs of the Union army met on the west bank of the Congaree opposite Columbia, and there Sherman held a brief council of war with Howard and Slocum, his wing commanders. Slocum was ordered to proceed to Zion Church, about thirteen miles up the Saluda River, where the left wing was to cross and move on Winnsboro. En route he was ordered to continue the destruction of railroads and bridges. Slocum's maneuver was designed to cut off Beauregard's evacuation should the Confederates linger in Columbia another day, while Howard was assigned the task of capturing Columbia.[1]

The heavy rainfall that had plagued the Union army since it entered South Carolina made crossing the high, swift-flowing Congaree at the burned-out bridge impossible, so Sherman decided upon a feint at that point, with the main force moving up the western bank of the Saluda. The decision allowed the Federals to cross the Saluda and then the Broad in separate maneuvers, thus

[1] *War of the Rebellion: A Compilation of the Official Records of the Union and Confederate Armies,* Ser. 1, XLVII, pt. 1: 20–21 (hereafter cited as *OR*); Rachel Sherman Thorndike, ed., *The Sherman Letters: Correspondence between General and Senator Sherman from 1837 to 1891,* pp. 268–269. The normal population of Columbia was slightly over eight thousand, but with the influx of refugees in late 1864 the population may have risen to as many as the twenty thousand reported by William Gilmore Simms in the *Columbia Phoenix* on March 21, 1865. With the approach of the Union army, however, it appears that many inhabitants and refugees fled the city, thus reducing the population to perhaps twelve or fourteen thousand by February 17.

alleviating some of the military problems and at the same time diminishing the natural hazard.[2]

After proceeding about a mile up the Saluda River, Howard's men arrived at the Saluda Factory, where they found the female operatives still scurrying through the building tearing cloth from the looms to take to their homes.[3] The nearby bridge had been burned, but with energy characteristic of the entire campaign in the Carolinas about one hundred men were ferried across the river to the narrow peninsula between the Saluda and Broad rivers. They quickly dislodged enough of the enemy to allow Captain C. B. Reese, the chief engineer, to construct a pontoon bridge across the Saluda River. As the engineers went about their task, Union sharpshooters located in the windows of the factory attempted to oust the remaining Confederates concealed in the underbrush on the peninsula. While the Rebel sharpshooters were able to delay completion of the bridge, the steadily increasing fire of the Union troops eventually drove them out of range of the engineers.[4]

Upon completion of the pontoon bridge, Howard's infantry, aided by some of Major General William B. Hazen's troops, rushed across the Saluda. The overwhelming Union pressure forced the Rebels to abandon their position rapidly, and it appeared for a time that the nearby Broad River bridge would be captured intact. The Confederates, however, anticipating that it would be impossible to hold the bridge, had prepared it for burning by coating it with resin. Once fire was applied to the bridge, it burst into such a mass of flames that some of the Confederate troops were unable to cross, being forced to make their escape up the peninsula.[5]

On the night of the sixteenth the final preparations for the capture of Columbia began. Colonel George A. Stone of the Twen-

---

[2] *OR*, Ser. 1, XLVII, pt. 1: 21, 197; George Ward Nichols, *The Story of the Great March: From the Diary of A Staff Officer*, p. 156.

[3] Nichols, *Great March*, pp. 156–158. To the eye of the New England critic, these people were "unkempt, frowzy, ragged, dirty, and altogether ignorant and wretched." Their living conditions were described as "dirty, wooden shanties" with "rotten steps" which "led to foul and close passage-ways, filled with broken crockery, dirty pots and pans, and other accumulations of rubbish. . . ."

[4] *OR*, Ser. 1, XLVII, pt. 1: 198, 271.

[5] Ibid., pp. 198, 227.

ty-Fifth Iowa Infantry Regiment, then commander of the Third Brigade, was assigned the task of crossing the Broad River with the anticipation that he would be in Columbia by daylight. The building of the pontoon bridge fell to Colonel William Tweeddale and the First Missouri Engineers. Tweeddale chose for the crossing a point about one-half mile above the destroyed bridge, but he immediately ran into difficulty. A number of efforts to get a rope across the Broad failed because the river was wider and the current swifter than had been expected. After much hardship and delay a lightweight cord found in the Saluda Factory enabled the engineers to get a ferry line across the river about 3:00 A.M. on the seventeenth. Shortly thereafter Stone launched two pontoon boats filled with sharpshooters with orders to take a defensive position on the eastern side of the river. When Stone arrived on the scene, however, he found that his men had landed on a small, crescent-shaped island about two hundred yards long, twenty-five yards wide, and only a few feet from the eastern bank. As Union troops continued to arrive on the island, Confederate opposition increased, and Stone, fearing that the enemy would be reinforced, eventually saw no alternative but to drive them from their positions. Stone's plan of attack was to send a regiment on a flanking movement to the northern end of the island, with the idea of crossing to the shore and then rolling up the Confederate right. It was daylight, or about seven o'clock, before the Union troops were of sufficient number and in a position to make their assault. The men plunged into the icy water and easily drove the Confederate troops from their position, whereupon Stone established a defense line and waited for his commanding officer, Brevet Brigadier General Charles R. Woods, to arrive. The pontoon bridge was not completed until about 9:00 A.M., at which time the remainder of Woods's division began to cross.[6]

Upon learning that reinforcements were at hand, Stone sent his skirmish line forward, and the Confederate rear guard of General Stevenson began to retreat eastward. Stone had proceeded little

---

[6] Ibid., pp. 198, 263–264; pt. 2: 457. The time is based on Mayor Goodwyn's estimate of Sherman's arrival in Columbia. Goodwyn to Colin Campbell Murchison, June 8, 1866, Thomas Jefferson Goodwyn Letter, South Caroliniana Library, University of South Carolina, Columbia.

more than a mile when he met, shortly after ten o'clock, Mayor Goodwyn and the three aldermen with a flag of truce. To their request for terms Stone could only offer unconditional surrender, to which the delegation acquiesced after a short discussion.[7] The mayor then presented the colonel the following letter addressed to Sherman: "The Confederate forces having evacuated Columbia, I deem it my duty, as Mayor and representative of the city, to ask for its citizens the treatment accorded by the usages of civilized warfare. I therefore respectfully request that you will send a sufficient guard in advance of the army to maintain order in the city and protect the persons and property of the citizens."[8] Stone sent the letter back to Sherman, who made no written acknowledgment.

After the surrender, Stone, accompanied by Major Albert R. Anderson and Captain William B. Pratt of General Logan's staff, joined Mayor Goodwyn and the aldermen in the carriage and proceeded toward Columbia. As they approached the intersection of Broad River Road and Winnsboro Road, about one-half mile north of Cotton Town, Stone noticed that some of his advanced skirmishers were being pushed back by what he termed a "battalion" of Confederate cavalry. Infuriated by this violation of the surrender, the Union officer placed the mayor and aldermen under three guards, who were instructed to shoot them if a single Federal soldier were killed or wounded by the advancing Confederates. Then Stone gathered about forty of his troops, who, with the retreating skirmishers, quickly dispersed the Southern cavalrymen. The advance resumed, and an ugly situation was avoided, but the Union troops had scarcely reached Cotton Town before potential trouble again developed. Scores of bewildered Columbians, both white and black, probably in an ill-conceived attempt to placate a dreaded conqueror, began distributing to the soldiers a number of varieties of alcoholic beverages which they had pilfered from the stores along Richardson Street.[9]

---

[7] *OR*, Ser. 1, XLVII, pt. 1: 264.

[8] *Columbia Phoenix*, March 21, 1865.

[9] *OR*, Ser. 1, XLVII, pt. 1: 264–265; pt. 2: 457; *Columbia Phoenix*, March 21, 1865; deposition of O. O. Howard, Dec. 10, 1872, No. 103, Wood and Heyworth *vs.* United States, No. 292, Cowlam Graveley *vs.* United States, *Mixed*

As the troops continued down Richardson they passed the stacks of cotton, some of which were smoldering ominously, that had been hauled out of storage. Upon reaching the town hall–market at about 11:00 A.M., they found a number of bales burning briskly.[10] Stone ordered his men to stack their arms and to begin extinguishing the flames. While his orders were being carried out, the Union officer placed a subordinate in charge, and he and Captain Pratt went to the capitol building with the intention of raising a United States flag.[11]

About one hour later Stone returned to his troops and discovered that a number were drunk. He later reasoned that since his men had slept little for two nights, and had not eaten for twenty-four hours, the liquor had an immediate debilitating effect. To prevent further complications because of intoxication, Stone ordered all alcohol destroyed. Within a matter of minutes numbers of barrels were burst open and poured into the streets, but later events would prove that much liquor went undestroyed. While disposing of the alcoholic beverages, Stone received orders from General Charles R. Woods to protect private property and the public buildings. This command, the colonel later reported, became

---

Commission on British and American Claims. Appendix: Testimony, XIV, 13; Anthony Toomer Porter, *The History of a Work of Faith and Love in Charleston, South Carolina, Which Grew Out of the Calamities of the Late Civil War, and a Record of God's Wonderful Providence,* p. 112; T. J. Goodwyn to Colin Campbell Murchison, June 8, 1866, Goodwyn Letter.

[10] Deposition of John McKenzie, April 9, 1872, No. 103, *Mixed Commission,* XIV, 9; deposition of William T. Sherman, March 30, 1872, No. 37, Joseph J. Browne *vs.* United States, *Mixed Commission,* III, 8; T. J. Goodwyn to Colin Campbell Murchison, June 8, 1866, Goodwyn Letter; J. P. Carroll, "Burning of Columbia," *Southern Historical Society Papers* 8 (May, 1880): 205; James Ford Rhodes, *History of the United States from the Compromise of 1850 to the Final Restoration of Home Rule at the South in 1877,* V, 91; affidavit of J. C. Abney, March 26, 1928, in U.S. Congress, Senate, *Destruction of Property in Columbia, S.C., by Sherman's Army. Speech of Hon. Cole. L. Blease, a Senator from the State of South Carolina, Delivered in the Senate May 15, 1930,* 71st Cong., 2d sess., 1930, Senate Doc. No. 149 (Serial 9220), p. 37; James Guignard Gibbes, *Who Burnt Columbia?,* p. 7.

[11] *OR,* Ser. 1, XLVII, pt. 1: 265; deposition of McKenzie, April 9, 1872, *Mixed Commission,* XIV, 9; deposition of William T. Sherman, Dec. 11, 1872, Nos. 103, 292, *Mixed Commission,* XIV, 81.

his next order of business, and he dispersed his five regiments throughout Columbia, with Lieutenant Colonel Jeremiah W. Jenkins of the Thirty-First Iowa Infantry as provost marshal.[12]

While Colonel Stone was moving on Columbia from the northwest, a small band of Federal soldiers, eager to be the first to enter the South Carolina capital, landed a leaky flatboat on the eastern bank of the Congaree River. Lieutenants Henry C. McArthur and William H. Goodrell, both of Brigadier General W. W. Belknap's staff, had found a dilapidated flatboat on the western side of the river near the burned bridge. After making hurried repairs on the boat, about twenty men crossed the Congaree directly in front of Columbia. Upon reaching the eastern shore they discovered that the Confederate pickets who had annoyed them during their repairs had withdrawn, and the rickety flatboat, along with another they had found, was sent back for more troops. When their number had been increased to about seventy-five, they began to advance toward the capitol building.[13]

From the river the Union troops rushed eastward along several streets toward the State House. After going some distance, the vanguard came upon a Columbian trying to escape southward in a one-horse buggy, whereupon the officers commandeered the vehicle and proceeded to outdistance their comrades. Near the State House a small force of Wheeler's cavalry attempted to stop them. After an exchange of shots by both sides, resulting in the death of one Southerner, the Confederates withdrew. Fear of further opposition led the Union officers to halt until they were joined by more of their troops. One of them, Captain A. E. Wood, would later report that he saw cotton bales burning along Gervais Street as he raced toward the capitol. When their troop strength was thought sufficient, the Federal officers moved on the State House, where they

[12] *OR*, Ser. 1, XLVII, pt. 1: 265. According to the calculations of Mark Mayo Boatner III, *The Civil War Dictionary*, pp. 611–612, five regiments would total approximately forty-five hundred men.

[13] *OR*, Ser. 1, XLVII, pt. 1: 417–418; Henry Clay McArthur, *Capture and Destruction of Columbia, South Carolina, February 17, 1865*, pp. 3–4. McArthur would later solicit a Medal of Honor for his activities in Columbia. H. C. McArthur to Secretary of War Newton D. Baker, June 24, 1916, copy, H. C. McArthur Collection, Iowa Archives, Des Moines.

planted the United States flag. They were the first Northern soldiers in Columbia; the time was approximately 10:30 A.M.[14]

Meanwhile, Sherman was sitting on a log talking with Howard and watching his engineers complete the pontoon bridge across
the Broad River when a messenger arrived from Colonel Stone an-
nouncing that Columbia had been surrendered by its mayor. Sherman's only reaction, he later wrote, was to turn to Howard and
remind him of Special Field Order No. 26, which had previously
been issued for the occupation of the South Carolina capital.[15]

The same messenger handed the Union commander a communication from the lady superior of the Ursuline Convent, a
Catholic school in Columbia. The lady superior, having heard
stories of the barbarity of the Northern invaders, hoped to protect
her charge by informing Sherman that she had been a teacher at
the Brown County, Ohio, convent when his daughter Minnie was
a pupil. She then proceeded in a straightforward manner to ask
the general to guarantee the safety of the convent. To alleviate her
fears, Sherman ordered his inspector general, Colonel Charles
Ewing, who was also his son-in-law, to visit the convent and assure
its inhabitants that private property would be respected and that
they had nothing to fear.[16]

Once the pontoon bridge was completed, Sherman led his
horse across, followed by Howard, John A. Logan, Charles R.
Woods, and eventually the entire XV Corps. Their route into Columbia, the same one that Stone followed, took them up a slight
but long hill to a plateau, where they found a wide road that ran
through old cotton and corn fields. After going about one mile
they arrived at Cotton Town, where the evidence of years of
handling cotton was everywhere apparent.[17]

The Union generals had ridden about a block and one-half
past Upper Boundary Street when they came upon cotton that had

14 A. E. Wood, "Burning of Columbia, S.C.," *North American Review* 146
(April, 1888): 402; *OR*, Ser. 1, XLVII, pt. 1: 418; deposition of Joseph H.
Marks, April 15, 1873, No. 236, David Jacobs *vs.* United States, *Mixed Com-
mission*, XXIII, 68; McArthur, *Capture and Destruction of Columbia*, pp. 4–5.

15 William Tecumseh Sherman, *Memoirs of General William T. Sherman*,
II, 277, 279.

16 Ibid., pp. 279–280.

17 Ibid., p. 280.

been piled in the street by the retreating Confederates. The bales were in bad condition; the cording had been slashed in some, and the bagging had been ripped open in places in others. The high wind that had been blowing out of the northwest since early morning had scattered the cotton over the ground. So much of it had snagged on the rough edges of buildings and lodged in trees on both sides of the street that Sherman turned to Howard and commented on its similarity to a northern snowstorm.[18]

Others were similarly impressed. In describing the occupation to a friend in a letter of March 3, 1865, an anonymous Columbian used the same simile: "The very elements seemed to conspire against us, for the wind blew a perfect gale. Bags of cotton were cut open in the streets & wind carried it even into the trees. The streets looked as if they were covered with snow."[19] Another inhabitant, Mary S. Whilden, noted Columbia's "peculiar appearance" caused by cotton "lodged in the leafless branches of the trees," and the "immense bundles" of cotton that rolled about the streets gathering dried leaves. By late afternoon, she wrote, streets and trees were covered with this "most combustible material."[20]

The situation that greeted the Union officers as they rode down Richardson Street was one of excitement, confusion, and disorder. The results of the pillage of the previous twenty-four hours were everywhere apparent, with pieces of broken furniture and abandoned merchandise strewn in the streets.[21] Jubilant Negroes and apprehensive but curious citizens jammed the street. Alcohol was liberally distributed to all who desired it by both blacks and whites.[22]

Sherman arrived at the town hall–market at approximately twelve noon. There he found that Colonel Stone's men had stacked their arms and that some were busy aiding citizens in putting out

[18] Deposition of Charlotte Goldstien, May 12, 1873, No. 236, *Mixed Commission*, XXIII, 12; deposition of Sherman, Dec. 11, 1872, *Mixed Commission*, XIV, 87; *OR*, Ser. 1, XLVII, pt. 1: 21; Sherman, *Memoirs*, II, 280.

[19] Anonymous letter, March 3, 1865, Anonymous Collection, South Caroliniana Library, University of South Carolina, Columbia.

[20] Mary S. Whilden, *Recollections of the War, 1861–1865*, p. 10.

[21] W. B. Hazen, *A Narrative of Military Service*, p. 349; Nichols, *Great March*, p. 161.

[22] *OR*, Ser. 1, XLVII, pt. 1: 198; pt. 2: 457; Sherman, *Memoirs*, II, 280.

a fire in the cotton with two old fire engines. The pile of cotton was three hundred to four hundred feet long, two or three bales high, and burning briskly. Because the flames made it difficult to pass the cotton, some of Stone's men were attempting to clear a path which would allow the XV Corps through. The size of the crowd steadily increased, but in Sherman's opinion, "general good order prevailed." In the crowd around Sherman was Mayor Goodwyn, who, upon reaching the general, gave the impression that he was "extremely anxious" about the safety of private property in Columbia. The Union commander assured him that private property would be respected.[23]

While conversing with the mayor, Sherman noticed several men attempting to push through the crowd. He ordered some "black people" to stand back to allow the men through, and he was soon surrounded by a group of the Federal soldiers who had been prisoners in Columbia. The men presented a pathetic picture in their tattered clothes; some were without hats and others without shoes, but all were obviously overjoyed at their liberation.[24] The Union commander told them that as soon as things "settled down" they were to report to General Howard, who would provide for their needs. One of the former prisoners handed Sherman a small piece of paper and asked him to read it at his leisure. The general placed the paper in his breast pocket and rode off with Howard toward the South Carolina Railroad station. There they found a detachment of Colonel Stone's brigade sifting through charred bags of corn and cornmeal, separating the good from the burned. Little remained of the depot but ashes.[25]

From the railroad station Sherman and Howard continued up the track for three hundred or four hundred yards toward a large foundry until they were hailed by a soldier who warned

[23] Deposition of Sherman, Dec. 11, 1872, *Mixed Commission*, XIV, 81; deposition of S. H. M. Byers, Dec. 12, 1872, Nos. 103, 292, *Mixed Commission*, XIV, 120; Samuel Hawkins Marshall Byers, "The Burning of Columbia," *Lippincott's Magazine* 29 (March, 1882): 258; Sherman, *Memoirs*, II, 280; *OR*, Ser. 1, XLVII, pt. 1: 21.

[24] Hazen, *Narrative of Military Service*, 350; Sherman, *Memoirs*, II, 280.

[25] Deposition of Sherman, Dec. 11, 1872, *Mixed Commission*, XIV, 67; Sherman, *Memoirs*, II, 280–281. The contents of the note are discussed in chapter 4.

them that Confederates were still lingering on the outskirts of town and that it would be dangerous to proceed further. They turned around and headed back for Richardson Street. Upon nearing the capitol building, Sherman noticed that some of the soldiers in the area were intoxicated. He called these men to Howard's attention and then rode off toward the town hall, where he again met Mayor Goodwyn and inquired about a house for himself and his staff. Goodwyn informed him that the house of the man who held the contract for printing Confederate money, Blanton Duncan, was available. At approximately 1:30 P.M. the two men proceeded to the location four blocks east of the capitol on Gervais Street, leaving Howard in charge of Columbia.[26]

Meanwhile, General Logan's XV Corps had begun to file through the city. The First Division, commanded by Charles R. Woods, with the exception of Stone's Third Brigade, marched through Columbia and made camp on the eastern side of the Charlotte and South Carolina Railroad. Woods's headquarters were at the residence of Mrs. Emma Stark on the corner of Senate and Barnwell streets, six blocks east of the State House. The Fourth Division, commanded by Brevet Major General John M. Corse, left its camp between the Saluda and Broad rivers and marched through Columbia to a site southeast of the college near the junction of the Charlotte and Charleston railroads.[27]

William B. Hazen's Second Division followed next, crossing the Saluda River about three o'clock, and marched down Richardson Street about 5:30 P.M. to a camp on the east side of Columbia about one mile beyond the Charlotte and South Carolina Railroad. General Hazen decided to make his headquarters in camp with his men.[28]

---

[26] Deposition of Sherman, Dec. 11, 1872, *Mixed Commission*, XIV, 67–68; Sherman, *Memoirs*, II, 281; deposition of Howard, *Mixed Commission*, XIV, 4–5; John G. Barrett, *Sherman's March through the Carolinas*, p. 79n; E. Merton Coulter, *The Confederate States of America, 1861–1865*, p. 214.

[27] Sherman, *Memoirs*, II, 281; *OR*, Ser. 1, XLVII, pt. 1: 335; pt. 2: 457; deposition of M. L. DeSaussure, April 22, 1873, No. 236, *Mixed Commission*, XXIII, 5–6.

[28] Hazen, *Narrative of Military Service*, p. 349; deposition of William B. Hazen, Dec. 14, 1872, Nos. 103, 292, *Mixed Commission*, XIV, 152; *OR*, Ser. 1, XLVII, pt. 1: 79, 272. Hazen mistakenly referred to his camp as being near the "Columbia and South Carolina" railroad.

The Third Division, the last of the XV Corps to enter Columbia, with Brevet Major General John E. Smith as commander, left camp on the Broad River around three o'clock and marched through Columbia to a location about one mile east of town. Smith also elected to make his headquarters in camp rather than in town. General Logan established his corps headquarters at the house of Confederate Brigadier General John S. Preston, which was located on Blanding Street.[29]

The XVII Corps, commanded by Frank P. Blair, Jr., the antislavery unionist from Missouri, did not enter Columbia. Instead, Major General Joseph A. Mower's First Division crossed the Broad River about three o'clock and marched in a northeasterly direction. They encamped about four miles north of town, as did the Third Division under the command of Brigadier General Manning F. Force. The Fourth Division, Brevet Major General Giles A. Smith commanding, followed the Third Division into camp north of Columbia, with the exception of the small part of the Third Brigade that had entered Columbia early on the morning of the seventeenth on the flatboat.[30]

During the four years of war, South Carolinians had witnessed the slow strangulation of the Confederacy and their own coast, but few dreamed when the fighting began that the heartland of the Palmetto State and its capital would be engulfed by the enemy. Having been abandoned by their defenders, Columbians found themselves on February 17, 1865, helplessly in the hands of their dreaded enemy. Before the night was over some of their fears had been realized.

[29] *OR*, Ser. 1, XLVII, pt. 1: 84, 317–318; deposition of John A. Logan, Dec. 21, 1872, Nos. 103, 292, *Mixed Commission*, XIV, 282.

[30] *OR*, Ser. 1, XLVII, pt. 1: 21, 104, 417; Sherman, *Memoirs*, II, 281–282.

4

The Burning of Columbia

IT had become a custom with Sherman's army that the first brigade to enter a town would serve as provost guard. The procedure generally followed was that one of the major public buildings such as the town hall or courthouse was appropriated as headquarters, and from there the provost marshal appointed by the commander of the brigade dispersed his men throughout the town.[1] As commander of the provost guard for the occupation of Columbia, the Third Brigade of the First Division, XV Corps, Provost Marshal Jenkins placed sentries at the intersections of the major streets and in front of public buildings and sent guards, when requested, to protect the property of private citizens. Following the establishment of the provost guard, the remainder of the First Division was allowed freedom of movement in Columbia to secure food, converse with citizens, or seek pleasure of one kind or another. This disposition of troops put a total of about 12,000 soldiers in Columbia, of whom 4,500 served as provost guard.[2] When Sherman and

[1] Deposition of William T. Sherman, Dec. 11, 1872, No. 103, Wood and Heyworth *vs.* United States, No. 292, Cowlam Graveley *vs.* United States, *Mixed Commission on British and American Claims. Appendix: Testimony*, XIV, 94, 102; Lloyd Lewis, *Sherman, Fighting Prophet*, p. 501.

[2] *War of the Rebellion: A Compilation of the Official Records of the Union and Confederate Armies*, Ser. 1, XLVII, pt. 1: 263, 265 (hereafter cited as *OR*); deposition of Sherman, Dec. 11, 1872, *Mixed Commission*, XIV, 94, 102; deposition of O. O. Howard, Dec. 10, 1872, Nos. 103, 292, *Mixed Commission*, XIV, 32; Lewis, *Sherman, Fighting Prophet*, p. 501; Mark Mayo Boatner III, *The Civil War Dictionary*, pp. 611–612.

his staff arrived at the town hall about noon on February 17, the routine of establishing security for the city was in operation.

From the outset of his thrust into South Carolina, if not before, Sherman appears to have been of two minds about the possibility of trouble when he reached Columbia. On the one hand, having heard since the time of the march to the sea that there were those in his army who had frequently issued threats against the state, he was aware that many of his troops seemed to hold a special antipathy for South Carolina.[3] Some, approximating the language of Old Testament prophets, spoke of the imminent "judgment day" in which the first state to secede would reap what it had sowed. "Fire and sword," camp talk declared, were the just penalties for precipitating secession and war. Others, omitting justifying jargon, stated bluntly that they "had it in" for South Carolina, which, they believed, was "bound to suffer."[4]

By the time the capture of Columbia was assured, however, Sherman appears to have dismissed these threats against the Palmetto State as mere rhetoric, the kind he himself was so prone to utter. What appears to have become foremost in the formulation of his thinking by mid-February was the overall success or failure of his movement into central South Carolina and whether or not General Slocum would meet determined opposition at Alston, South Carolina, a small town on the Broad River twenty-four miles to the northwest, through which he would have to pass to get to Winnsboro. Therefore, when Sherman routinely placed Howard in charge of occupying the South Carolina capital with no special orders, it was not from lack of concern; the more important matters of victory or defeat simply dominated his thinking.[5]

It was, then, General Howard's responsibility to maintain security in the "home of secession," and from the very beginning

---

[3] Deposition of Sherman, Dec. 11, 1872, *Mixed Commission*, XIV, 74.

[4] *Story of the Fifty-Fifth Regiment Illinois Volunteer Infantry in the Civil War, 1861–1865*, pp. 404, 409; Paul M. Angle, ed., *Three Years in the Army of the Cumberland: The Letters and Diary of Major James A. Connolly*, p. 384; Henry J. Aten, *History of the Eighty-Fifth Regiment, Illinois Volunteer Infantry*, pp. 266–267; George S. Bradley, *The Star Corps; or, Notes of an Army Chaplain During Sherman's Famous March to the Sea*, pp. 258–259.

[5] Deposition of Sherman, Dec. 11, 1872, *Mixed Commission*, XIV, 93, 95.

he was aware that there would be more than just the typical problems of occupation. Howard, like Sherman, was cognizant of the threats against South Carolina, and he knew that there were those in any army of thirty thousand men who would perpetrate any imaginable crime. To prevent wanton acts of destruction, Howard realized that he would have to take "unusual precautions" during the army's stay in Columbia. Under normal conditions he would have placed Charles R. Woods, commander of the First Division, XV Corps, in charge of the town without "positive, specific instructions." But Howard decided to retain command in Columbia as a precautionary measure.[6]

Upon entering the South Carolina capital, Howard's first act was to evaluate security. He found that some of the troops of the Third Brigade had already been stationed along Richardson Street in front of important public buildings and at the principal intersections. A large portion of the brigade was yet unassigned, and many troops milled around, some awaiting orders. Howard, too, noted the men who were assisting citizens with old fire engines as they attempted to extinguish the blaze in the cotton piled near the town hall. Howard was satisfied that the situation was under control and rode off with Sherman toward the South Carolina Railroad depot.[7] It was about 1:30 P.M., as they retraced their steps toward the town hall, that Sherman pointed out to Howard the intoxicated soldiers in the vicinity of the capitol building. Discerning that the troops were indeed drunk, Howard rode up to Charles R. Woods, who was at that moment leading the First Division through Columbia, and ordered him to have the inebriated troops placed under guard.[8]

The drunken soldiers disturbed Howard. He wondered how widespread the drinking was and whether or not the sentinels assigned to guard property were conscientious in their tasks. As evidence of his concern, the general decided to ascertain for him-

[6] Deposition of Howard, *Mixed Commission*, XIV, 28–32, 56–57. Howard was careful to point out that while he was worried about disorders in Columbia, he had no reason to believe the town would be burned.

[7] Ibid., p. 4; *OR*, Ser. 1, XLVII, pt. 1: 198.

[8] Deposition of Howard, *Mixed Commission*, XIV, 4–5.

self the status of security by a quick survey of the provost guards. It is impossible to state the extent of his scrutiny, but Howard later recorded that he "tested" numerous guards with respect to their orders and drinking. Satisfied that the provost guard was functioning properly, he decided to seek lodging for the night. He was able to secure several rooms for himself and his staff in the McCord home at the northwest corner of Pendleton and Bull streets near South Carolina College, and they arrived there before dark.[9]

Meanwhile, Sherman had ridden to the Duncan house, which was to be his headquarters during the occupation of Columbia. Located on Gervais Street about seven blocks from the town hall, it was a spacious, modern, completely furnished building with a large yard and stable. It was two o'clock before Sherman was settled in his room, and, as was his custom upon making camp, he began to rummage through his pockets, laying out all communiques for review. From his breast pocket he pulled the crumpled note handed him on his arrival at the town hall by the escaped Union prisoner. He was, he wrote later, quite surprised and pleased to find a poem, "Sherman's March to the Sea," which Captain S. H. M. Byers of the Fifth Iowa Infantry Regiment had written while a prisoner in Columbia. The Union commander was moved by the poem and sent word to Byers that he was being attached to his staff, thus beginning a lifelong friendship between the two.[10]

Sherman then lay down for a rest, but was shortly aroused by a visit from Mayor Goodwyn. A lady in Columbia, the mayor explained, had informed him that she was an old friend of the general. A few queries revealed that her maiden name was Poyas, a family Sherman had known well between 1842 and 1846 when, as a young lieutenant, he had been stationed at Fort Moultrie near Charleston. During those happy years Sherman had enjoyed

---

[9] Ibid., pp. 5, 8–9; *OR*, Ser. 1, XLVII, pt. 1: 198; Oliver Otis Howard, *Autobiography of Oliver Otis Howard, Major General, United States Army*, II, 121.

[10] William Tecumseh Sherman, *Memoirs of General William T. Sherman*, II, 281–282; M. A. DeWolfe Howe, ed., *Home Letters of General Sherman*, p. 333.

Charleston society and had often visited the Poyas plantation about forty miles from Fort Moultrie.[11]

Within a matter of minutes Sherman and Goodwyn began walking to his old friend's residence, which was located some eight or nine blocks away in the northern part of Columbia beyond the Charlotte depot. As they entered the yard, Sherman noticed chickens and ducks scurrying about and was impressed with the tranquil appearance of the home. After inquiring about the health of her relatives, Sherman informed the lady that he was surprised, but pleased, that her premises had not been disturbed by troops out looking for food. "I owe it to you, General," she began, and proceeded to explain how a group of troops entered her yard and began appropriating her poultry. Armed with a book that Sherman had given her during one of his visits to her home, she approached the leader of the party and showed him the inscription the Northern general had written: "To Miss ——— Poyas, with the compliments of W. T. Sherman, First Lieutenant Third Artillery." The leader of the Union troops recognized the signature, she continued, and ordered his men not to disturb her property. The troops moved on down the street, leaving a guard behind until the regular provost guard arrived.[12]

After a pleasant visit with his old friend, Sherman and the mayor returned to the Duncan house and remained there until about sundown.[13] During their conversations Sherman, noticing the anxiety of Goodwyn, an elderly man who had been under a tremendous strain for the past week,[14] sought to calm his frayed

[11] Earl Schenck Miers, *The General Who Marched to Hell: William Tecumseh Sherman and His March to Fame and Infamy*, pp. ix–x; Sherman, *Memoirs*, II, 284.

[12] Sherman, *Memoirs*, II, 284–285; affidavit of T. J. Goodwyn, Nov. 3, 1866, in *The Burning of Columbia. I. A Letter to Gen. Wade Hampton, June 24, 1873, With Appendix. II. Report of Committee of Citizens, Ex-Chancellor J. P. Carroll, Chairman, May 1866*, p. 7 (hereafter cited as *Burning of Columbia, Letter and Report*).

[13] Deposition of T. J. Goodwyn, April 27, 1872, No. 103, *Mixed Commission*, XIV, 14.

[14] Edwin J. Scott, *Random Recollections of a Long Life, 1806 to 1876*, p. 194; R. W. Gibbes to Andrew G. Magrath, Feb. 28, 1865, Robert Wilson Gibbes Papers, South Caroliniana Library, University of South Carolina, Columbia.

nerves. He assured the mayor that there was no need for apprehension about the safety of Columbia since no destruction of private property would occur.[15] The only property to be destroyed,
Sherman continued, would be arsenals, machine shops, foundries, and other war matériel. This burning would be done the
next day after the wind diminished and with the fire engines,
which Goodwyn assured him were in satisfactory condition, standing by. With this exchange the mayor left for home. The time was
approximately 6:00 P.M.[16]

If Mayor Goodwyn was alarmed, it was because events were
already transpiring that proved his fears were indeed well found-
ed. Shortly after the entrance of the Union troops into Columbia,
the superabundance of alcohol became an insurmountable problem. After the very first troops of Colonel Stone had been met by
whites and blacks who foolishly provided them with whiskey, those
who wanted more liquor had little trouble finding it in the stores
or homes of citizens.[17] The presence of drunken soldiers in the
streets of Columbia led, shortly, to the order that all liquor be
destroyed, but the task proved impossible since many of the troops
and some of the citizens were hesitant to smash the highly desired
beverages.[18]

As the Union army filed through Columbia during the afternoon on its way to camp, many men dropped out of line to accept
whiskey, and some did not return to the ranks. Between two and
four o'clock, General Hazen, a man who was an admirer of South
Carolina's aristocracy and a strict disciplinarian, rode around Columbia. He later testified that there were "a great many straggling

[15] Deposition of Sherman, Dec. 11, 1872, *Mixed Commission*, XIV, 79–80.

[16] Deposition of Goodwyn, *Mixed Commission*, XIV, 14–15; affidavit of
Goodwyn, Nov. 3, 1866, in *Burning of Columbia, Letter and Report*, p. 7.

[17] *OR*, Ser. 1, XLVII, pt. 1: 227; deposition of Maxwell Woodhull, Dec.
17, 1872, Nos. 103, 292, *Mixed Commission*, XIV, 246; *Columbia Phoenix*,
March 25, 1865; Oscar Lawrence Jackson, *The Colonel's Diary: Journals Kept
Before and During the Civil War by the Late Colonel Oscar L. Jackson, Sometime Commander of the Sixty-Third Regiment Ohio Volunteer Infantry*, p. 183.

[18] Deposition of Woodhull, *Mixed Commission*, XIV, 235; *OR*, Ser. 1,
XLVII, pt. 1: 265; Mrs. W. K. Bachman to Kate Bachman, March 27, 1865,
copy, W. K. Bachman Papers, South Caroliniana Library, University of South
Carolina, Columbia.

soldiers in the city," though he maintained that "few" of his men fell out of line or returned to the city during the evening.[19]

Other Union commanders witnessed this accumulation of troops and the deterioration of discipline. When John E. Smith led his men through town between 4:00 and 4:30 P.M., he noted that soldiers were "obtaining liquor freely," and consequently he decided to confine his troops to camp. Smith remained in camp to enforce his order.[20] Other officers were not so conscientious, or certainly not as successful in keeping their men in camp. As the various brigades encamped on the northern and eastern sides of Columbia, there was a steady flow of men back into town. They had seen liquor literally flowing in the streets as they marched through, and many returned to claim their share while others were merely curious sightseers.[21] The accumulation of soldiers in town was gradual throughout the afternoon, and the evidence is clear that as the day progressed there was an ever increasing amount of drunkenness.[22] It was also true that many of the Union troops were foraging throughout the city during the afternoon and that some of them were without doubt drunk. They entered the stores on Richardson Street, some of which had already been raided by retreating Confederates and townspeople, and they roamed through some of the residential streets, entering yards and taking bacon, chickens, ducks, pigs, and other food supplies.[23]

Yet there were those, both Union officers and local citizens, who were not disturbed by the situation that existed during that afternoon, apparently believing that what they saw was "normal" for the occupation of towns during war. As Sherman and Goodwyn walked back to the Duncan house late in the afternoon, the general noticed that there were numbers of soldiers strolling through

[19] Deposition of William B. Hazen, Dec. 14, 1872, Nos. 103, 292, *Mixed Commission*, XIV, 152; W. B. Hazen, *A Narrative of Military Service*, p. 349.

[20] *OR*, Ser. 1, XLVII, pt. 1: 318.

[21] Deposition of Sherman, Dec. 11, 1872, *Mixed Commission*, XIV, 95.

[22] Deposition of Howard, *Mixed Commission*, XIV, 38; deposition of Hazen, *Mixed Commission*, XIV, 152.

[23] Sherman, *Memoirs*, II, 285; Peter J. Shand to Mrs. Howard Kennedy, March 9, 1868, Peter J. Shand Papers, South Caroliniana Library, University of South Carolina, Columbia. Shand described the goods taken from his home as "provisions."

the streets, but he later stated that he saw nothing that could be classified as "disorder" or "out of the way."[24] Logan subsequently testified that he rode through many of the streets of Columbia during the afternoon and was not adversely impressed by the accumulation of stragglers or the consumption of alcohol,[25] and Hazen reported that he saw no disorders such as looting.[26]

While Columbians found it more difficult to exculpate the Northern invaders from the charge of immediate pillage, there were those who were impressed by the relative calmness of the afternoon. The Reverend Robert Wilson, a Charleston refugee, stated that he walked freely through the streets of Columbia and was not molested in any way.[27] And James G. Gibbes, a prominent resident, stated that while numerous stores were "sacked" during the afternoon, the Union soldiers were "generally civil and pleasant spoken."[28] The young and intelligent Emma LeConte added her testimony of what she had heard, and to some degree observed, when she recorded in her diary that everything was "quiet and orderly" during the afternoon.[29] These statements are corroborated by William Gilmore Simms, who referred to the afternoon as having "few shows of that drunkenness which prevailed" during the night.[30]

In the confusion of the evacuation and occupation of Columbia, the city endured a series of fires, the first of which occurred during

[24] Depositions of William T. Sherman, March 30, 1872, No. 37, Joseph J. Browne *vs.* United States, *Mixed Commission*, III, 6; Dec. 11, 1872, *Mixed Commission*, XIV, 83.

[25] Deposition of John A. Logan, Dec. 21, 1872, Nos. 103, 292, *Mixed Commission*, XIV, 282–283.

[26] Hazen, *Narrative of Military Service*, p. 349; deposition of Hazen, *Mixed Commission*, XIV, 151–152. For an interesting comparison of the entry of the Federal army into a town, see Edwin B. Coddington, *The Gettysburg Campaign: A Study in Command*, pp. 225–226.

[27] Yates Snowden, *Marching with Sherman: A Review by Yates Snowden of the Letters and Campaign Diaries of Henry Hitchcock*, p. 29.

[28] James Guignard Gibbes, *Who Burnt Columbia?*, pp. 7–8.

[29] Earl Schenck Miers, ed., *When the World Ended: The Diary of Emma LeConte*, p. 42.

[30] *Columbia Phoenix*, March 23, 1865. Harriott Horry Ravenel referred to the streets in her neighborhood as being "deserted" before the fire began.

the early hours of the morning of February 16 when the Congaree River bridge was burned against Beauregard's orders. That action can with little doubt be attributed to a diligent soldier who was uninformed of Beauregard's intent or to a straggler bent upon delaying the enemy. The next fires, of unaccountable origin, were those of the burning cotton which Major Chambliss reported were illuminating Columbia at three o'clock on the morning of February 17. That same morning before daylight there was the enormous explosion at the South Carolina Railroad station, generally attributed to the recklessness of greedy plunderers carrying torches; when the Federal army entered the capital, the terminal was still smoldering. Also burning when the Federal troops entered the city was the Charlotte Railroad station, which Beauregard had ordered Hampton to burn as he withdrew his last forces. There was one other fire in Columbia when the Union army entered, the fire in the cotton on Richardson Street. When Sherman arrived at the town hall about noon, two of Columbia's volunteer fire companies, the Independent commanded by John McKenzie and the Palmetto of William B. Stanley, aided by several of Stone's men, were working to extinguish the fire in the 100 to 150 cotton bales in the area. Near one o'clock, as the blaze was almost extinguished, it was learned that a fire had broken out in the town jail a short distance away on Washington Street between Assembly and Richardson streets. While the Palmetto engine continued to fight the cotton fire, McKenzie, with the aid of ten or twelve Union soldiers, hurried his engine to the jail and within a short period of time had the fire under control; the damage was confined to only one cell. No one knew the cause of the fire in the jail, but it seems quite clear that great damage to the city could have occurred if it had gotten out of control.[31]

See Ravenel, "Burning of Columbia," March 12, 1898, manuscript article from letter of March, 1865, Harriott Horry Ravenel Papers, South Caroliniana Library, University of South Carolina, Columbia.

[31] Depositions of John McKenzie, April 29, 1872, No. 37, *Mixed Commission*, III, 26, 28–29; April 9, 1872, No. 103, *Mixed Commission*, XIV, 9, 11; deposition of Milo H. Berry, March 16, 1872, No. 37, *Mixed Commission*, III, 20; deposition of Goodwyn, *Mixed Commission*, XIV, 14; *Columbia Phoenix*, March 23, 1865.

Fires in cotton are notoriously difficult to extinguish,[32] and though it was believed by those present that no danger remained from the cotton near the town hall, the smoldering bales were rekindled again later in the day, probably by the wind. Alderman Orlando Z. Bates later testified that he saw a small amount of cotton burning on Richardson Street about three o'clock in the afternoon,[33] and as Colonel John E. Tourtelotte rode through town toward camp between 3:00 and 4:00 P.M., he noticed several bales of cotton still on fire.[34]

During the afternoon, fires continued to break out. James G. Gibbes saw a fire consume about thirty cotton bales that had been removed from J. H. Kinard's stable at the corner of Plain and Richardson streets. He also witnessed the burning of "a few bales" near Richard O'Neale's warehouse in Cotton Town, but on neither occasion could he pinpoint the cause. At about the same time, between three and five o'clock in the afternoon, there occurred several fires two to five miles east of Columbia. The fine homes of Wade Hampton, Confederate Treasurer George A. Trenholm, Dr. John Wallace, J. U. Adams, and several other well-known citizens were deliberately burned.[35] Accident can be ruled out in this case, though the task of identifying the guilty is complicated. The most plausible answer is that Union troops or possibly escaped prisoners were led to these homes by disgruntled townspeople or blacks.

Shortly after five o'clock, just before sunset, John McKenzie's Independent Fire Company was called to fight another fire in some cotton stacked in the middle of Sumter Street between Washington and Lady streets. Captain McKenzie and his firemen extinguished the blaze, but not before the cotton was consumed. The cause of the fire was never learned.[36] At approximately the same

[32] *Columbia Tri-Weekly South Carolinian*, Jan. 21, 1864.

[33] Deposition of O. Z. Bates, April 8, 1872, No. 103, *Mixed Commission*, XIV, 6.

[34] Deposition of John E. Tourtelotte, Dec. 17, 1872, Nos. 103, 292, *Mixed Commission*, XIV, 256.

[35] Gibbes, *Who Burnt Columbia?*, p. 7; Henry S. Nourse, "Burning of Columbia, S.C., February 17, 1865," in *Operations on the Atlantic Coast 1861–1865; Virginia 1862, 1864; Vicksburg*, IX, 436.

[36] Depositions of McKenzie, April 29, 1872, *Mixed Commission*, III, 26, 29; April 9, 1872, *Mixed Commission*, XIV, 9.

time, Major T. W. Osborn later testified, the cotton on Richardson Street appeared to be still burning.[37]

The fire on Sumter Street had scarcely been extinguished when, as night approached, another accidental fire broke out two blocks west of the capitol on Gervais Street in the area where Captain A. E. Wood had seen cotton burning around 10:00 A.M. The houses in that vicinity were wooden, apparently not well kept, and "occupied mostly as brothels." When McKenzie heard of the Gervais Street fire, he rushed his engine to the scene and within a short space of time was joined by other volunteer companies; in spite of their efforts, all of the houses were destroyed.[38]

About eight o'clock that night another fire broke out and soon developed into a general conflagration which was not extinguished until two or three o'clock the next morning. It was this fire, the last in a long series of mostly inexplicable blazes, that destroyed about one-third of Columbia.[39] The fire spread rapidly, nourished by scattered cotton, wooden buildings with common walls, and a very strong wind blowing out of the northwest.[40]

During the afternoon, as the men of the XV and XVII Corps entered Columbia and as drunkenness mounted, it became increasingly apparent that stronger security measures would have to be taken. Consequently, shortly after five o'clock Howard ordered Logan to remove Stone's troops and replace them with a fresh brigade. This was the first occasion that Howard had been forced to take such action during the entire march through Georgia and South Carolina.[41] It indicated that the situation was indeed serious

[37] Deposition of T. W. Osborn, Dec. 16, 1872, Nos. 103, 292, *Mixed Commission*, XIV, 222. Osborn would later serve as United States senator from New Jersey.

[38] *Columbia Phoenix*, March 23, 1865; A. E. Wood, "Burning of Columbia, S.C.," *North American Review* 146 (April, 1888): 402; deposition of Philip S. Jacobs, Feb. 9, 1872, No. 37, *Mixed Commission*, III, 5; deposition of McKenzie, April 29, 1872, *Mixed Commission*, III, 26.

[39] Deposition of McKenzie, April 29, 1872, *Mixed Commission*, III, 27.

[40] Rachel Sherman Thorndike, ed., *The Sherman Letters: Correspondence between General and Senator Sherman from 1837 to 1891*, p. 266; *OR*, Ser. 1, XLVII, pt. 1: 252; B. H. Liddell Hart, *Sherman: Soldier, Realist, American*, p. 367.

[41] Howard, *Autobiography*, II, 121; Lewis, *Sherman, Fighting Prophet*, p. 504.

and that he was making an effort to prevent any untoward events from occurring in Columbia.[42] Nevertheless, Howard was not without fault in handling the matter. He had firsthand information of the deteriorating situation in Columbia, and he had been delegated the authority to take whatever measures were needed. There is no doubt that he should have acted earlier, and he obviously should have made it clear that immediate action was necessary.[43]

Logan was at his quarters in the Preston house when his assistant adjutant general, Major Maxwell Woodhull, brought Howard's order for a change in the provost guard. Logan chose Charles R. Woods to relieve Stone and restore order, and it was just before dark, nearly six o'clock in the evening, when Woodhull informed Woods of his orders. They were quite specific, not only instructing Woods to send in fresh troops to relieve Stone's brigade, but also directing him to detail fifty mounted men and infantry patrols of "sufficient strength" to sweep drunken and disorderly soldiers from the streets. It was left to Woods's discretion to determine the need for a new provost marshal.[44]

Charles R. Woods was at his headquarters on Senate Street, three-quarters of a mile east of the State House, when Woodhull arrived with his orders. Woods's choice of his brother, Brevet Brigadier General William B. Woods, to lead the relief troop is generally considered a sound decision. Word was sent to William

[42] Liddell Hart, *Sherman*, p. 367. Howard was considered by his fellow officers as a man of high character.

[43] Both David P. Conyngham, a newspaper correspondent for the *New York Herald*, and Colonel George A. Stone, to whom Mayor Goodwyn surrendered, would later claim that it was obvious that troops should have been brought into Columbia much earlier. See Conyngham, *Sherman's March Through the South, with Sketches and Incidents of the Campaign*, p. 332, and Stone's letter to the *Chicago Tribune*, Jan. 2, 1873, quoted in U.S. Congress, Senate, *Destruction of Property in Columbia, S.C., by Sherman's Army. Speech of Hon. Cole. L. Blease, a Senator from the State of South Carolina, Delivered in the Senate May 15, 1930*, 71st Cong., 2d sess., 1930, Senate Doc. No. 149 (Serial 9220), p. 100.

[44] Deposition of Woodhull, *Mixed Commission*, XIV, 236; deposition of Charles R. Woods, Dec. 16, 1872, Nos. 103, 292, *Mixed Commission*, XIV, 187; deposition of Logan, *Mixed Commission*, XIV, 286. It appears that there was a short delay between the time the order arrived and the time it was actually placed in Logan's hand, since he was apparently out of the room when the note arrived. It is not clear what firsthand information Woods had to determine "sufficient strength."

B. Woods, who was encamped with his men about one and one-half miles east of Columbia, to enter town as a new provost guard. By the time Woods had put the forty-five hundred men of the First Brigade, First Division, XV Corps into motion and marched into town, about two hours had elapsed, a not inordinate amount of time considering the fact that speed had not been emphasized. When the troops arrived at Richardson Street about 8:00 P.M., they found it in flames.[45]

As the flames climbed skyward in the center of Columbia, they soon became visible to the scattered Union officers at their headquarters. About the time that the new provost guard arrived at Richardson Street, Charles R. Woods, who as division commander was attempting to keep in touch with the situation, noticed the flames. He had his horse saddled and rode to Richardson Street to investigate, arriving at approximately 8:30 P.M. He found that William B. Woods, having walked into an inferno, had ordered his troops "to stop the fire," thus losing sight of his original orders of purging the streets of disorderly soldiers.[46] It seemed to both officers the natural action to take. Six hours would pass before a second decision would be reached to send in more troops to suppress the increasing disorders, another fatal lapse of time.

Logan, the corps commander, was at his headquarters on Blanding Street when he learned of the fire six or seven blocks to the west. He summoned his staff, and they hurried to the scene, where he began giving orders to both soldiers and citizens in an attempt to prevent the spreading of the fire.[47]

For General Howard the day had been long and tiring, and upon arriving at the McCord House near the college he lay down for a rest. Shortly after dark, probably about 8:30 P.M., he was awakened by one of his aides, Captain Frederick W. Gilbreth, and informed of a large fire in town. Howard then dressed and went to Richardson Street, where he found Logan directing the fire fighting.[48]

[45] *OR*, Ser. 1, XLVII, pt. 1: 243; Lewis, *Sherman, Fighting Prophet*, p. 504. The time given here differs slightly from that of the source.
[46] Deposition of Woods, *Mixed Commission*, XIV, 187.
[47] Deposition of Logan, *Mixed Commission*, XIV, 283, 286.
[48] Deposition of Howard, *Mixed Commission*, XIV, 5–7, 20.

Of Columbia's four fire company leaders, only John Mc-
Kenzie, captain of the Independent Fire Company, left a record of
his activities during the conflagration. McKenzie had spent the
early afternoon fighting fires, and "being nearly tired out," he
went to his home on Richardson Street to rest. Apparently very
concerned about the safety of Columbia, McKenzie later went up
on his roof, from which he had a good view of the city. During the
afternoon his worst apprehensions were realized as he saw a number of fires on the outskirts of town and several within the city.
The latter were eventually extinguished, but after dark he saw a
fire break out at Phillips's Warehouse on Taylor Street, about a
block from his home. McKenzie left his roof for Richardson Street,
where he found fires burning all around him. Upon walking toward his firehouse about a block away, he found his men at the
corner of Richardson and Washington streets spraying water on
Athenaeum Hall. Apparently believing that the hall could not be
saved, McKenzie ordered that the engine be moved to the corner
of Richardson and Plain streets in an attempt to save Lieber and
Agnew's store. While the engine was spraying water on the front
of the store, the rear caught fire, and then the store across the
street burst into flames. When other stores on the block caught fire
and it soon became apparent that they were making no headway,
McKenzie and his men gave up.[49]

Shortly after Mayor Goodwyn left Sherman's headquarters,
the Union commander had decided to lie down for a rest. He had
not been asleep long when he was awakened by an unsteady light
shining on the walls of his room. Upon inquiring about its cause,
Sherman was informed by a member of his staff, Major George W.
Nichols, that there was a fire in the business district near the town
hall. Nichols was dispatched to the scene and shortly returned to
report that the block of buildings opposite the place where they
had seen the cotton burning earlier in the day was afire. General
Charles R. Woods was on the scene with plenty of men trying to
contain the fire, Nichols continued, but the high wind was negating
their efforts. Sherman seemed satisfied with Nichols's report at the
time, but as the night passed and "the heavens became lurid," his

49 Deposition of McKenzie, April 29, 1872, *Mixed Commission*, III, 26–27.

After the fire: Richardson Street north from the State House grounds. The path of the fire was toward the viewer, slightly from left to right.

1 Alexander's Foundry
2 Arsenal Academy
3 Athenaeum Hall,
 Government Office
4 W. K. Bachman Home
5 Baptist Church
6 Bayonet Factory
7 Blacksmith shop-Kraft,
 Goldsmith, and Kraft
8 Campbell Bryce Home
9 Button Factory
10 Camp, First Div. XV
 Corps
11 Camp, Second Div. XV
12 Camp, Third Div. XV
 Corps
13 Camp, Fourth Div. XV
 Corps
14 Camp, First Div. XVII
 Corps
15 Camp, Third Div. XVII
 Corps
16 Camp, Fourth Div. XVII
 Corps
17 Catholic Church
18 Charlotte Railroad Depot
19 Columbia Canal
20 Columbia Theological
 Seminary
21 Commandant of Prisoners
 Office
22 Commissary Stores
 (5 locations)
23 Confederate Armory of C. C.
 McPhail (2 locations)
24 Confederate Government
 Offices (4 locations)
25 Confederate, State Military
 Offices
26 Congaree Hotel
27 Cotton Card Factory
28 Cotton Town
29 Enrolling Officer
 (2 locations)
30 Evans and Cogswell
31 Fair Grounds, Medical
 Purveyor Lab
32 Gas Works
33 Robert W. Gibbes Home
34 T. J. Goodwyn Home
35 Government Stables
36 Government Stores, Warehouses
 (7 locations)
37 O. O. Howard Hdq.
38 Independent Fire Company
 of John McKenzie
39 Insane Asylum
40 Jail
41 Joseph LeConte Home
42 John A. Logan Hdq.
43 John McKenzie Home
44 Medical Purveyor's Office

45 Methodist Church
46 Methodist Female College
47 Naval Agent Office
48 New State House
49 Niter Bureau Office
50 Old State House
51 Palmetto Fire Company of
 William B. Stanley
52 Palmetto Iron Works
53 Phillips Warehouse
54 Pottersfield
55 Powder Mill
56 Provost Marshal Hdq.
57 Harriott H. Ravenel Home
58 William Reynolds Home
59 St. Mary's College,
 Government Warehouse

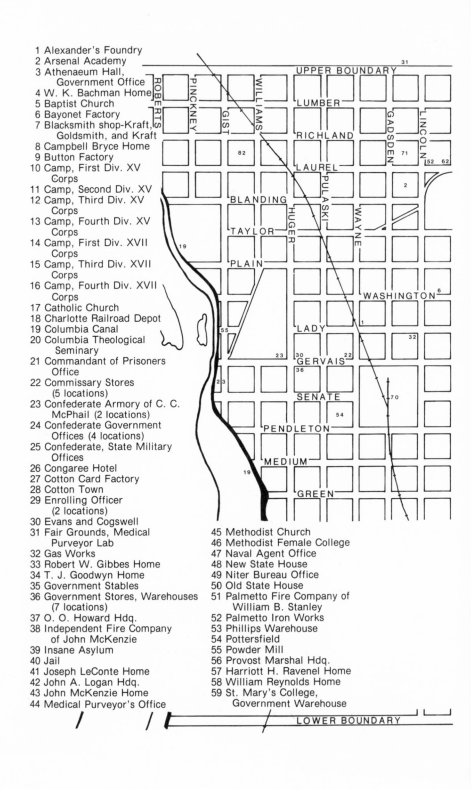

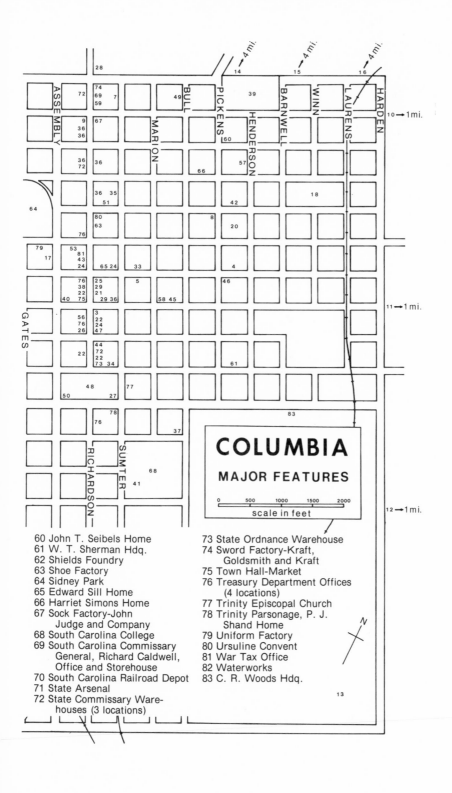

COLUMBIA

MAJOR FEATURES

scale in feet

60 John T. Seibels Home
61 W. T. Sherman Hdq.
62 Shields Foundry
63 Shoe Factory
64 Sidney Park
65 Edward Sill Home
66 Harriet Simons Home
67 Sock Factory-John
   Judge and Company
68 South Carolina College
69 South Carolina Commissary
   General, Richard Caldwell,
   Office and Storehouse
70 South Carolina Railroad Depot
71 State Arsenal
72 State Commissary Ware-
   houses (3 locations)

73 State Ordnance Warehouse
74 Sword Factory-Kraft,
   Goldsmith and Kraft
75 Town Hall-Market
76 Treasury Department Offices
   (4 locations)
77 Trinity Episcopal Church
78 Trinity Parsonage, P. J.
   Shand Home
79 Uniform Factory
80 Ursuline Convent
81 War Tax Office
82 Waterworks
83 C. R. Woods Hdq.

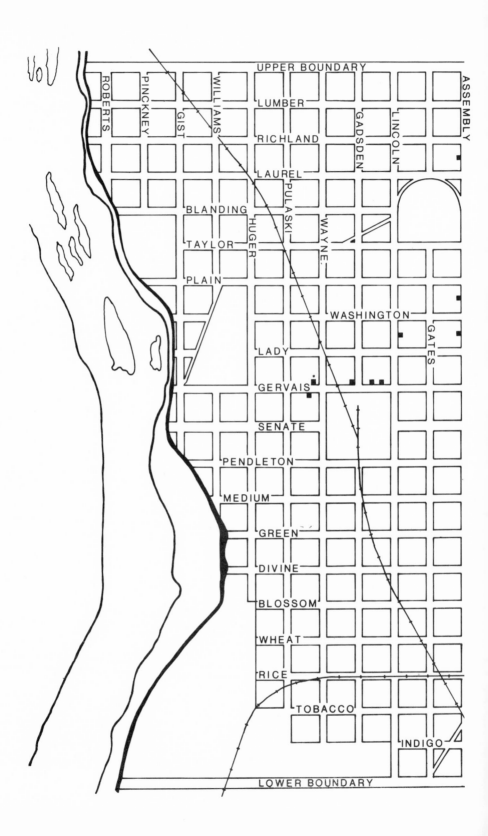

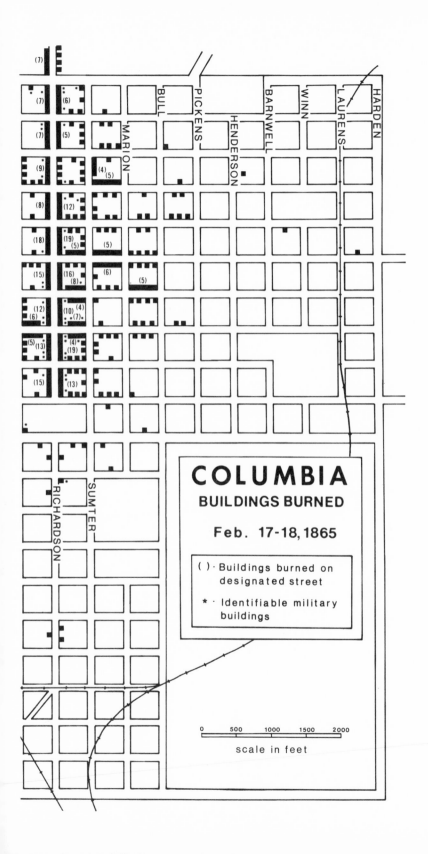

COLUMBIA
BUILDINGS BURNED

Feb. 17-18, 1865

( ) · Buildings burned on
designated street

* · Identifiable military
buildings

0   500   1000   1500   2000

scale in feet

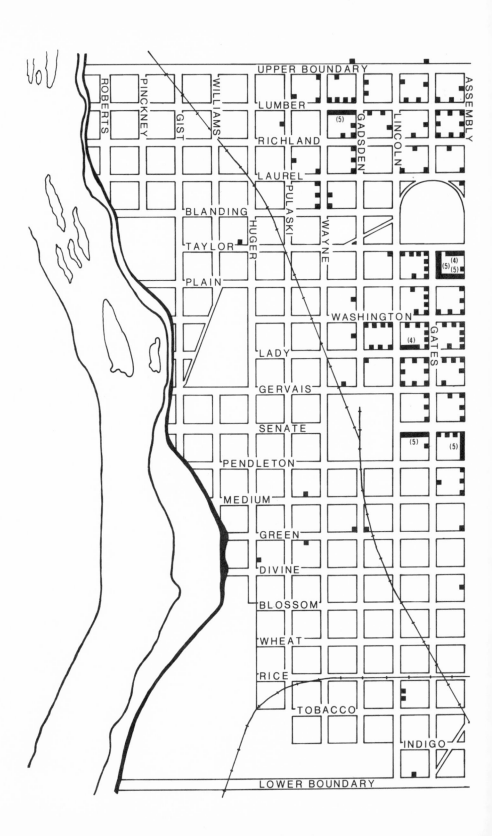

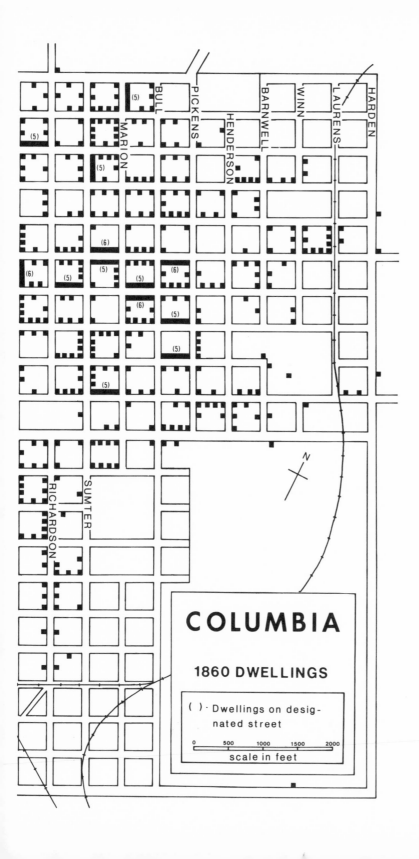

COLUMBIA

1860 DWELLINGS

( ) · Dwellings on desig-
nated street

scale in feet
0   500   1000   1500   2000

After the fire: Ursuline Convent at the southeast corner of Richardson and Blanding streets.

concern increased. Other messengers were sent to inquire about the prospects of stopping the fire. Each found Howard, Logan, and Charles R. Woods battling the fire with their men, but all feared that the fire could not be contained as long as the wind raged.[50]

Reports from the Federal generals indicate that strenuous efforts were made to prevent a conflagration that would destroy the entire town. When Howard arrived on Richardson Street he found Logan already directing troops in fighting the flames. In a quick consultation the two generals apparently agreed that there was little possibility of extinguishing the fire and that their only hope lay in tearing down sheds and buildings in the fire's path to prevent its spreading. Most of the available soldiers were placed at this task, though some were sent to the tops of buildings, where water was passed to them in order to snuff out fires. Still others were assigned to guard citizens and assist them in protecting their property when it was taken into the streets.[51]

Logan's account of his activities indicates that he made arduous efforts to combat the fire. According to his testimony, he directed troops in fire fighting up and down Richardson Street, "wherever the fire was." While trying to contain the flames, he said, he saw other Union officers directing similar efforts, all of which were nullified by the strong wind, which spread the flames.[52]

Like Logan, Charles R. Woods had arrived early and engaged in fighting the fire all during the night. On several occasions he ordered men to tear down houses and other buildings in an effort to stop its progress, but in each case the debris could not be removed fast enough to prevent the flames from spreading. Woods later estimated that at least two thousand Union soldiers were engaged in fighting the fire.[53]

Once the fire began, it moved so rapidly that there was often scarcely time to escape. The hotel that Brevet Major General William F. Barry and his staff had chosen for headquarters was one of the first buildings to which the flames spread, and only a

[50] Sherman, *Memoirs*, II, 286.
[51] Deposition of Howard, *Mixed Commission*, XIV, 5–6.
[52] Deposition of Logan, *Mixed Commission*, XIV, 283, 298.
[53] Deposition of Woods, *Mixed Commission*, XIV, 189–190.

concerted effort enabled them to flee with their lives, though much of their property was lost. Barry moved to a nearby house, which he saved by placing three of his staff on the roof to put out fires set by sparks.[54]

It was about eleven o'clock before Sherman decided to go to the business district to ascertain conditions for himself. By then the flames had been raging for almost three hours. While surveying the situation, he noticed that the fire was creeping toward the home of Mrs. Harriet Simons, whom he had visited during the afternoon. He went to the house, advised the inhabitants to move to his headquarters at the Blanton Duncan house, and provided wagons for their baggage. The Simonses were indeed fortunate, for when they returned to their home the next morning, they found it had not been burned. Sherman remained in the streets of Columbia until about three o'clock the next morning, when the wind subsided and the fire was brought under control. During that time he had ample opportunity to view the performance of his men in fighting the fire and was apparently satisfied with their efforts.[55]

The greatest problem in combating the fire was the powerful wind that blew out of the northwest but that gusted in all directions. Almost every account, from both Southern and Northern writers, tells of sparks, carried high into the air by the flames, falling all over town. Columbian James McCarter described the scene as one of burning boards and shingles wafted in the air by the wind and then falling in a "perfect shower of fire," spreading the flames beyond the power of "mortal men to arrest."[56] Another inhabitant, the locally prominent John T. Seibels, remembered how the "air was filled with sparks and small pieces of blazing shingles," the effect of which was to light the "entire city."[57] Ed-

[54] Deposition of James C. McCoy, Dec. 17, 1872, Nos. 103, 292, *Mixed Commission,* XIV, 265–266; deposition of Joseph C. Audenried, Dec. 13, 1872, Nos. 103, 292, *Mixed Commission,* XIV, 133.

[55] Sherman, *Memoirs,* II, 286; Harriet H. Simons, "Burning of Columbia" [1865?], manuscript, Harriet H. Simons Papers, South Caroliniana Library, University of South Carolina, Columbia.

[56] James McCarter, "The Burning of Columbia Again," *Harper's Magazine* 33 (Oct., 1866): 643.

[57] Quoted in Snowden, *Marching with Sherman,* p. 35.

ward Sill, writing in 1868, spoke of "great sheets of flames" being swept by the wind "from one side of Main [Richardson] street to the other."[58]

Mrs. J. J. Pringle Smith and William Gilmore Simms added their testimony of "sparks" carried by the wind falling in "showers" on contiguous buildings.[59] An anonymous writer, telling of the burning of the Ursuline Convent, wrote that the convent, located one block north of the spot John McKenzie reported the first fire began, quite early became endangered from the falling sparks. When the nuns finally abandoned the convent about eleven o'clock, "sparks and pieces of burning wood" were falling "so thick" that many of the nuns had holes burned in their veils and dresses.[60]

Union observers were equally impressed with the effect of the wind in spreading the fire. Charles R. Woods saw "masses of flaming material" blown "on and over roofs, in windows and doors, and against fences,"[61] and Hazen observed "blazing siding and shingles" blown onto the roofs of buildings.[62] General Logan stated that "the wind was blowing shingles that were on fire in nearly every direction," Major George W. Nichols wrote of the air being "filled" with sparks,[63] and S. H. M. Byers reported seeing sparks ignite houses.[64] Sherman's testimony corroborated these

[58] Edward Sill, "Who is Responsible for the Destruction of the City of Columbia, S.C., on the Night of 17 February, 1865," *Land We Love* 4 (March, 1868): 364.

[59] Daniel E. Huger Smith et al., eds., *Mason Smith Family Letters, 1860–1865*, p. 176; *Columbia Phoenix*, April 6, 1865.

[60] A. T. Smythe, M. B. Poppenheim, and Thomas Taylor, eds., *South Carolina Women in the Confederacy*, I, 294–295, 302. The Catholic priest in Columbia stated that the convent and St. Mary's College were not deliberately burned, but the college, which was used by the Confederate government to store commissary supplies, was sacked. J. J. O'Connell, *Catholicity in the Carolinas and Georgia: Leaves of its History*, pp. 268, 279–280.

[61] U.S. Congress, Senate, *Congressional Globe*, 39th Cong., 1st sess., May 1, 1866, 36, pt. 3: 2301.

[62] Hazen, *Narrative of Military Service*, p. 351.

[63] Deposition of Logan, *Mixed Commission*, XIV, 286; George Ward Nichols, *The Story of the Great March: From the Diary of a Staff Officer*, p. 165; George Ward Nichols, "The Burning of Columbia," *Harper's Magazine* 33 (Aug., 1866): 364.

[64] Samuel Hawkins Marshall Byers, "The Burning of Columbia," *Lippincott's Magazine* 29 (March, 1882): 259.

witnesses when he reported seeing "flames carried sometimes two blocks by the force of the wind."[65]

A vivid picture of the effect of the blowing sparks and burning shingles can be imagined from the events that transpired on the campus of South Carolina College. Shortly after the capture of Columbia the provost marshal assigned guards to protect the college buildings, which were encompassed by an eight-foot wall. The afternoon passed without disturbance at the college, but upon the outbreak of fire in the center of town the appearance of "a copper colored sky" on the northwestern horizon created apprehension on the campus. At Joseph LeConte's home, the present Lieber College, Emma LeConte watched the fire rage but hoped that the college would be spared. During the night, however, the "fearful gale" pushed the "flames from house to house," encroaching ever closer upon the campus, until eventually the buildings were threatened with "showers" of burning debris.[66] When the "crashing of timbers and the thunder of falling buildings" appeared to be opposite the campus wall, Mrs. LeConte decided to abandon her house to the flames. Bedding, clothing, and food were removed to the garden behind the house and covered with an old carpet to shelter them from the "sparks and flakes of fire." The LeContes thought it inevitable that their home would be lost, but it was not. "By what miracle it was saved I cannot think," Emma recorded in her diary the next day. "No effort could be made—no one was on the roof, which was old and dry, and all the while the sparks and burning timbers were flying over it like rain."[67]

Others on the campus were less fortunate. Professors J. L. Reynolds and W. J. Rivers spent much of the night on their roofs putting out fires started by sparks, and during the first hours of February 18 the roof of Dr. Maximilian LaBorde's house, located near a building being used for a hospital, ignited. A potentially disastrous situation was avoided when a number of Federal soldiers

[65] Deposition of Sherman, Dec. 11, 1872, *Mixed Commission*, XIV, 66, 87; Thorndike, *Sherman Letters*, p. 266; Sherman, *Memoirs*, II, 286; *OR*, Ser. 1, XLVII, pt. 1: 21.

[66] Miers, *When the World Ended*, pp. 42, 45–46; *Columbia Phoenix*, April 6, 1865.

[67] Miers, *When the World Ended*, pp. 46–47.

who had been fighting the fire nearby were successful in extinguishing the flames in LaBorde's roof. As it turned out, the only danger to the campus was from the wind-blown sparks, and fortunately the college was saved without the loss of a single building. The major part of the fire stopped about two blocks from the college, though ten structures were consumed within that two-block area.[68]

One fact seemed clear to many observers during the night: as long as the powerful wind continued it was impossible to stop the spread of the flames. William Gilmore Simms, writing about the effect of the wind, stated that even if the fire engines had been employed to capacity, they would have been useless "against such a storm of fire." If the flames had reached the college campus, he continued, "the destruction of any one building would to a certainty have led to the loss of all."[69] Fireman McKenzie, a veteran of thirty years' service, concurred that once the flames blew out of control, there was little hope in controlling the fire.[70] James G. Gibbes, who spent the entire night in the streets, was similarly impressed: "There is no doubt but that the city was burned by the wind spreading the flames...."[71]

The testimony of the Northern generals corroborates that of the inhabitants. Sherman stated that as long as the high winds prevailed, controlling the fire was "beyond human possibility,"[72] a belief shared by Charles R. Woods.[73] Logan thought that subjugating the flames under existing wind conditions was an "impossibility,"[74] and Hazen stated that the "wind was so overpowering" that all his efforts to prevent the spread of the flames came to naught.[75]

[68] William Alexander Nicholson, *The Burning of Columbia*, p. 6; *Columbia Phoenix*, April 6, 1865; Daniel Walker Hollis, *University of South Carolina: South Carolina College*, p. 227. The proximity of the fire to the college can be seen on the map depicting the burned district.

[69] *Columbia Phoenix*, March 23, April 6, 1865.

[70] Deposition of McKenzie, April 9, 1872, *Mixed Commission*, XIV, 12.

[71] Deposition of James G. Gibbes, July 29, 1872, No. 236, David Jacobs *vs.* United States, *Mixed Commission*, XXIII, 11.

[72] Sherman, *Memoirs*, II, 286.

[73] Deposition of Woods, *Mixed Commission*, XIV, 190; Senate, *Congressional Globe*, 39th Cong., 1st sess., May 1, 1866, pt. 3: 2301.

[74] Deposition of Logan, *Mixed Commission*, XIV, 283.

[75] Deposition of Hazen, *Mixed Commission*, XIV, 161–162.

As it turned out, these judgments were correct, for it was not until between two and three o'clock on the morning of the eighteenth, when the wind abated, that the fire fighters were able to control the holocaust.[76]

The fire, of course, was a great tragedy, but it was not until the flames reached such proportions that they were observed by the men of the XV and XVII Corps encamped on the perimeter of the city that conditions reached their nadir. The raging fire was the invitation to stragglers, sightseers, and the curious that all such calamities attract, and consequently a steady stream of troops began to drift into town.[77] Liquor was everywhere abundant, as it had been during the entire day, and new supplies were discovered readily.[78] Soon an assortment of drunken citizens and refugees, both white and black, and "the vilest vagabond soldiers, the veriest scum of the entire army," roamed the streets. The appearance of this rioting mob, which continued to accumulate in intensity until it reached a crescendo between 2:00 and 4:00 A.M. on the morning of the eighteenth, greatly hampered the already hopeless attempts to control or localize the flames.[79]

The rioting in the streets of Columbia resulted in three basic kinds of misconduct: citizens were taunted by roving gangs which stole or destroyed property; acts of physical violence were performed against citizens; and, finally, the fire was extended through incendiarism. Responsibility for these deeds has been attributed to a number of sources, and while Negroes, escaped Union prisoners, and the local criminal element have received a share of the blame,[80] the major burden of criticism has been placed upon the occupying Federal army. It is certain that all of these groups participated to some degree in the riot, and it is possible that some

[76] Deposition of Howard, *Mixed Commission*, XIV, 6.

[77] Deposition of Woodhull, *Mixed Commission*, XIV, 246; Allen Diary [Feb., 1865], Edward W. Allen Papers, Southern Historical Collection, University of North Carolina, Chapel Hill.

[78] Deposition of Howard, *Mixed Commission*, XIV, 38–39; *OR*, Ser. 1, XLVII, pt. 1: 227.

[79] *OR*, Ser. 1, XLVII, pt. 1: 243; pt. 2: 457; Howard, *Autobiography*, II, 121.

[80] Deposition of Howard, *Mixed Commission*, XIV, 6; *OR*, Ser. 1, XLVII, pt. 1: 199; Senate, *Congressional Globe*, 39th Cong., 1st sess., May 1, 1866, pt. 3: 2301.

were guilty of all types of charges. A number of general accounts include stories of intoxication, pillage, and even burning by Negroes, though incidents identifying blacks as being the primary cause of the riot, pillage, or fire are nonexistent. Only one witness reported having seen Negroes fire buildings in Columbia.[81] References to the culpability of escaped Federal prisoners are also numerous, but the charges cannot be sustained because of the absence of eyewitness accounts.[82] Evidence is clearer about the part played by one of Columbia's criminals in spreading the fire. Bill Morris, who escaped from jail during the confusion of the entrance of the Union army, was recognized by several citizens during the night as he set fire to houses and outbuildings. The extent of his involvement, however, is unknown.[83] Evidence of the participation of Federal troops in the riot, pillage, and burning of buildings is far more abundant,[84] and it was from bands of drunken soldiers, stragglers and rabble who roamed the streets during the night that the greatest danger to Columbians arose. Numerous eyewitness accounts of these activities exist.

One extensive account was that of Dr. Robert W. Gibbes, antiquarian, naturalist, and an old and distinguished citizen of Columbia who resided in a brick house on the north side of Plain between Sumter and Marion streets. He possessed in his home a large number of copies of fine portraits, an extensive group of Southern fossils, a fine collection of sharks' teeth, relics of aboriginal Americans, many South Carolina historical documents relating to the Revolution, and an outstanding assemblage of coins from around the world. The flames had swept down Plain Street past Dr. Gibbes's house, the dwelling having been saved only by the presence of men on his roof with buckets of water. Around midnight, however, after the crisis seemed to be over, a band of drunken,

[81] R. W. Gibbes to W. A. Gibbes, March 14, 1865, Gibbes Papers; Mrs. W. K. Bachman to Kate Bachman, March 27, 1865, copy, Bachman Papers.

[82] *Story of the Fifty-Fifth Illinois*, p. 409; Henry Clay McArthur, *Capture and Destruction of Columbia, South Carolina, February 17, 1865*, pp. 13–14.

[83] *Columbia Phoenix*, March 23, 1865; Mrs. S. McCam to daughter, March 5 [1865?], in "Burning of Columbia," miscellaneous manuscripts and printed materials, Yates Snowden Collection, South Caroliniana Library, University of South Carolina, Columbia; *The State* (Columbia), March 4, 1893.

[84] An evaluation of this evidence will be made in chapter 6.

carousing soldiers entered his house. In the confusion which followed a fire was set in the parlor, and when Dr. Gibbes and a
companion, Robert McCollough, attempted to extinguish the
flames, the intruders interfered, saying, "Let the damned house
burn." As the flames spread the soldiers broke open and robbed a
trunk of silver plate, and upon leaving they took some of Dr.
Gibbes's clothes. Realizing the hopelessness of the situation, Gibbes
abandoned his home to the flames, which consumed all his possessions except for his "bonds and money."[85]

Another case of plunder and revelry was witnessed by two
escaped Federal prisoners, Captain Byers and Lieutenant Devine,
who had found refuge in the home of an unidentified Northern-
born family. Before the inhabitants realized the danger, the fire
had leaped from across the street and ignited the house. The ladies
were escorted to the garden along with several trunks, while Byers
and Devine reentered the house for more valuables. Upon returning with their arms full, they found that about six intoxicated
soldiers had smashed open the trunks and were parading around
in the ladies' petticoats and bonnets. After much difficulty Byers
and Devine secured the arrest of the drunken soldiers, but they
were unable to save anything else from the house.[86]

A. Toomer Porter, a strongly secessionist Episcopal minister
who had recently fled the siege of Charleston, had found refuge
for his wife and two children in the home of Dr. William Reynolds on Washington Street.[87] About 10:00 P.M., when it appeared
that the flames would engulf them, Reynolds and Porter, with the
aid of Lieutenant John A. McQueen, a young officer from Howard's
staff, led the ladies and children to an area near the Blanton Duncan house, which they heard was not threatened. With the women

---

[85] R. W. Gibbes to W. A. Gibbes, March 14, 1865, Gibbes Papers; Gibbes,
Who Burnt Columbia?, p. 19; James Ford Rhodes, *History of the United States
from the Compromise of 1850 to the Final Restoration of Home Rule at the
South in 1877*, pp. 95–96. It has been impossible to determine what happened
to Dr. Gibbes's guard or who was on his roof with water buckets. Seventeen
days after the fire Gibbes recovered some of his silver and one hundred bottles
of alcoholic beverages from the ruins.

[86] Byers, "Burning of Columbia," p. 259.

[87] Anthony Toomer Porter, *Led On! Step By Step: Scenes from Clerical,
Military, Educational, and Plantation Life in the South, 1828–1898*, p. 168.

safely situated, Reynolds, accompanied by McQueen, decided to return to his home in an attempt to save some of his property. After Reynolds had been gone for what seemed like an inordinate length of time, and when soldiers making threatening remarks appeared at the doors of the house where they had taken refuge, Mrs. Reynolds became frantic about her husband's safety. Porter had decided to go in search of Reynolds when McQueen returned to inform him that the house had been saved and that the doctor desired the return of the ladies. Unsure of what was happening, and suspicious of the Union officer, Porter decided to talk with Reynolds before taking the ladies into the burned district. Upon arriving in the neighborhood of Reynolds's home, Porter saw a burning building which he mistook for the doctor's dwelling; certain of foul play, he hurried back to the ladies.[88]

While retracing his steps, Porter was attacked by a drunken Union soldier, who gave him a staggering blow to the temple and stole his shawl. Seeing the attack, another soldier pursued the assailant and forced him to return the shawl and apologize to his victim. Finally reaching his destination, Porter was astonished to learn that the officer had moved the women to Dr. Reynolds's house. Convinced that Lieutenant McQueen was guilty of perfidy, Porter for a second time sought out the Reynolds home, where he found, to his amazement, the women safe and the house unburned. He learned further that McQueen had emptied the house of plunderers and had posted a guard at the front and rear.[89]

Charles D. Bateman, an immigrant from Cork, Ireland, who had moved from Charleston to Columbia in 1862, told of similar occurrences. A group of rowdy Union soldiers forced their way into his home and proceeded to steal his watch, chain, and gold key and several pieces of jewelry belonging to his wife. Trunks were burst open and vandalized, and household utensils and

[88] Anthony Toomer Porter, *The History of a Work of Faith and Love in Charleston, South Carolina, Which Grew Out of the Calamities of the Late Civil War, and a Record of God's Wonderful Providence*, pp. 114–116.

[89] Ibid., pp. 116–119, 122–123, 125. Porter reciprocated McQueen's kindness when he later learned that the lieutenant was wounded and captured at Darlington, S.C. Porter visited McQueen and secured a pass for him into Union lines in North Carolina. The men remained lifelong friends.

clothes were scattered throughout the residence. Shortly thereafter Bateman was thrown into the street and his house was burned.[90]

Once again, the testimony of the Northern observers corroborates that of the Columbians. In his *Autobiography* General Howard, always quite frank, stated that "drunken soldiers ran through house after house and were doubtless guilty of all manner of villainies," including setting fires and insulting and roughly handling citizens.[91] Sherman, somewhat less candidly, admitted that all these activities may have happened.[92]

Major G. W. Nichols was on the scene during the entire night, and he observed intoxicated men pillaging and burning houses, leaving a "heart-rending sight" of "men, women, and children huddled about the few articles of clothing and household wares which were saved from their ruined homes."[93] Elijah P. Burton, a Union medical doctor, recorded what he observed in his diary: "After dark I saw the town on fire. Walked down & found a general riot, Boys drunk & scattering the tobacco & other plunder profusely. . . . I picked up a nice white double blanket, at a big hotel just ready to burn."[94] Vett Noble, another Union soldier, described in a letter to his mother his own participation in the events in Columbia:

> Houses and such were not touched until after the whole city was on fire and such stuff taken because it would have been in the ruins otherwise. . . .
> I have got a splendid silver teapot for you, been used of course but yet it is a nice one. I did have a lot of trinkets, knives, forks and spoons, goblets etc. all silver, but the mess kept growing larger . . . so most of the things are in use by mess as mess property. . . . I had a dozen silver plated dessert knives, quite nice. I broke into them and I guess all will go, some of the forks are lost, spoons ditto, goblets getting jammed up etc etc but the teapot I laid away.[95]

[90] Deposition of Charles D. Bateman, June 11, 1872, No. 190, Charles D. Bateman *vs.* United States, *Mixed Commission*, XX, 1–3.

[91] Howard, *Autobiography*, II, 122.

[92] Deposition of Sherman, Dec. 11, 1872, *Mixed Commission*, XIV, 91.

[93] Nichols, "Burning of Columbia," p. 364.

[94] Elijah P. Burton, *Diary of E. P. Burton, Surgeon, Seventh Regiment Illinois, Third Brigade, Second Division, Sixteenth Army Corps*, II, 63.

[95] Donald W. Disbrow, ed., "Vett Noble of Ypsilanti: A Clerk for General Sherman," *Civil War History* 14 (March, 1968): 36.

Edward W. Allen, a lieutenant in a Wisconsin regiment, described the "heart rending" sight during the night of "women down on their knees with hands clasped in prayer," begging for relief. It made him think of home and how he would react if his family had to go through a similar event. "Our brigade," he continued,

> lay close by so that many of the men went two and three times to the city—for things and when morning came, every conceivable article that one could imagine, most, was to be found in our camp, clothing, bed clothing, such splendid coverlids, quilts, and sheets, musical instruments—violins, guitars, music box, and had not pianos been quite so heavy you might have seen many of them there. . . . Silver plate, plates, knives, forks, spoons, but it would take too much time, candle and paper to mention or even try to mention all that was there, most all was left—destroyed except small articles of value easily carried by one of the boys. I got a nice vase which I will try to get home—(It's broke now).[96]

Articles "picked up" in Columbia were for many years exhibited by former Union soldiers in their Northern homes after the war, as victorious soldiers are disposed to do.[97] Some items, however, such as the church plate taken from the Reverend P. J. Shand, were returned as soon as they were discovered by officers. Reverend Shand recorded that while attempting to make his way to the college green with a trunk of church service plate, he was approached by five soldiers who pushed him and stole the trunk.[98] Later, after the Federal army left Columbia, Logan found the trunk in one of his headquarters wagons and had it returned.[99] At least one stolen item, a bracelet, was restored to its proper owner when it was recognized by Columbians visiting in the North after the war.[100] A copy of Robert Mills's *Atlas of South Carolina*, clearly marked as property of the State of South Carolina, was picked

---

[96] Allen Diary [Feb., 1865], Allen Papers.

[97] John T. Trowbridge, *The Desolate South, 1865–1866: A Picture of the Battlefields and the Devastated Confederacy*, pp. 303–304.

[98] Peter J. Shand, "Burning of Columbia," Jan. 8, 1866, manuscript, Shand Papers; J. P. Carroll, "Burning of Columbia," *Southern Historical Society Papers* 8 (May, 1880): 208.

[99] Deposition of Logan, *Mixed Commission*, XIV, 302.

[100] Trowbridge, *Desolate South*, p. 304.

up on the night of the fire and, after passing through the hands of two Northern generals, was placed in the National Archives in Washington, D.C., where it is presently housed.[101]

With drunken men roaming the streets, it was almost inevitable that some acts of personal violence against inhabitants of Columbia would occur. One such instance occurred when Edward Sill confronted a group of about six brawling soldiers who entered his yard. One of the soldiers gave Sill a "violent push" which threw him to the sidewalk. When Sill regained his composure, he found that he had suffered a dislocated thumb, a cut on his hand that bled profusely, and the loss of a tooth.[102] In addition to the attack on the Reverend A. Toomer Porter and the Reverend P. J. Shand, William Gilmore Simms reported that the Catholic priest, the Reverend Doctor J. J. O'Connell, was "knocked down and severely handled by the soldiers," though the priest did not include this information in his own account of the events.[103] The only other account of a similar occurrence was one given by R. W. Gibbes, in which he stated that "one Col. Hayne and Mr. Alfred Huger were treated very roughly and pulled about and struck" during the conflagration.[104] These are the only recorded cases of physical violence against Columbians, and there were no reported cases of rape or murder during the series of events in Columbia.

Extension of the fire through incendiarism is one of the most disputed issues in the events surrounding the burning of Columbia, and it is greatly complicated by the lack of reliable eyewitness accounts. While a small number of persons involved in the fire saw direct acts of incendiarism, others in the streets who were reliable witnesses and in a good position to observe witnessed few cases or none at all.

Robert W. Gibbes and his son, James G. Gibbes, witnessed the burning of the distinguished doctor's house, and Mrs. Agnes

[101] Brevet Brigadier General Orlando M. Poe was given a copy of Mills's *Atlas* by a Union soldier after the evacuation of Columbia. Poe sent it to Sherman, who apparently sent it to the National Archives, where it is now in section P-14.

[102] Sill, "Who is Responsible," pp. 364–365.

[103] *Columbia Phoenix*, March 23, 1865. See also O'Connell, *Catholicity*, pp. 268–282.

[104] Gibbes to Andrew G. Magrath, Feb. 28, 1865, Gibbes Papers.

Law, in 1884 at the age of seventy-two, testified in an affidavit that when the fire began in Columbia the four guards protecting her house suddenly ran up to the third floor of her brick home and set it on fire.[105] A. Toomer Porter wrote in 1882 that he "saw men with balls of cotton, dipped in turpentine, enter house after house, . . . throw the liquid over the furniture, and then set it on fire."[106] D. H. Trezevant, in an account of the burning of Columbia written in 1866, listed six people who had told him that they saw Union troops setting fires to houses or outbuildings.[107] William B. Stanley and O. Z. Bates, both well-known Columbians, also claimed to have seen soldiers fire one or more buildings, as did Emeline Squire, Malcolm A. Shelton, R. Cochran, John A. Civil, and Milo H. Berry, the latter a pro-Union man living in Columbia.[108]

On the point of incendiarism the Union generals are unanimous. None admitted later that he saw Federal soldiers actually set fires, but all acknowledged that such acts were entirely possible or even probable.[109] However, fireman John McKenzie, who was in the streets of Columbia much of the night, stated, "I saw no Federal soldiers apply the torch."[110] Another Columbian, Francis W. Wing, gave the same testimony: "I saw no person or persons, United States soldiers or any other, set fire to any building on that night."[111] And James G. Gibbes, who reported that he was in the

[105] "The Burning of Columbia—Affidavit of Agnes Law," *Southern Historical Society Papers* 12 (May, 1884): 233.

[106] Porter, *Work of Faith*, p. 114.

[107] Daniel Heyward Trezevant, *The Burning of Columbia, S.C.: A Review of Northern Assertions and Southern Facts*, p. 22.

[108] Deposition of William B. Stanley, Feb. 6, 1872, No. 37, *Mixed Commission*, III, 5; deposition of Bates, *Mixed Commission*, XIV, 4; deposition of Emeline Squire, April 30, 1872, No. 103, *Mixed Commission*, XIV, 18; deposition of Malcolm A. Shelton, April 30, 1872, No. 103, *Mixed Commission*, XIV, 20; deposition of R. Cochran, July 31, 1872, No. 236, *Mixed Commission*, XXIII, 24; affidavit of John A. Civil in *Burning of Columbia, Letter and Report*, p. 6; deposition of Berry, *Mixed Commission*, III, 18; affidavit of Berry in *Burning of Columbia, Letter and Report*, p. 6.

[109] Deposition of Sherman, Dec. 11, 1872, *Mixed Commission*, XIV, 89–91; deposition of Logan, *Mixed Commission*, XIV, 298–299; deposition of Hazen, *Mixed Commission*, XIV, 167; deposition of Howard, *Mixed Commission*, XIV, 6.

[110] Deposition of McKenzie, April 29, 1872, *Mixed Commission*, III, 29.

[111] Deposition of Francis W. Wing, April 29, 1872, No. 37, *Mixed Commission*, III, 31. Wing did not leave his home until 11:00 P.M.

streets throughout the disaster, stated that he "saw no fire applied" by soldiers except in the burning of his father's house.[112] Charles D. Bateman corroborated these accounts.[113]

It would be difficult to exaggerate the horrors of that night for those whose houses were entered by drunken mobs, for those who suffered physical attack, or for those whose homes were burned. To minimize their fright, their suffering, their loss, would be unforgivable. As General Slocum later pointed out, "a drunken soldier with a musket in one hand and a match in the other is not a pleasant visitor to have about the house on a dark, windy, night. . . ."[114] But to exaggerate the number of Columbians who experienced such visits would also be an injustice. While the record clearly reveals that there was an intoxicated, rioting mob in the streets of Columbia during the fire, the evidence is equally lucid that for the most part the prevailing mood was not malevolent.

Mrs. Mary Leverett found both humanity and hatred in the conduct of Union soldiers during the fire. "My poor sister's house was burnt down—some houses were set afire, & some caught—the latter was the case with hers," she wrote a friend on March 18, 1865, "but a Captain of an Iowa company & his men were very kind, and assisted her, Mary Heyward & Annie Hanckel in moving their things, that is provisions, bedding & clothes, but all of their furniture was burned." She concluded from her experiences that "some of the soldiers of Sherman were demons, [while] others were very humane. . . . As far as I could learn," she continued, "no actual personal insult was inflicted on any lady besides rude and violent attempts to search them for gold."[115]

W. D. Meister, a Columbian who left for the Up Country shortly after the Union army departed, wrote a vivid account of the treatment of citizens during the fire. "No cases of personal violence, with one exception, were heard of," he told the readers

---

[112] Deposition of James G. Gibbes, May 1, 1872, No. 103, *Mixed Commission*, XIV, 25.

[113] Deposition of Bateman, *Mixed Commission*, XX, 3.

[114] Henry W. Slocum, "Sherman's March from Savannah to Bentonville," in *Battles and Leaders of the Civil War*, ed. Robert Underwood Johnson and Clarence Clough Buel, IV, 686.

[115] Mary Leverett to Caroline, March 18, 1865, Mary Leverett Letter, South Caroliniana Library, University of South Carolina, Columbia.

of the *Yorkville Enquirer* three weeks after the event. "The Yankee soldiers were made drunk on the whiskey left in the Medical Purveyor's Store, and from this cause ensued much of the mischief." As to their comportment, he stated that "the Yankees were boisterous and bullying, but not actually violent to persons, except to steal everything from them, they could get."[116]

Another home entered by drunken soldiers during the night was that of Mrs. Harriott H. Ravenel, who also recognized the absence of viciousness in their activities. A constant "stream of drunkards poured through the house, plundering and raging," she stated two weeks after the event, yet they were "curiously *civil*, and abstaining from personal insult. . . . They generally spoke to us as 'Lady', and although they swore horribly, they seldom swore at us. . . . They were all more or less excited by drink, but in the early part of the night it was not as bad as later on."[117] Mary Janney concurred with these opinions. "The Yankees were just as gentlemanly as rough men could well be," she wrote. "I didn't see any bad behavior."[118]

The youthful Malvina S. Gist, who had fled the South Carolina capital before the arrival of the invading army, received a letter from her parents describing their ordeal during the fire, and on March 4, 1865, she recorded its contents in her diary: "My father and mother made friends even among their enemies, and through their exertions and old Maum Nancy's the family were fed and protected during the whole time." She was pleased to learn also that their home and furniture had been saved from the fire and that her new Steinway piano had come through "without a scratch."[119] And when Professor Joseph LeConte returned home after the withdrawal of Sherman's army, having lost all the items he had tried to evacuate, he learned, to his surprise, that not one of the enemy had "crossed the threshold" of his house.[120]

Probably one of the most important reasons why the rioters

---

[116] *Yorkville Enquirer*, March 9, 1865.
[117] Ravenel, "Burning of Columbia," Harriott Horry Ravenel Papers.
[118] Smythe, Poppenheim, and Taylor, *South Carolina Women*, I, 250.
[119] Ibid., p. 278.
[120] Joseph LeConte, *The Autobiography of Joseph LeConte*, ed. William Dallam Armes, p. 227; Miers, *When the World Ended*, p. 45.

were relatively moderate in maliciousness was that many more
guards assigned to protect citizens remained faithful to their posts
than traditionally has been believed. A number of Columbians
have left records of the activities of their guards on the night of the
fire, some of which indicate that their protectors not only were
kindly disposed but also apparently were appalled at the turn of
events. One such account was that of Melvin M. Cohen, who described the guards sent to protect his home as both "gentle and
unobtrusive." During the crisis of the night they prevented a gang
of marauding soldiers from entering or destroying Cohen's property, while at other times they even comforted and amused his children.[121] John T. Seibels, writing his reminiscences years after the
event, recalled how as a teenager he had witnessed the entry of a
group of Union troops into his home during the fire. Some items,
such as food, were taken by the plunderers, though he remembered
that the family silver was not stolen. Furthermore, their guard
was faithful and helpful throughout the night, and when the ordeal
was over the Seibelses' house, one of the oldest in Columbia, had
survived the flames.[122]

The daughters of E. V. Ravenel, who were in Columbia during
its occupation, described their many trials on that fateful night in
a letter to their father. The provost marshal had provided them
with a guard, they related, who had performed his duty faithfully.
Ravenel was relieved to hear that his daughters had endured the
entire nightmare "in safety & without loss."[123] Another well-known
citizen, Alfred Huger, in an August 22, 1866, letter to the *New
York World*, told how his house, where several members of his
family were ill and bedridden, was endangered by a nearby burning building. He ran into the streets, where he found, Huger communicated, two volunteers—"soldiers in the true sense of the
word"—who assisted him and his servants in saving the house.[124]

About three o'clock on the afternoon of February 17 Mrs.

---

[121] *Columbia Phoenix*, April 1, 1865.

[122] Snowden, *Marching with Sherman*, pp. 33, 36.

[123] E. V. Ravenel to Allan Macfarlan, March 21, 1865, Allan Macfarlan
Papers, South Caroliniana Library, University of South Carolina, Columbia.

[124] Alfred Huger to *New York World*, Aug. 22, 1866, quoted in Gibbes,
Who Burnt Columbia?, pp. 50–51.

Catherine P. Ravenel obtained a guard from a generous neighbor who had acquired three guards from the provost marshal. In the hours that followed, Mrs. Ravenel's sentinel proved to be both energetic and alert. During the height of the riot the guard rushed from one part of the house to another, driving off possible intruders in addition to consoling and protecting her family.[125]

When Mrs. Campbell Bryce and a friend went to the provost marshal seeking protection for their property, several troops volunteered, but before their offer could be accepted a young captain stepped forward, saying he would lead them to some faithful guards. Hesitatingly, the women followed the captain to his headquarters near the town hall, where he asked his men for volunteers. Mrs. Bryce chose two of the men and was not disappointed in their conduct. It was their faithfulness and efficiency, she later wrote, that prevented the flames from engulfing her home. The friendship between Mrs. Bryce and the soldiers became so cordial that when a corporal appeared the next day to relieve the guards, they elected to remain, as Mrs. Bryce believed, "where they were well fed and cared for."[126]

It was through the efforts of Dr. Elias Marks, the proprietor of Barhamville Female School located two miles north of Columbia, that guards were secured for protection of that institute. Dr. Marks, who resided in town and was not on the school premises during the fire, had barely managed to pack off the last group of girls to the Up Country before Sherman's forces entered the South Carolina capital. It was Madame Sophie Sosnowski, an immigrant from Baden and the operator of Barhamville School, who received and placed the guards. Madame Sosnowski was not impressed with the "dogged, mean looking men," though one soldier seemed kindly disposed and appeared to commiserate with her plight. Engaging in conversation with the young soldier, Madame Sosnowski learned that he was from Knoxville, Tennessee, and that he had known a former friend of hers there, a coincidence which she found greatly

---

[125] James Conner et al., eds., *South Carolina Women in the Confederacy*, II, 147–148.

[126] Campbell Bryce, *The Personal Experiences of Mrs. Campbell Bryce During the Burning of Columbia, South Carolina by General W. T. Sherman's Army, February 17, 1865*, pp. 20, 23.

reassuring. While the other guards were none too active during the night, the Tennessean and Madame Sosnowski managed to diminish the virulence of two groups of drunken soldiers who approached Barhamville and threatened to do violence.[127]

There are other accounts of faithful guards—some anonymous; some fragmentary, like those of Robert McDougal, E. J. Scott, A. F. Carroll, Dr. John Lynch, Mrs. St. Julien Ravenel, the F. H. Elmore family, and Mrs. Stratton;[128] and still others that are more complete, such as that of the Mason Smith family, of James C. Janney, or the account of the saving of South Carolina College.[129] Not all guards remained faithful, however, for there are reports, though the number is not large, of some who abandoned their charge or even participated in the riot. Mayor Goodwyn, who made friends with several "Christian soldiers" during the occupation, wrote that when the fire commenced his guard "left immediately," an action that was duplicated by a captain who was billeted at the home of A. Toomer Porter. Agnes Law blamed her guards for igniting the third floor of her residence, and Emma Le-Conte described her aunt's guard as being only "tolerably faithful."[130] How many guards placed duty over the lure of personal

127 Sophie Sosnowski, "Burning of Columbia," manuscript, Sosnowski-Schaller Papers, South Caroliniana Library, University of South Carolina, Columbia.

128 Anonymous, "Burning of Columbia" [1865?], manuscript, Anonymous Collection, South Caroliniana Library, University of South Carolina, Columbia; deposition of Robert McDougal, Aug. 23, 1872, No. 458, George Collie *vs.* United States, *Mixed Commission*, XXXVII, 3; Scott, *Random Recollections*, p. 180; deposition of A. F. Carroll, Feb. 6, 1872, No. 37, *Mixed Commission*, III, 3; *The State* (Columbia), Feb. 17, 1932; Mrs. St. Julien Ravenel, "Burning of Columbia," undated manuscript, St. Julien Ravenel Papers, South Carolina Historical Society, Charleston; Smythe, Poppenheim, and Taylor, *South Carolina Women*, I, 209; *New York Times*, March 19, 1865.

129 Smith et al., eds., *Mason Smith Family Letters*, pp. 174–177; Smythe, Poppenheim, and Taylor, *South Carolina Women*, I, 248; William James Rivers, "Saving of South Carolina College Library," 1906–1907 [?], manuscript, William James Rivers Papers, South Caroliniana Library, University of South Carolina, Columbia; Edwin L. Green, *A History of the University of South Carolina*, p. 78; Nicholson, *Burning of Columbia*, p. 6.

130 Goodwyn to Colin Campbell Murchison, June 8, 1866, Thomas Jefferson Goodwyn Letter, South Caroliniana Library, University of South Carolina, Columbia; Porter, *Led On!*, pp. 159–160; "Burning of Columbia—Affidavit of Agnes Law," p. 233; Miers, *When the World Ended*, pp. 48–49.

plunder and profit, a differentiation which many have failed to distinguish, is impossible to say. William Gilmore Simms, a man not inclined to be generous to the invaders, estimated that probably one-half of the guards remained at their posts on that extraordinary night.[131] When shortly after the war Columbians sought to determine how many guards actually ignited the homes they were assigned to protect, only three citizens responded with affidavits.[132]

What, then, was the "typical" experience of a citizen of Columbia whose house was invaded by soldiers on the night of the fire? A possible example might be found in the experiences of Mrs. W. K. Bachman, as described in her letter to Miss Kate Bachman dated March 27, 1865. The Bachmans, who resided on Plain Street between Pickens and Henderson streets, had heard tales of avarice and destruction brought into Columbia by the refugees, and they belatedly prepared for occupation by removing everything of value. Upon the entry of the Union army the next morning, Mrs. Bachman's aunt Jane, who resided next door, made a request for guards for both families. When they did not arrive at the appointed hour, the ladies walked four blocks to Richardson Street, where they obtained "one poor little guard." Returning home, they found a Union officer, who advised them that the large supply of wine each family possessed must be destroyed. The officer proceeded to accomplish his task with no small difficulty, being quite "tired out" when he finished. It was sad, indeed, Mrs. Bachman wrote, to see "bottle after bottle" of spirits so necessary to the "sick" destroyed.

Mrs. Bachman's first encounter with misconduct on the part of Union troops began shortly before she acquired her guard. A "young officer" pounded on her door to inquire if the structure across the street were a military college. Upon learning that the edifice was a Methodist Female College, the soldier demanded and got "spirits," a small amount of which was undestroyed, and then rode away. By dusk Mrs. Bachman noticed a definite increase in

131 *Columbia Phoenix*, March 23, 1865.

132 Daniel Heyward Trezevant, "Notes on the Burning of Columbia," miscellaneous manuscripts and copies of letters, Daniel Heyward Trezevant Papers, South Caroliniana Library, University of South Carolina, Columbia.

drunkenness as soldiers entered her yard and storehouse readily. About dark an intoxicated "Indian" walked into the house through her open front door, but another soldier followed and persuaded the intruder to leave.

After the fire began, a Private Davis of an Iowa regiment, who had been guarding a house that had burned, appeared at the steps of Mrs. Bachman's house. Informed that the ladies had been frightened by the prowlers and the Indian, Private Davis agreed to remain as their guard. Shortly thereafter, the Indian reentered the house, walked through the hall to the rear door, which he unlocked, and then proceeded to leave with the key. Davis pursued the Indian and forced him to relinquish the key, an act which increased Mrs. Bachman's confidence in her guard. The private next evicted from the cellar some soldiers who Mrs. Bachman was convinced were about to burn the house, and then, after an argument with the persistent Indian, Davis struck him, knocking him unconscious. When the Indian awoke, the argument continued, which led Private Davis to hit him with his musket, a blow which knocked the Indian unconscious for a second time in addition to breaking the private's gun. During the remainder of the night four more soldiers appeared at the front door of Mrs. Bachman's house, and one actually entered, though he left voluntarily after a few minutes.

There are several conclusions that can be reached from the experiences of the Bachman family. That the night, indeed, the entire occupation, was an ordeal is unquestionable. Soldiers, sober and intoxicated, came to Mrs. Bachman's door, and two entered her house. But she "met no insult" nor was she forced to use "exasperating language," though there did occur what might be called a confrontation of cultures with occasional Union troops in which she defended her "principles." When the crisis was over and the Union army marched out, Mrs. Bachman insisted that Private Davis accept a "small silver cup," not as remuneration for his faithfulness, but as a gift from one friend to another. As he walked off, Mrs. Bachman wrote, he "seemed really sorry to go." After three trying days, she could be thankful that her house was standing, as well as that of her aunt, that her cow was not taken, and that, thanks to the wit of Private Davis, much of the meat from the smokehouse was not appropriated by the Union quarter-master.[133]

The fire raged in Columbia for five hours, accompanied by a riot that had built steadily in confusion and intensity so that most control was lost over the city. While it is true that many soldiers were fighting the fire during the night, the rushing to and fro of frightened citizens and the drunkenness of the rioting mob made direction of the troops exceedingly difficult.[134] Finally, and belated-ly, between one and two o'clock on the morning of February 18, Howard and Logan decided that the confusion which prevailed in the streets had to be contained. About 1:30 A.M. Logan sent an order to Hazen, who had returned to camp a few minutes before, having given up the town as hopelessly lost, telling him to send another brigade to clear rioters from the streets. Authority was given to meet resistance with force, with only citizens who were orderly and soldiers who were fighting the fire or guarding houses to be allowed to remain in the streets.[135]

The task of restoring order was assigned to Brigadier General John M. Oliver, who entered Columbia about 2:00 A.M. and pro-ceeded to patrol the streets for the next two hours.[136] By five o'clock Oliver had returned to Hazen's camp to announce that the mission was accomplished. A month later in his official report Oliver summed up his activities in Columbia succinctly: "February 18, at 4 a.m. the Third Brigade was called out to suppress riot; did so, killing 2 men, wounding 30, and arresting 370. . . ." Among those arrested were officers, soldiers, civilians, and Negroes.[137]

Coincidence, as in so much of what happened in Columbia, played a major role in the final conquest of the fire. About 3:00 A.M. the strong wind that had been blowing out of the northwest since early on the previous morning subsided, eliminating the greatest impediment to controlling the flames, and by the time that Oliver had completed his operation and reported to Hazen, the fire

[133] Bachman to Bachman, March 27, 1865, Bachman Papers.
[134] Deposition of Sherman, Dec. 11, 1872, *Mixed Commission*, XIV, 101–102; deposition of Howard, *Mixed Commission*, XIV, 6.
[135] Deposition of Hazen, *Mixed Commission*, XIV, 152–153, 163.
[136] *OR*, Ser. 1, XLVII, pt. 1: 273, 310.
[137] Deposition of Hazen, *Mixed Commission*, XIV, 153, 163; *OR*, Ser. 1, XLVII, pt. 1: 310. The two men killed were Union soldiers.

had "virtually ceased."[138] General Sherman, looking back in later years, said that the option which lay before the Federal officers was clear: they could have suppressed the riot by sweeping the mob from the streets, or they could have fought the fire.[139] They chose to attempt to contain the fire, an act which cannot be condemned, though with the number of troops at their command it does appear that an attempt to terminate the riot might have been made much sooner. Control of the situation in Columbia was lost, and that fact was only belatedly realized by the Federal officers in charge. To have ended the riot would have eliminated much of the confusion, but it seems certain that there was no possibility of stopping the fire until the wind diminished.

[138] Deposition of Hazen, *Mixed Commission,* XIV, 153.
[139] Deposition of Sherman, Dec. 11, 1872, *Mixed Commission,* XIV, 101–102.

5

The Extent of the Devastation

F RIDAY morning, February 18, 1865, dawned upon a smoldering, blackened Columbia. Quiet had replaced the revelry, drunkenness, and confusion of the previous night. Many citizens, driven
by the flames, had sought refuge on the periphery of town, in Sidney Park, on the college green, in Columbia Theological Seminary,
and in the State Insane Asylum. Others had gathered their families
and what possessions they had rescued from the flames in empty
lots or in the center of streets. Morning light revealed these people
huddled on bundles of clothing and pieces of furniture they had
saved, a sad picture indeed. "This A.M. I took a walk around town
and saw a sight I hope to never see again," Union surgeon Elijah
P. Burton wrote in his diary. "All around the outskirts of the city
were groups of women and children sitting on . . . all that was left
them. All looked tired. Many crying and despondent. Some all
patient, submissive and quiet, and some complaining terribly about
the Yankees. . . . I talked with some but it made me feel too bad
to be endured. . . ."[1]

The first task of the Union commanders on the morning of the
eighteenth was to find housing for the citizens who had been
burned out, at first glance an apparently hopeless task. A quick
survey, however, revealed that the fire had been confined chiefly

---

[1] Elijah P. Burton, *Diary of E. P. Burton, Surgeon, Seventh Regiment
Illinois, Third Brigade, Second Division, Sixteenth Army Corps*, II, 63; William
Tecumseh Sherman, *Memoirs of General William T. Sherman*, II, 287.

to the business district and that the destruction of residences was not as extensive as it had appeared during the zenith of the fire. After consultation with Sherman, Howard, aided by Mayor Goodwyn, began seeking shelter for the homeless. By using the houses that had been vacated by fleeing refugees, the officers' quarters of Arsenal Academy, and the buildings at the college campus, Howard and Goodwyn were able to place the homeless before the end of the day.[2]

After conferring with Howard, Sherman visited the Catholic Church on Assembly Street near Sidney Park, where the young ladies of Ursuline Convent had taken refuge. He found the girls lodged in the church and an adjoining house. To ameliorate their discomfort, Sherman offered the Lady Superior the use of the abandoned Methodist Female College as a replacement for the destroyed convent. The general placed two of his aides, Colonel Ewing and Captain Joseph C. Audenried, at the ladies' service and provided ambulances to transport the girls to the Methodist buildings. The young girls were impressed with the kindness of the Union officers, who supplied them with cotton pads and blankets for bedding, some hardtack rations, and a small amount of groceries in addition to surrounding the building with a strong guard. Later, the Lady Superior, upon learning that the nearby home of John S. Preston was slated for destruction when the Federals resumed their march northward, requested that the building be contributed to her as a convent. Sherman complied with her request. On the twentieth, when the Union army left Columbia, the Ursuline girls received ten days' supply of rations.[3]

[2] J. P. Thomas to James L. Orr, Dec. 8, 1865, James L. Orr Papers, South Carolina Archives, Columbia; George Ward Nichols, *The Story of the Great March: From the Diary of a Staff Officer*, pp. 166, 169; Robert W. Barnwell to Board of Trustees of the University of South Carolina, May 9, 1866, Robert W. Barnwell Papers, South Caroliniana Library, University of South Carolina, Columbia. Many of the citizens who took lodging in the college dormitories later refused to leave, and the state had to resort to forcible eviction in mid-1866.

[3] Deposition of William T. Sherman, Dec. 11, 1872, No. 103, Wood and Heyworth *vs.* United States, No. 292, Cowlam Graveley *vs.* United States, *Mixed Commission on British and American Claims. Appendix: Testimony*, XIV, 92; A. T. Smythe, M. B. Poppenheim, and Thomas Taylor, eds., *South Carolina Women in the Confederacy*, I, 304–307.

In addition to the task of trying to house the citizens, Howard was also engaged in establishing a tight security throughout Columbia. Cognizant of the role of Federal troops in the riot, and having been informed that some "lawless and evil-disposed soldiers" were still making threats to citizens, he determined to prevent a "recurrence of the horrors" of the previous night. Therefore, he divided Columbia into two sections and placed Frank P. Blair, the commander of the XVII Corps, in charge of everything north of Taylor Street and William B. Woods in command of the area to the south. Each general was told to appoint a provost marshal who was authorized to use any number of troops or any force necessary "to prevent burning, pillaging, and all other acts subversive of good order and military discipline." Though Blair left no record of his specific activities on the eighteenth, General Woods placed eight regiments on guard duty in his section of Columbia and ordered the arrest of any enlisted man found on the streets after five o'clock in the afternoon who was not on duty. The next three days, the term of the Union occupation, passed without difficulty for the provost guards.[4]

Two other pressing problems had to be dealt with, the first of which was to provide food for the burned-out citizens. Howard ordered that after the commissary chief had taken all the supplies needed by the army from the railway depots and the local merchants, the remainder was to be turned over to the mayor for distribution among the homeless citizens. The new capitol building was chosen by Howard to store the supplies left for the inhabitants. Enough salt was placed there for the citizens and the hospitals on the college campus. Since it apparently would be some time before Columbia would recover from the conflagration, Howard urged Goodwyn to advise destitute citizens to leave for the countryside as soon as possible. Howard also suggested that foraging parties be organized under the leadership of reliable citizens to go into the surrounding area to acquire food. On the morning of the twentieth Howard had five hundred head of cattle driven to the college green, where they were left for the use of the people of Columbia under

[4] *War of the Rebellion: A Compilation of the Official Records of the Union and Confederate Armies*, Ser. 1, XLVII, pt. 2: 475–476 (hereafter cited as *OR*).

Mayor Goodwyn's control, a gift which proved extremely benefi-
cial in the succeeding weeks.[5]

Finally, Howard attempted to provide for the protection of
Columbia after the Union army left. Both Howard and Goodwyn
were aware that as the Civil War passed into its final months a certain potential for lawlessness existed among the desperate, vagabond Confederate troops and Union stragglers.[6] To deal with this
threat, Howard provided Mayor Goodwyn with one hundred rifles
and a supply of ammunition. The mayor took an oath that the guns
would never be used against the government of the United States.[7]

While providing housing, food, and protection for the citizens,
Sherman's officers were also busily engaged during the eighteenth
and nineteenth in their primary task of destroying the war matériel and commissary stores abandoned in Columbia as well as railroads and bridges in the area that might be used by the Confederacy. Their work began at the three railroad stations, where they
found an extensive amount of railroad supplies and rolling stock,
including nineteen locomotives and twenty freight cars, which they
destroyed by breaking all moveable parts and setting the remainder on fire. In the tool and freight sheds at the depots the Union
army found and destroyed 60 six-mule team harnesses, one thousand pounds of trace chains, forty barrels of nails, and twenty-five
kegs of railroad spikes. Another five tons of repair machinery were
destroyed, as were 650 train wheels. To these stores can be added a
"large" collection of miscellaneous parts, tools, and implements.[8]

On Saturday, February 18, the Evans and Cogswell Company,
which possessed the contract for printing Confederate money, was
burned. Located in a large brick structure on Gervais Street two

[5] Ibid., pp. 476, 485; Earl Schenck Miers, ed., *When the World Ended:
The Diary of Emma LeConte*, p. 57; Mrs. W. K. Bachman to Kate Bachman,
March 27, 1865, copy, W. K. Bachman Papers, South Caroliniana Library, Uni-
versity of South Carolina, Columbia; James Guignard Gibbes, *Who Burnt
Columbia?*, p. 16. Not all Columbians lost their cows to Union foragers. Both
the LeContes and the Bachmans were able to retain their cattle.

[6] *Columbia Phoenix*, May 3, 1865; I. S. Black to W. P. Miles, Dec. 19,
1864, William Porcher Miles Papers, Southern Historical Collection, University
of North Carolina, Chapel Hill.

[7] *OR*, Ser. 1, XLVII, pt. 2: 488.

[8] Ibid., pp. 502–503. The twenty freight cars were only part of the rolling
stock left in Columbia, the others having been destroyed on the seventeenth.

blocks from the Congaree River, Evans and Cogswell was described by Simms as "perhaps the most complete establishment of its kind in the Confederacy."[9] Sherman later stated that sixty hand presses were destroyed in the building, and while the Confederates had saved the plates, an "immense quantity" of Confederate money was carried off by the Union soldiers. Two other buildings which contained printed Confederate forms, stationery, envelopes, pens, penholders, and ink, amounting to about two tons of material, were also burned.[10]

More destruction of Confederate property occurred on Saturday when the machinery in the powder mill on the Congaree River and its supplier plants clustered along the riverbank was wrecked and the buildings were blown up. The machinery in the Confederate government's armory, also located near the Congaree River, was smashed, and the warehouses, machine shops, foundry, and offices were burned. Destroyed in the armory buildings were a large number of files and other implements for manufacturing guns which had been crated for evacuation by the Confederate officials. Another ten tons of machinery discovered in boxes "under a shed on the common" were smashed, and the smokestacks of six factories were blown up. The gasworks was also destroyed on Saturday, as was Alexander's foundry. The work of devastation continued on Sunday, when, after the ordnance stores had been removed, the arsenal building was burned, as was the building at the fairgrounds which had been used by the Confederate government as a mobilization camp early in the war and, later, as a medical laboratory.[11]

Considering the desperate condition of the Confederate armies, the quantity of ordnance stores captured in Columbia was astounding. It included 1.3 million rounds of small-arms ammunition, 26,150 pounds of gunpowder, and 9,069 rounds of artillery ammunition. While some of these stores were used by the Union

[9] *Columbia Phoenix*, April 8, 1865; Jane Kealhofer Simons and Margaret Babcock Meriwether, *A Guide to Columbia, South Carolina's Capital City*, p. 76.

[10] Sherman, *Memoirs*, II, 288; *OR*, Ser. 1, XLVII, pt. 2: 503.

[11] *Columbia Phoenix*, April 8, 1865; *OR*, Ser. 1, XLVII, pt. 2: 503; Gibbes, *Who Burnt Columbia?*, p. 15.

army, most were hauled from the arsenal and thrown into the Congaree River under the direction of Sherman's chief of ordnance, Colonel T. G. Baylor. During one trip several percussion shells detonated as they hit the water, causing a wagon to explode and resulting in the death of sixteen men.[12] Also captured were 10,210 muskets and rifles, which were destroyed, along with six thousand musket barrels and stocks of unfinished weapons. Forty-three bronze and iron cannon, some rifled and others smooth-bore, were also destroyed. A sample of other matériel demolished included 3,095 cutlasses and sabers, nine gun carriages, fourteen gun caissons, three hundred cavalry pistol holsters, four thousand bayonet scabbards, more than three thousand cartridge boxes of various caliber, 3,700 belts, and nine hundred haversacks.[13]

Another important military operation being carried out on February 18–19 was the demolition of the railroads around Columbia. The troops of Generals Hazen and Corse disrupted the railroad toward Charleston as far as Cedar Creek, about fifteen miles from Columbia, where Corse's mounted men burned the trestle. This activity forced the Confederates operating in the area to retreat behind the Wateree River bridge and then burn it. When the Union troops had completed their mission, they had laid waste to fifteen miles of track and damaged forty more. At the same time, Blair's men were wrecking the railroads north of Columbia, attempting to destroy all track within fifteen miles of the South Carolina capital.[14]

One final work of destruction remained—disposing of the cotton that had not burned in the holocaust. During Saturday and Sunday the troops of Charles R. Woods were sent throughout Columbia in search of cotton. A total of 1,370 bales was found, with 820 bales in the streets and the remainder stored in outbuildings, warehouses, and basements. This cotton was cautiously burned without accident.[15]

---

[12] *OR*, Ser. 1, XLVII, pt. 1: 180–181; Sherman, *Memoirs*, II, 288. For a complete list of ordnance stores captured in Columbia, see Appendix A.

[13] *OR*, Ser. 1, XLVII, pt. 1: 181–182.

[14] Ibid., p. 199; pt. 2: 476–477.

[15] Ibid., pt. 1: 243; deposition of Charles R. Woods, Dec. 16, 1872, Nos. 103, 292, *Mixed Commission*, XIV, 197; Mrs. W. K. Bachman to Kate Bachman, March 27, 1865, copy, Bachman Papers.

On Monday, February 20, 1865, the right wing of the Union army resumed its march northward. Logan's XV Corps moved out first, followed by the XVII Corps of Blair. Charles R. Woods's command was the last to leave the South Carolina capital, marching out at about 1:00 P.M.[16] Thus ended the fateful eight days of the defense, evacuation, and occupation of Columbia.

One of the major disputes to arise from Sherman's capture of the Palmetto State capital was that of the magnitude of the fire on the night of February 17–18. In an attempt to answer this question, William Gilmore Simms, the well-known South Carolina writer, made a survey of the city shortly after the fire and published in the *Columbia Phoenix* what proved to be the most complete list of buildings destroyed.

However, Simms's account, "The Sack and Destruction of the City of Columbia, S.C.," in which he attempted to enumerate every building destroyed between February 16 and 20, was not without its controversial points. One difficulty was that he often repeated names of property owners several times, while failing to clarify the purpose for such repetition. One example is the listing on Richardson Street of "H. Hess. Store and dwelling," which is followed by "H. Hess. Store filled with furniture."[17] Do these two listings mean that H. Hess owned a store, a furniture store, and a dwelling? Probably not. The 1860 *Columbia Directory* listed one Henry Heiss, a "clothing and dry goods" dealer on Richardson Street with his residence at the same address.[18] Apparently, the elaboration of "Store filled with furniture" was for emphasis. One other illustration will suffice. "L. Carr. Bank of South Carolina" is followed by "L. Carr. Rooms occupied by D. Wadlow and others," which evidently represented a two-story building with renters living on the second floor. Yet the separate entries might be interpreted as two buildings.[19]

Another factor that confuses the determination of the build-

---

[16] Sherman, *Memoirs*, II, 288; *OR*, Ser. 1, XLVII, pt. 2: 485, 503–504.

[17] A. S. Salley, ed., *Sack and Destruction of the City of Columbia, S.C., by William Gilmore Simms*, p. 89.

[18] *The Columbia Directory, Containing the Names, Business and Residence of the Inhabitants*, p. 19.

[19] Salley, *Sack and Destruction*, p. 95.

ings burned was the unusually large number of buildings listed on some of the streets. While twelve or thirteen buildings on one side of each block appears to have been about average, five blocks were listed by Simms as having between seventeen and twenty-one structures per side, an inordinately large number.[20] Finally, to ascertain as nearly as possible the exact extent of the general conflagration, those buildings burned during the evacuation of the Confederates, in addition to those destroyed intentionally on February 19–20, must be subtracted from Simms's list.[21]

The fire swept down both sides of Richardson Street from Cotton Town to the State House, burning every structure with the exception of one building located between Upper Boundary and Lumber streets.[22] Forty-four of the 212 buildings burned on Richardson were in Confederate service. The fire did the least amount of damage in the western portion of the city. Between Richardson and Assembly streets 43 buildings were burned, only 2 of which were used for Confederate governmental purposes. From Assembly to the river only 9 buildings were consumed, 6 of which were within a block of the South Carolina Railroad depot.[23]

On the eastern side of Richardson Street the damage to the city was much more extensive. Seventy-five structures, four of which were used by the Confederate government, were burned in the area between Richardson and Sumter streets. Another fifty-eight buildings burned on the blocks between Sumter and Marion

20 Ibid., pp. 88–95.

21 The map of buildings burned contains a plotting of the burned buildings on Simms's list. Those buildings burned before the main fire, those destroyed by the Union army after the conflagration, and those listings which have been determined not to be separate houses have been deleted. They are the second-story rooms of the estate of J. J. Kinsler, the second-story rooms of Gibbes and Guignard, the second-story rooms of L. Carr, the second-story rooms occupied by Southern Express, the government armory, Evans and Cogswell, nine residences between Lincoln and Gates on Lumber Street, the State Arsenal and Academy, the powder works, Shields's foundry, and the Charlotte and South Carolina Railroad Station. See Salley, *Sack and Destruction*, pp. 91, 94–95, 98–99, 101–102.

22 Deposition of John McKenzie, April 9, 1872, No. 103, *Mixed Commission*, XIV, 10; deposition of T. J. Goodwyn, April 27, 1872, No. 103, *Mixed Commission*, XIV, 15; deposition of William B. Stanley, April 30, 1872, No. 103, *Mixed Commission*, XIV, 22. See map of buildings burned.

23 Salley, *Sack and Destruction*, pp. 88–106. See also Appendix B.

streets, but only three of those buildings were south of Gervais Street. Moving eastward to the area between Marion and Bull streets, thirty buildings were consumed, twenty-two of which were on three adjoining blocks. Of the remaining eight houses destroyed between Marion and Bull, six were on adjoining blocks, and the other two were scattered. Between Bull and Pickens streets nine houses, five of which were located on the same block, were burned in the fire. East of Pickens three isolated buildings were consumed.[24]

This survey demonstrates that the greatest damage occurred between the west side of Richardson Street and Bull Street, where the fire virtually ceased. From the pattern of destruction depicted on the map of structures burned, it is clear that most of the damage was done on contiguous blocks over a thirty-six-block area approximately nine squares long and four wide. The path cut by the flames ran from the northwest, beginning in Cotton Town, to the southeast, halting at the State House. The greatest devastation was in the center of the burned district.[25]

Determining the number of dwellings in Columbia in 1865 is one of the most crucial and difficult problems in analyzing the extent of the devastation. The 1860 *Columbia Directory* was obviously incomplete in that it listed only 600 homes for a city of over eight thousand, of whom about thirty-five hundred were unlisted Negroes. Since the average occupancy was about five persons per house, this would indicate, even if there had been no new construction between 1860 and 1865, that there were at least 1,100 residences and 200 stores. The number of dwellings burned consisted of 36 on Richardson Street and 176 on other streets. Fifty-five of the 156 stores burned on Richardson, as well as 4 on other streets, also served as residences. The total number of residences burned was 265.

A map taken from the 1860 *Columbia Directory*, however, incomplete as it is, indicates that the major residential sections of Columbia were outside the burned district. From Assembly Street —one of Columbia's widest—westward, the residential areas were most fortunate. In the region north of Sidney Park, only four houses

[24] Ibid.
[25] See map of buildings burned.

were burned, three of which were on the east side of Assembly. Though not quite so fortunate, the section south of the park escaped with the loss of only sixteen buildings, with seven of them on the east side of Assembly. A third residential area east of Richardson Street suffered the greatest loss.[26]

While residences in the center of town were hard hit, the business community was virtually wiped out. On Richardson Street alone 101 stores burned, in addition to 34 structures on various streets which served as stores, offices, and warehouses and another fourteen used exclusively as warehouses. Two fire stations, one machine shop, two factories, one meeting hall, one schoolroom, and two hotels were also consumed. To this must be added eleven churches, seven stables, two mills, one carpenter shop, seven public buildings, two blacksmith shops, two printing companies, two barbershops, and one stoneyard office. In all, 193 business and public structures were burned. Thus, the total number of buildings burned was 458,[27] or approximately one-third of Columbia.

[26] Compare maps of buildings burned and 1860 dwellings.

[27] The figure of 458 buildings destroyed has been derived from Simms's list.

6

Who Burned Columbia?

THE smoke over Columbia had scarcely cleared before the controversy over who had burned the city began. A scant ten days after the event Wade Hampton hurled the first charges, indicting General Sherman for the destruction of the South Carolina capital: "You have permitted, if you have not ordered, the commission of these offenses against humanity and the rules of war; you fired into the city of Columbia without word of warning; after its surrender by the mayor, who demanded protection to private property, you laid the whole city in ashes, leaving amidst its ruins thousands of old men and helpless women and children, who are likely to perish of starvation and exposure."[1]

Sherman did not reply to this charge of barbarism until April 4, 1865, when he made his report of the campaign in the Carolinas. In this first official statement Sherman countered Hampton's accusation with a denial and a recrimination of his own: "I disclaim on the part of my army any agency in this fire, but, on the contrary, claim that we saved what of Columbia remains unconsumed," Sherman wrote, "and without hesitation I charge General Wade Hampton with having burned his own city of Columbia, not with a malicious intent, or as the manifestation of a silly 'Roman stoicism,' but from folly and want of sense, in filling it with lint, cotton, and tinder."[2]

[1] *War of the Rebellion: A Compilation of the Official Records of the Union and Confederate Armies,* Ser. 1, XLVII, pt. 2: 597 (hereafter cited as *OR*).
[2] Ibid., pt. 1: 21–22.

With the charge of barbarism on one side and that of poor judgment on the other, the controversy over the burning of Columbia was under way, and South Carolinians quickly seized the initiative in attempting to compile evidence to prove their point. The first effort to produce an extensive account of the events that transpired in Columbia between February 13 and 20, 1865, was made by William Gilmore Simms, Charleston's prolific writer of poetry and prose, who is primarily remembered as a protagonist of the "Southern way of life." Forced by the advance of the Union army to leave his Woodlands plantation fifty miles south of Columbia, Simms took refuge in the South Carolina capital, where he remained to witness the evacuation, occupation, and burning of the city. His memory was supplemented by information he collected from other inhabitants. The culmination of Simms's efforts was a series of articles which began in the first issue of the *Columbia Phoenix* on March 21, 1865, and concluded on April 10. In this polemical account, entitled "Sack and Destruction of the City of Columbia, S.C.," Simms spared no effort in laying the blame at the feet of Sherman.[3] These articles were slightly edited and published in a book in late 1865.

In April, 1867, a public meeting of citizens at Carolina Hall began a second major effort to ascertain who burned the city. A committee of prominent Columbians, including Chancellor J. P. Carroll, William F. DeSaussure, E. J. Arthur, Dr. John Fisher, Dr. William Reynolds, Dr. Daniel H. Trezevant, Dr. A. N. Talley, Professor W. J. Rivers, Professor Joseph LeConte, Colonel J. T. Sloan, and Colonel L. D. Childs, was created to investigate and collect testimony regarding the events of February 17–18, 1865. The committee resolved to accept only the testimony of those who could swear to events which they had personally observed.[4]

[3] William Gilmore Simms was editor of the *Columbia Phoenix* from its beginning on March 21, 1865, until October of the same year. Julian A. Selby was the publisher. The paper began as a triweekly and was published Tuesday, Thursday, and Saturday until April 10, when it became a daily. On May 15 the title was changed to *Columbia Daily Phoenix* and on July 31 to *Daily Phoenix*. See Mary C. Oliphant, Alfred Taylor Odell, and T. C. Duncan Eaves, eds., *The Letters of William Gilmore Simms*, IV, 499n.

[4] James Parsons Carroll, *Report of the Committee Appointed to Collect Testimony in Relation to the Destruction of Columbia, S.C., on the 17th of February, 1865*, p. 3.

After an extensive campaign, the Carroll committee was able to accumulate about sixty affidavits from respondents of "high-toned and elevated character" whose "unpretending and sterling probity" was beyond doubt. From these depositions twenty-five accusations were constructed to indict Sherman and the Union army. Fourteen affidavits stated that "soldiers were seen setting fire to houses." Only one citizen, however, testified that he personally observed families being "driven from their dwellings and the latter fired." Two of the depositions contended that "citizens were robbed, when escaping from their burning houses." On one crucial point four respondents signed affidavits stating that "soldiers broke into stores and private dwellings"; the same number also testified that "soldiers stole silver, clothing, etc." The affidavits were more abundant on general, sweeping assertions, such as the charge that "General Sherman's march through the State before entering Columbia was marked by burning, robbery and outrages on old men, women, children and negroes" to which seventeen Columbians deposed that they were eyewitnesses.[5] The committee concluded that "although actual orders for the burning of the town may not have been given, the soldiers of General Sherman certainly believed that its destruction would not be displeasing to him."[6] Dr. Trezevant also collected a small amount of testimony which he published shortly after the war in a pamphlet. His account contained six eyewitness descriptions of Union soldiers starting fires.[7]

[5] Ibid., pp. 4–5; Daniel Heyward Trezevant, "Notes on the Burning of Columbia," miscellaneous manuscripts and copies of letters, Daniel Heyward Trezevant Papers, South Caroliniana Library, University of South Carolina, Columbia. The official affidavits, said by the Carroll committee to be "more than sixty," were given to the city council of Columbia during the term of Mayor John McKenzie, November 17, 1868, to April 5, 1870. In April, 1870, the Republicans under Mayor John Alexander gained control of the municipal government, which they retained until 1878. When William B. Stanley was elected mayor in 1878, a thorough search of the city council archives failed to uncover the affidavits, of which there were no duplicates. An analysis of the various charges brought against Sherman and his army in the affidavits, however, was retained by Wade Hampton and later given to Dr. Trezevant. This analysis indicated that there were fifty-six affidavits.

[6] Carroll, *Report of the Committee*, p. 14.

[7] Daniel Heyward Trezevant, *The Burning of Columbia, S.C.: A Review of Northern Assertions and Southern Facts*, p. 22. It has been impossible to determine how many of Trezevant's affidavits duplicated those of the Carroll

By far the greatest amount of evidence collected on the conflagration in Columbia resulted from the Treaty of Washington between the United States and Great Britain. Article XII of the 1871 treaty created the Mixed Commission on British and American Claims to gather evidence regarding the destruction of United States property by Confederate raids from British soil, or with the aid of British subjects, and the destruction of property of British citizens living in the seceded states as a result of the invasion of the South. The Mixed Commission was composed of a representative from the United States, James S. Frazer, formerly a justice of the Supreme Court of Indiana, and a representative from Great Britain, Russell Gurney, a member of Parliament and a recorder at London. In an attempt at impartiality, a third member, Count Louis Corti, the minister plenipotentiary to the United States from the King of Italy, was chosen by the United States and British governments.[8]

The Mixed Commission made a sincere effort to consider all points of view arising out of the burning of Columbia by appearing at a number of locations throughout the United States to hear testimony. Anyone who claimed knowledge of the sequence of events in Columbia from February 12 to 20, 1865, apparently had ample opportunity to submit it to the tribunal. Those who were unable to appear before the Mixed Commission were allowed to present sworn depositions. Cross-examination by attorneys representing the claimants and defendants was allowed. Though time had dulled the memory of some, the result was six volumes of extremely valuable testimony.

The eighteen claims of British subjects stemming from the

---

committee. Though present during the fire, Trezevant did not include himself as an eyewitness to incendiarism or misconduct, possibly because he spent much of the night of the seventeenth attending a woman giving birth to a child. See Mrs. W. K. Bachman to Kate Bachman, March 27, 1865, copy, W. K. Bachman Papers, South Caroliniana Library, University of South Carolina, Columbia.

[8] U.S. Congress, House, *Report of Robert S. Hale, Esq., Agent and Counsel of the United States before the Commission on Claims of Citizens of the United States Against Great Britain, and of Subjects of Her Britannic Majesty Against the United States, Under the Twelfth Article of the Treaty of 8th May, 1871, Between the United States and Great Britain*, 43d Cong., 1st sess., 1873–1874, III, pt. 2, House Exec. Doc. No. 1 (Serial 1596), p. 7.

burning of Columbia were based on the allegation that the "city was wantonly fired by the army of General Sherman,"[9] with his "consent and connivance," resulting in the destruction of their property. This assertion was based on the belief that Sherman hated Columbia and that his men, fully aware of his enmity, were determined to see the city destroyed. The claimants further contended that Federal officers viewed acts of pillage without reprimand, that rockets signaled the commencement of the destruction, that no *bona fide* effort was made to stop the destruction, and that Union soldiers were observed setting fires and looting houses.[10]

The attorneys defending the United States contended that Sherman had neither ordered nor insinuated that the South Carolina capital be burned. The destruction of Columbia, the government maintained, was the result of the carelessness of the retreating Confederates, who burned the Congaree River bridge, the railway stations, and the cotton, which had been piled in the streets and from which the flames spread throughout the city. The defense admitted that acts of pillage and violence may have been perpetrated by straggling, lawless soldiers, but argued that the Union officers made a sincere effort to contain the fire and repress disorders.[11]

On September 25, 1873, The Mixed Commission on British and American Claims announced its decision. The agent of the United States, Robert S. Hale, was informed by the commissioners that they had unanimously concluded that the conflagration "was not to be ascribed to either the intention or default of either the Federal or confederate officers,"[12] a kind of nondecision which seemed to say that the results of the war could not be changed.

[9] Ibid., p. 50.
[10] Great Britain, *Parliamentary Papers*, "Foreign Office Report by Her Majesty's Agent of the Proceedings and Awards of the Mixed Commission on British and American Claims Established Under the XII Article of the Treaty between Great Britain and the United States of America Concluded at Washington, May 8, 1871," 1874 (no. 2), 75: 54.
[11] Ibid., pp. 52–53. The United States government maintained before the tribunal that the defense of Columbia would have made the city's destruction a legal act of war had Sherman been inclined to burn it.
[12] House, *Report of Robert S. Hale, Esq.*, 43d Cong., 1st sess., 1873–1874, III, pt. 2, House Exec. Doc. No. 1 (Serial 1596), p. 50.

The final effort to collect data relative to the burning of Columbia was made during 1929 and 1930 by South Carolina's Senator Coleman L. Blease. In an attempt to secure reparations for the burning of Ursuline Convent and Washington Street Methodist Church, Blease gathered over one hundred pages of testimony. Most of it consisted of old affidavits or recently written remembrances, which he presented to the Senate Committee on Claims. Blease's presentation was essentially a perfunctory survey of the events of February 17–18, 1865, and contained no new evidence. No action was taken by the Senate committee.[13]

In sifting through the mass of testimony, affidavits, charges, countercharges, memoirs, reminiscences, and histories that grew out of the burning of Columbia, few facts are self-evident. One conclusion that becomes evident, however, was that from beginning to end both sides held certain positions which never altered. South Carolinians were convinced that they had been invaded by barbarians who treated them in an uncivilized manner and that Sherman was "morally responsible for the burning of Columbia."[14] Conversely, the Union officers and troops, for the most part, accepted the invasion of South Carolina and the events which transpired in Columbia as regrettable but little different from what had been happening increasingly as the nature of the war steadily changed.

Attempting to reconcile these two diametrically opposed positions is, of course, no easy matter. The events in Columbia occurred during the last stages of a desperate civil war that had grown increasingly cruel as new measures were taken in an effort to end the bloodshed as rapidly as possible.[15] The Union army's superiority enabled it to move over the enemy's countryside at will, while the

[13] U.S. Congress, Senate, *Destruction of Property in Columbia, S.C., by Sherman's Army. Speech of Hon. Cole. L. Blease, A Senator from the State of South Carolina, Delivered in the Senate May 15, 1930,* 71st Cong., 2d sess., 1930, Senate Doc. No. 149 (Serial 9220).

[14] James Wood Davidson, "Who Burned Columbia? A Review of General Sherman's Version of the Affair," *Southern Historical Society Papers* 7 (April, 1879): 192.

[15] It is my belief that at least one belligerent will generally do what is necessary to win a war. To achieve victory it is therefore possible to attach a humanitarian argument to each escalation of hostilities, since these measures are designed to end the war quickly, thus saving lives in the long run. The Vietnam War affords numerous excellent examples of how this logic works.

South, possessing a certain chivalrous tradition and having pledged to fight to the death, humiliatingly saw its armies wither away in the face of the enemy. The result was that Northern soldiers and generals, flushed with victory, often grossly overstated their destructiveness. In the South the story of Sherman's march was reported primarily by elderly men and by women who were, as Clement Eaton and Frank Vandiver have pointed out, probably the fiercest protagonists of the Confederacy.[16] Fed by years of propaganda and a firm belief in the superiority of Southern civilization —and convinced that only a supermonstrous army could defeat their gallant sons and husbands—Southerners also tended to exaggerate the destructiveness of the Union forces. The task, then, is to separate charge from guilt and to disentangle denial from responsibility. Events must be placed in their proper historical perspective by isolating the charges against Sherman, analyzing his motives and activities, and evaluating the reactions of Columbians.

The first and perhaps the major charge against Sherman was that he desired the destruction of Columbia and entered the state solely for that purpose, a thought which only belatedly entered the minds of the military men defending South Carolina. Primary evidence in the Southern brief is the statements uttered by Sherman as the war against the South progressed. These remarks, always short and seemingly unfeeling, though never clearly pointed at Columbia, have been quoted repeatedly. One of the first came on December 13, 1864, as Sherman stood poised with his army before the defenses of Savannah and his thoughts anticipated the campaign in the Palmetto State. "The whole army is crazy to be turned loose in Carolina," he wrote Major General H. W. Halleck, "and with the experience of the past thirty days I judge that a month's sojourn in South Carolina would make her less bellicose."[17] In a sec-

---

[16] Clement Eaton, ed., "Diary of an Officer in Sherman's Army Marching Through the Carolinas," *Journal of Southern History* 9 (May, 1943): 239; Frank E. Vandiver, *Their Tattered Flags: The Epic of the Confederacy*, pp. 63–64.

[17] *OR*, Ser. 1, XLIV, 702. Note that Sherman's harsh statements which might suggest vengeance were almost always directed to Halleck, the armchair general who was notoriously famous for failing to marshal the forces at his disposal, and seldom to Grant, the field general. I believe that such distinctions

ond letter almost two weeks later Sherman responded to a sug-
gestion by Halleck that *"some* accident"[18] might occur to destroy
Charleston should it be captured:

> I will bear in mind your hint as to Charleston, and don't think
> salt will be necessary. When I move the Fifteenth Corps will be
> on the right of the Right Wing, and their position will bring
> them, naturally, into Charleston first; and if you have watched
> the history of that corps you will have remarked that they gen-
> erally do their work up pretty well. The truth is the whole army
> is burning with an insatiable desire to wreak vengeance upon
> South Carolina. I almost tremble at her fate, but feel that she de-
> serves all that seems in store for her. . . . I look upon Columbia as
> quite as bad as Charleston, and I doubt if we shall spare the pub-
> lic buildings there, as we did at Milledgeville.[19]

In addition to these declarations the Carroll committee found
numerous citizens who were convinced by what they saw, heard,
or surmised that Columbia was Sherman's primary target. Mrs.
L. Catherine Joyner, having reached her conclusions after conversing with men of the XIV and XX Corps, told the Carroll committee that "they seemed to gloat over the distress that would result
from their march through the State." A friend of hers, she continued, was warned by Sherman, apparently in Georgia, to "go off
the line of railroad, for I will not answer for the consequences
where the army passes."[20] Mrs. Rosa J. Meetze told the Carroll committee that in Lexington, South Carolina, a small town

---

are often made by generals in the field who realize the need of zealots on the
home front for ever increasingly hostile statements.

[18] U.S. Congress, Senate, *Supplemental Report of the Joint Committee on
the Conduct of the War, 39th Cong.,* 1st sess., 1866, I, Senate Reports (Serial
1241), 287.

[19] *OR,* Ser. 1, XLIV, 799.

[20] J. P. Carroll, "Burning of Columbia," *Southern Historical Society Pa-
pers* 8 (May, 1880): 202–203; Harriott Horry Ravenel, "Burning of Columbia,"
March 12, 1898, manuscript article from letter of March, 1865, Harriott Horry
Ravenel Papers, South Caroliniana Library, University of South Carolina, Co-
lumbia. It is interesting that when communicating with the Carroll committee,
Rachel Susan Cheves, to whom the statement is attributed, indicated that her
husband preferred that her name not be attached to the document. Cheves to
John LeConte [March ?, 1866], Rachel Susan Cheves Papers, Manuscript Divi-
sion, Duke University Library, Durham, N.C. During the occupation Mrs.
Cheves questioned both Howard and Orlando M. Poe about the possibilities of

twelve miles southwest of Columbia occupied by General H. J. Kilpatrick, it was "common talk" among the Union soldiers that "Columbia was to be burned." Another Lexingtonian quoted Kilpatrick as saying that Sherman would lay Columbia in ashes, a story often reported to have been repeated by Federal troops taken prisoner.[21] These statements led citizens like James G. Gibbes and Edward Sill to the inescapable conclusion that the destruction of Columbia was a "prearranged affair."[22]

Though Sherman had been contemplating an invasion of South Carolina since early October, it was not until Savannah was in his grasp that his plans were finalized. "I have now completed my first step," he wrote Grant on December 22, 1864, "and should like to go on to you *via* Columbia. . . ."[23] In making the decision to invade South Carolina, which ultimately resulted in the destruction of Columbia, it seems clear that Sherman, the apostle of modern war, was motivated primarily by military, economic, political, and psychological factors. From the standpoint of military strategy, there were excellent reasons for marching through central South Carolina. Columbia, as has been shown, was an important war manufacturing center—one of the few still in Confederate hands—producing munitions, equipment, and uniforms.[24] In addition, central South Carolina contained the last Confederate sources of food untouched by the war. Meat and vegetables flowed through Colum-

---

getting to Philadelphia. Her husband had instructed her to flee to the North should she be overtaken by the war. Cheves to J. K. Cheves, March 2, 1865, Cheves Papers.

[21] Carroll, "Burning of Columbia," p. 204; Trezevant, "Notes on the Burning of Columbia," Trezevant Papers. The left wing, which went through Lexington, did not enter Columbia.

[22] James Guignard Gibbes, *Who Burnt Columbia?*, p. 9; Edward Sill, "Who is Responsible for the Destruction of the City of Columbia, S.C., on the Night of 17 February, 1865," *Land We Love* 4 (March, 1868): 368.

[23] Deposition of William T. Sherman, Dec. 11, 1872, No. 103, Wood and Heyworth *vs.* United States, No. 292, Cowlam Graveley *vs.* United States, *Mixed Commission on British and American Claims. Appendix: Testimony*, XIV, 74; Senate, *Supplemental Report*, 39th Cong., 1st sess., 1866, I, Senate Reports (Serial 1241), 235, 281, 285.

[24] George Ward Nichols, *The Story of the Great March: From the Diary of a Staff Officer*, pp. 152–153; deposition of William T. Sherman, March 30, 1872, No. 37, Joseph J. Browne *vs.* United States, *Mixed Commission*, III, 11.

bia daily en route to the Army of Northern Virginia. Furthermore, the city was a vital rail center with lines that led to Augusta, where there was an important powder works,[25] Charleston, upstate South Carolina, and Virginia.

The importance of maintaining communications between South Carolina and Virginia was recognized by many alert Southerners. In January, 1865, William Porcher Miles, a South Carolina representative in the Confederate Congress, wrote Governor Magrath that "the question recurs—as you have forcibly put it—how can we hold Richmond indefinitely—or even for any considerable period—unless we preserve our Southern communications? How can Genl. Lee's army be fed if Sherman holds or destroys or greatly injures the Rail Roads through South Carolina?"[26] Confederate Commissary General L. B. Northrop, who had the almost impossible assignment of feeding Lee's army, was fully aware of the importance of Sherman's raid on Virginia's southeastern supply lines, but like so many others he was unable to alter the situation.[27]

Sherman's strategic maneuver, then, had far-reaching military and economic results. By breaking up the railroads of central South Carolina, he cut vital supply lines and stopped the flow of supplies to Virginia. In marching through the interior of the South Atlantic states, the evacuation of the last major Confederate ports became inevitable. It was "Sherman's rear attack" more than any other campaign of the Civil War, wrote the noted military historian B. H. Liddell Hart, that led to the final collapse of the Confederacy.[28]

Of equal importance in Sherman's campaign in South Carolina were the political and psychological effects, which were inseparably intermingled. Sherman, aware of the war weariness and disintegrating morale on the Southern home front, as well as the desperate military condition of the Confederacy, and cognizant of the bellicose condemnation of the Northern armies that had emanated from South Carolina for years, believed that a moral victory

25 Vandiver, *Their Tattered Flags*, p. 241.

26 William Porcher Miles to Andrew Gordon Magrath, Jan. 15, 1865, Andrew Gordon Magrath Papers, South Caroliniana Library, University of South Carolina, Columbia.

27 *OR*, Ser. 1, XLIV, 980–981.

28 B. H. Liddell Hart, *Strategy, the Indirect Approach*, pp. 151, 153–154.

could be gained by the capture of Columbia. "If you place an army where the enemy say you cannot, you gain an object," he told a Saint Louis, Missouri, audience on July 20, 1865. "And therefore, when I could place my army in Columbia, I fought a battle—reaped the fruits of a victory—bloodless, but still produced military results."[29] Emphasizing the political and psychological importance of Columbia to the Confederacy, Sherman later wrote: "From the hour that the army under my command entered Columbia, the fate of the Southern Confederacy was sealed."[30]

The ultimate effect of a policy that took a marauding army through the heart of a virtually undefended country was disastrous on Confederate troop morale, their will being weakened by loyalties divided between nation and family.[31] At the same time, civilian morale was shattered by Sherman's concept of war.[32] "We are not only fighting hostile armies, but a hostile people," Sherman wrote Halleck in December, 1864, "and must make old and young, rich and poor, feel the hard hand of war, as well as their organized armies."[33] His aim was to make the Southern people who had for almost four years supported a distant war realize that their continued fighting was useless, that the hope of eventual victory held out by Jefferson Davis was futile. Sherman was convinced, as T. Harry Williams put it, that an "overwhelming display of strength that nobody could misread" was the only way to destroy the will of the Southern people and get what he wanted—a rapid end to the war.[34]

It was in his psychological attempt to get at the mind of the Southern people, "to humble their pride, to follow them to their inmost recesses,"[35] that Sherman's new concept of warfare in South

---

[29] Grenville M. Dodge, *Personal Recollections of President Abraham Lincoln, General Ulysses S. Grant and General William T. Sherman*, pp. 175, 181.

[30] Deposition of Sherman, March 30, 1872, *Mixed Commission*, III, 11.

[31] Liddell Hart, *Strategy*, p. 152.

[32] T. Harry Williams, *McClellan, Sherman and Grant*, p. 75.

[33] *OR*, Ser. 1, XLIV, 799.

[34] Williams, *McClellan, Sherman and Grant*, pp. 72–73. The instructions for the Union armies in the field, General Orders No. 100, were written by a former Columbia resident, Francis Lieber, and allowed the interpretation applied by Sherman. See *OR*, Ser. 3, III, 148–164.

[35] Williams, *McClellan, Sherman and Grant*, p. 74.

Carolina proved to be a colossal miscalculation. His harsh, abrasive statements were taken literally and inevitably interpreted to mean hatred for Columbia specifically. South Carolinians would remember his remark that he viewed "Columbia as quite as bad as Charleston" and probably would not spare the public buildings in the capital. They would not accept the statement for what it was—an afterthought. When Sherman, or some of his officers, told the lady in Savannah to stay away from the railroads, the emphasis was on the destruction of transportation. Indeed, virtually every mention of the havoc to be wreaked on South Carolina was coupled with threats of disruption of the state's transportation system, with the emphasis on the latter.[36] Columbians, however, viewed these statements as "personal" threats. The failure of Sherman's psychological warfare, a new kind of war which Southern civilians did not understand, was that the hatred generated during the invasion did not terminate with the war's end. The trauma of the invasion and burning of Columbia lived on in the minds of South Carolinians in the form of an undying hatred of Sherman and a worship of the "lost cause." They misinterpreted Sherman and were never willing to revise their opinions. Sherman's dictum, "war is war, and not popularity seeking," proved true in South Carolina.[37] E. Merton Coulter, a man who has sometimes been chided in the

---

[36] *OR*, Ser. 1, XLIV, 702, 798–799; Senate, *Supplemental Report*, 39th Cong., 1st sess., 1866, I, Senate Reports (Serial 1241), 291, 301, 306, 310, 314–333.

[37] Quoted in James M. Merrill, *William Tecumseh Sherman*, p. 258. The record is clear that Confederates adopted degrees of the same policy as the war progressed. In the Gettysburg campaign Jeb Stuart burned a lumberyard, the gasworks, and government barracks in Carlisle, Pennsylvania, and then shelled the town when the inhabitants did not raise the provisions levied upon them. Major General Jubal Early assessed levies of $200,000 on Hagerstown and Frederick, Maryland, during the 1864 Washington raid, in addition to burning Chambersburg, Pennsylvania, when the town did not produce the required ransom. The raid on Saint Albans, Vermont, in 1864 turned out to be little more than common robbery and thievery, with the participants belatedly identifying themselves as Confederate soldiers. See Edwin B. Coddington, *The Gettysburg Campaign: A Study in Command*, pp. 201–202; Frank E. Vandiver, *Jubal's Raid: General Early's Famous Attack on Washington in 1864*, pp. 92, 107, 118; Mark Mayo Boatner III, *The Civil War Dictionary*, p. 136; Robin W. Winks, *Canada and the United States: The Civil War Years*, pp. 299–301.

historical profession for his pro-Southern proclivities, best described Sherman:

> Cruelty was not remotely concerned with his makeup; it was the great American god efficiency which Sherman was servant. . . .
>
> Some defense for Sherman rests in this very weakness of his for making extravagant statements; for he announced policies he did not act upon, and said things he did not believe, though he did not realize it at the time. . . .
>
> Plainly enough he was not an enemy of the South apart from his four years of warring against it to preserve the Union. . . .
>
> Sherman's war record was not nearly so cruel as some of his widely expressed intentions would indicate. There is no evidence that in his most destructive moments he ever permitted his army to slay non-combatants or that his army ever desired to do so, although he had solemnly written Sheridan that the correct method was to kill the people rather than conquer the territory. To repeat, it was not inborn cruelty that prompted Sherman in his war measures; it was his idea of effective warfare. It was his conception of the best method by which to perform a given duty. He firmly believed that his system would win the war in the shortest time, and therefore be a blessing to both North and South.[38]

A second tenet in the indictment of Sherman was that the Union army, in spite of the fact that the Confederate authorities made no attempt to defend Columbia, indiscriminately and mercilessly bombarded the town although they knew it was filled with women, children, and elderly men.[39] William Gilmore Simms presented the position of Columbians succinctly in his newspaper: "The enemy's shells . . . fell fast and thick about the town. They had commenced shelling the evening before [February 15], and

---

[38] Ellis Merton Coulter, "Sherman and the South," *North Carolina Historical Review* 8 (Jan., 1931): 42, 49.

[39] Gibbes, *Who Burnt Columbia?*, pp. 5–6; Anna Tillman Swindell, *The Burning of Columbia: Prize Essay of Wade Hampton Chapter, U.D.C.*, p. 7; Anthony Toomer Porter, *The History of a Work of Faith and Love in Charleston, South Carolina, Which Grew Out of the Calamities of the Late Civil War, and a Record of God's Wonderful Providence*, p. 110.

continued it throughout the night. No summons for surrender had been made; no warning of any kind was given. The shelling continued throughout the day, and new batteries were in rapid progress of erection on the West side of the Congaree, the more effectually to press the work of destruction."[40]

That some shells fell in residential areas of Columbia is beyond question, but the intent of the Union army's cannonade and the extent of the damage done to private homes has been vehemently disputed. Simms listed only one illustration of shells falling in a residential area,[41] and James G. Gibbes recorded that two houses were struck, one of which was located near the arsenal.[42] One other citizen, Mrs. W. K. Bachman, noted that a cannonball fell harmlessly near the Methodist Female College gate.[43]

From these and other general accounts presented by Columbians, certain conclusions can be drawn about the shelling of the city. First, little actual damage was done to residential areas. Simms stated flatly that "the damage was comparatively slight,"[44] and Mrs. Bachman spoke of the destruction as "a few bricks dislodged here and there."[45] Second, it seems clear that few civilians, if any, were injured in those residences which were struck. Gibbes reported "no casualties,"[46] as did Anna T. Swindell,[47] while Mrs. Bachman wrote that "two persons are said to have been killed."[48] Simms also reported hearing of two deaths from the shelling, one of which had occurred near the South Carolina Railroad depot.[49]

It is clear that a large number of shells were thrown into Columbia; it is equally apparent that most, aimed at military in-

[40] *Columbia Phoenix*, March 21, 1865; T. J. Goodwyn to Colin Campbell Murchison, June 8, 1866, Thomas Jefferson Goodwyn Letter, South Caroliniana Library, University of South Carolina, Columbia.
[41] *Columbia Phoenix*, March 21, 1865.
[42] Gibbes, *Who Burnt Columbia?*, pp. 5–6.
[43] Bachman to Kate Bachman, March 27, 1865, copy, Bachman Papers. See also A. T. Smythe, M. B. Poppenheim, and Thomas Taylor, eds., *South Carolina Women in the Confederacy*, I, 328.
[44] *Columbia Phoenix*, March 21, 1865.
[45] Bachman to Kate Bachman, March 27, 1865, copy, Bachman Papers.
[46] Gibbes, *Who Burnt Columbia?*, pp. 5–6.
[47] Swindell, *Burning of Columbia*, p. 7.
[48] Bachman to Kate Bachman, March 27, 1865, copy, Bachman Papers.
[49] *Columbia Phoenix*, March 21, 1865.

stallations, were on target, as is illustrated by the fact that Confederate officers and state officials who were evacuating war matériel and supplies cited the bombardment as the chief cause of their loss of property. Federal artillery records indicate that 325 rounds were fired during the capture of Columbia, though the target is not clearly designated in each case. The First Illinois Light Artillery reported firing 110 rounds into "the main street in the city of Columbia in which the rebel cavalry were moving" and into the "woods" opposite where the Union army crossed the Broad River. The Twelfth Wisconsin Battery reported that it "shelled the city, expending thirty-one rounds," on February 16, and the next day fired 49 shells into the "woods" on the east bank of the Broad River. The First Missouri Light Artillery, from its position on the Congaree River, reported shelling "rebel works, expending 135 rounds" on February 16.[50]

The fact is, Columbia was not an open city. The accepted international law of the period stated that whenever acts were taken to defend a town, it could not then be called an open city.[51] As has been shown, Sherman's advance had been contested by the Confederates, though unsuccessfully, to the extent that they attacked the force that had received Mayor Goodwyn's surrender. In addition, the rules of war under which Sherman operated gave him the right—even the duty—to shell Columbia to protect his own force.[52] Southerners recognized that they had attempted a defense of Columbia, and they were also aware that no attempt was made to declare the city open. Consequently, the shelling of the South Carolina capital resulted not from an overzealous General Sherman, but from the bad judgment of Beauregard and Hampton in not declaring the city to be open when they knew it could not be defended.

If South Carolinians appeared to have reacted emotionally to

[50] *OR,* Ser. 1, XLVII, pt. 1: 371–373.

[51] Quincy Wright, "The American Civil War, 1861–65," in *The International Law of Civil War,* ed. Richard A. Falk, p. 64; Charles G. Fenwick, *International Law,* pp. 473–474; Charles Cheney Hyde, *International Law Chiefly as Interpreted and Applied by the United States,* II, 303.

[52] *OR,* Ser. 3, III, 150. This code of conduct was reissued in the Spanish-American War and used in preparing the *U.S. Rules of Land Warfare* published in 1917 and 1940. It was replaced by *Law of Land Warfare* in 1956. See Wright, "The American Civil War," p. 55.

the shelling of Columbia—which is certainly understandable—
they differed little from Sherman, who responded with equal irra-
tionality to the shelling of his troops on the west side of the Congaree River on the night of February 15. Aware that he was
changing the nature of warfare, though much of his contribution
would not be recognized until after World War I,[53] Sherman did
not always comprehend the multifarious ramifications of his inno-
vations. The result was that he applied a double standard—as
South Carolinians did—to much of what transpired. The same
Sherman who was responsible for the concept of "total war" could
not accept the land mines used by Confederates to impede his
progress, referring to them as "uncivilized warfare" and marching
Southern prisoners in front of his columns to explode them.[54] He
assigned the shelling of his camp at least partially to the same cate-
gory of barbarity. "In war you do everything that will produce a
good result," Sherman told the Mixed Commission in accordance
with his usual pragmatism, but merely spending the lives of "a few
miserable soldiers, rolled up in their blankets asleep," was not only
"bad warfare [sic], but very bad policy." Such wanton mischief,
for which he unjustly held Wade Hampton responsible, was not
carried out with the hope of stopping his army, Sherman believed,
and could only provoke "retaliation," which he at first contem-
plated but later decided against. Sherman also maintained that the
bombardment of his camp increased the bitterness of his officers
and men against South Carolina;[55] on this point, however, he stood
alone. Both Logan and Charles R. Woods testified that they and
their men accepted the shelling as the normal act of soldiers attempting to defend their homes.[56]

A third criticism leveled against Sherman by Columbians was
that he purposely sent the XV Corps into the city as the occupying
force, knowing their proclivities for destruction. The "vile and des-

[53] Liddell Hart, *Strategy*, pp. 143–144.
[54] William Tecumseh Sherman, *Memoirs of General William T. Sherman*, II, 194; M. A. DeWolfe Howe, ed., *Home Letters of General Sherman*,
p. 161.
[55] Deposition of Sherman, Dec. 11, 1872, *Mixed Commission*, XIV, 95–98.
[56] Deposition of John A. Logan, Dec. 21, 1872, Nos. 103, 292, *Mixed Commission*, XIV, 294; deposition of Charles R. Woods, Dec. 16, 1872, Nos. 103,
292, *Mixed Commission*, XIV, 201.

perate character" of the "diabolical 15th" was such, Emma Le-
Conte wrote on the afternoon following the fire, that Sherman had
never before permitted it to enter a captured city.[57] "The first regiment sent into the city was what Sherman calls his 'Tigers,'" a
Columbian wrote two weeks after the fire. "Whenever he sends
these men ahead, he intends to do his worst. He says he would not
be afraid to go to the lower regions with this regiment in the lead.
They had the toes of their shoes covered with steel & would kick
open the strongest locks."[58] It was, therefore, very easy for Simms
and other Columbians to conclude that once the XV Corps entered
the South Carolina capital, the city was doomed to destruction.[59]

Proving the barbaric composition of the XV Corps and their
determination to burn Columbia was an important part of the case
presented by lawyers representing claimants before the Mixed
Commission. Verbal sparring was constant, especially when Sherman was testifying. When asked about the activities of the XV
Corps in Columbia, Sherman mentioned that one division was given
freedom of movement, whereupon the counsel for the claimant
queried: "You allowed the 15th corps, then, to walk the streets of
Columbia?" When Sherman replied that Howard had given orders
regarding the disposition of troops in Columbia, counsel for the
claimant persisted: "I understood you to say that, knowing the
character of the 15th corps, knowing its desire to burn Columbia,
you yet suffered your officers. . . ." At this point Sherman inter-
rupted: "I do not think I said I knew of any desire on their part to
burn Columbia; I knew they had a deep-seated feeling of hostility
to Columbia, but I do not think I said they had a desire to burn
it." When Sherman was reminded that only a short while before
he had said his soldiers were "likely" to burn Columbia, the general responded candidly: "I could have had them stay in the ranks,
but I would not have done it, under the circumstances, to save
Columbia."[60]

[57] Earl Schenck Miers, ed., *When the World Ended: The Diary of Emma
LeConte*, p. 43; Porter, *Work of Faith*, p. 114.

[58] Anonymous letter, March 3, 1865, Anonymous Collection, South Caroliniana Library, University of South Carolina, Columbia.

[59] *Columbia Phoenix*, March 21, 1865.

[60] Deposition of Sherman, Dec. 11, 1872, *Mixed Commission*, XIV, 102–
103.

Throughout the proceedings Sherman insisted that the men of the XV Corps were typical citizens, for the most part farmers and mechanics from Ohio and Illinois, who were subject to good discipline and who carried out their orders thoroughly, doing no more destruction than necessary. He presented as evidence the fact that he had heard of only two cases of rape within his army. The XV Corps was, the Union general maintained, no different from any other corps.[61]

The XV Corps' reputation for destructiveness was built on two factors: actual destruction of property and verbal bombast. That the XV Corps engaged in the destruction of property throughout Sherman's march cannot be disputed. Private dwellings were burned simply because they were abandoned, and others were torn down, as were fences and barns, to be used as firewood for cooking or for heating rails that were then bent around trees to make "Sherman's neckties." In evaluating the damage done by Sherman's army, it is impossible to determine which corps was the most ruinous, though it is safe to say that there was a large gap between what was claimed and what was accomplished. As T. Harry Williams points out, the thirty-five-day march in South Carolina could scarcely have touched more than a fraction of the total resources still available to the Confederacy.[62] Indeed, the only distinction made by Columbians in their criticism of the different corps was that the XV Corps burned the city. The second ingredient in the reputation of the XV Corps was its boasts of its strength and accomplishments, and credit here must be given to both Sherman and his troops. The general believed in all his men and bragged on them frequently, as he did when writing Halleck about what the XV Corps would do to Charleston when they entered that city. Stories are abundant which tell how Sherman's soldiers shouted to the Confederates in front of them, "you'd better get out, this is the

[61] Ibid., pp. 75–77; see also deposition of O. O. Howard, Dec. 10, 1872, Nos. 103, 292, *Mixed Commission*, XIV, 28–29, 32. The assessment of the Catholic priest in Columbia was not strikingly different from Sherman's: "All the men were not equally desperate and abandoned; there were many humane and religious men among them; a fact that refutes the charge of universal depravity, frequently urged against this [XV] corps" (J. J. O'Connell, *Catholicity in the Carolinas and Georgia: Leaves of Its History*, p. 272).

[62] Williams, *McClellan, Sherman and Grant*, pp. 72–73.

Fifteenth Corps!" causing them to retreat.[63] The XV Corps also possessed a natural pride which Sherman's praise did not diminish. What made all this propaganda so effective was that both the Confederate army and the civilian population in South Carolina believed it, thus creating an undying hatred for the XV Corps.

Another accusation in the controversy over the burning of Columbia was that Sherman, upon entering the city, promised its inhabitants that private property would be protected. After lulling them into a sense of false security, the charge continued, Sherman ordered the town burned.[64] When Mayor Goodwyn surrendered the city on the morning of the seventeenth, he reported that Colonel Stone had promised its safety "until Gen. Sherman arrived." During the afternoon Goodwyn met with the Northern commander and was promised, the mayor later reported, that there would be no destruction of private property. "Go home and rest assured that your city will be as secure in my hands as if you had control!" the mayor quoted Sherman as saying.[65]

The general's remarks were widely circulated, and the stationing of guards throughout the town doubtless reassured many. As a result, Columbians apparently believed that Sherman had promised protection of the city. One Columbian wrote:

> The city was at an early hour of the morning surrendered by the mayor to [Sherman's] *tender mercies* and *protection* which latter he promised upon his honor should be given to the helpless inhabitants; and furthermore he promised, that beyond the *State House, City Hall* and some *other public buildings*—none others should be burned. How *faithfully* he kept that promise—*We all know to our sorrow!* . . . We had relied so implicitly upon Sherman's solemn promise to the mayor, whom we knew, that we had not made the slightest effort to save anything.[66]

---

[63] Lloyd Lewis, *Sherman, Fighting Prophet*, p. 489.

[64] Sill, "Who is Responsible," p. 362.

[65] Goodwyn to Colin Campbell Murchison, June 8, 1866, Goodwyn Letter; affidavit of Goodwyn, Nov. 3, 1866, in *The Burning of Columbia. I. A Letter of Gen. Wade Hampton, June 24, 1873, With Appendix. II. Report of a Committee of Citizens, Ex-Chancellor J. P. Carroll, Chairman, May 1866*, p. 7 (hereafter cited as *Burning of Columbia, Letter and Report*); *Columbia Phoenix*, March 21, 1865.

[66] Anonymous, "Burning of Columbia" [1865?], manuscript, Anonymous Collection.

"Strange as it may seem," Emma LeConte lamented in her diary on the eighteenth, "we were actually idiotic enough to believe Sherman would keep his word! A *Yankee*—and *Sherman*! It does seem incredible, such credulity, but I suppose we were so anxious to believe him—the lying fiend!"[67]

Sherman's position concerning whether or not he promised the protection of private property in Columbia is somewhat clouded. When testifying before the Mixed Commission in December, 1872, he emphatically denied on two occasions that he had in any way made such a commitment. However, when asked for a third time by counsel for the claimant, Sherman modified his answer, bringing it into agreement with the statements of Mayor Goodwyn and other Columbians, but he maintained that he "made no promise; it is very probable I may have said that there was no necessity for being frightened, that we were not going to burn anything except arsenals, machine shops, and foundries; but it was not in the form of a promise; if it was said it was a mere conversational remark, probably to the mayor or some of the people who came to me very much alarmed, as they naturally would be at the fall of their city."[68] Three years later, when writing his memoirs, Sherman said that he met Mayor Goodwyn, who was quite apprehensive about the fate of his fellow citizens, "and it is probable I told him then not to be uneasy, that we did not intend to stay long, and had no purpose to injure the private citizens or private property."[69] Sherman's denial before the Mixed Commission is not convincing. Without belaboring a fairly obvious point, it appears that Sherman was trying to say that since he did not protect private property, as he had said he would, it was therefore not a promise, thus exculpating him for any failure to perform his duty.

A fifth indictment of the Northern army was that soon after Columbia was occupied a number of citizens were warned that the city would be put to the torch. The signal for commencing the burning, they were told, would be rockets ascending into the sky. A number of versions of this story have been recorded, two of

[67] Miers, *When the World Ended*, p. 44.
[68] Deposition of Sherman, Dec. 11, 1872, *Mixed Commission*, XIV, 79–80.
[69] Sherman, *Memoirs*, II, 280.

which were published by the Carroll committee. Mrs. L. S. McCord told the committee that on the morning of the seventeenth one of her maids brought her an ill-spelled note which, the maid said, had been left by a Union soldier. "Ladies," the kindly intruder had written, "I pity you; leave this town; go anywheres to be safer than here." That night, Mrs. McCord's testimony proceeded, the arson began.[70] Another Columbian received a similar warning from a Union officer who, accompanied by a group of soldiers, visited William H. Orchard's home shortly before the fire began. As the men were leaving, Orchard related to the Carroll committee, the officer called him aside and said: " 'You seem to be a clever sort of a man, and have a large family, so I will give you some advice; if you have anything you wish to save, take care of it at once, for before morning this d----d town will be in ashes—every house in it.' My only reply was: can that be true? He said, 'yes, and if you do not believe me, you will be the sufferer; and if you watch you will see three rockets go up soon, and if you do not take my advice you will see h-ll.' "[71] Mrs. John Thompson related a similar story to Dr. Trezevant in 1866. Upon the arrival of her guards, she was informed that three rockets would soon signal the sack and burning of Columbia, thus making their services unnecessary.[72] Catherine P. Ravenel wrote years later that her guard told her of a regiment that had sworn to burn Columbia when signaled to do so by rockets.[73]

Mayor Goodwyn reported that upon returning home after having spent most of the afternoon with Sherman, he saw three rockets—red, white, blue—fired into the air from in front of his residence. His guard, whom he characterized as "quiet and good," promptly exclaimed, "My God, is it coming to this!" and walked off without saying another word. In fifteen minutes, the mayor wrote,

[70] Carroll, "Burning of Columbia," pp. 206–207; Trezevant, "Notes on the Burning of Columbia," Trezevant Papers.

[71] Carroll, "Burning of Columbia," p. 207; Carroll, *Report of the Committee*, pp. 11–12.

[72] Trezevant, *Burning of Columbia*, p. 23.

[73] James Conner et al., eds., *South Carolina Women in the Confederacy*, II, 147. Mrs. Ravenel reported seeing the rockets about 7:00 P.M., but gave no location.

he heard the cry of fire.[74] Two ministers, William Yates and A. Toomer Porter, reported virtually the same experience as the mayor's.[75]

The question of the location of the rockets fired skyward, which were "considered" by those who saw them to be the signal for the burning,[76] adds to the confusion. Edward Sill, corroborating Mayor Goodwyn's account, saw red, white, and blue rockets ascend "in the direction" of the State House.[77] O. Z. Bates viewed several rockets near the capitol at about 8:00 or 9:00 P.M.[78] The Reverend Peter J. Shand reported seeing numerous rockets ascending "every now and then" during the conflagration near his home, which was several blocks from the State House.[79] From this testimony it seems clear that rockets were fired skyward in the vicinity of the State House, but James G. Gibbes saw rockets in the "northern part" of town, after which he noticed three fires in Cotton Town.[80] Still another citizen, in a letter written two weeks after the event, quoted her mother as saying she observed four rockets, "one at each corner of the town, all at the same moment."[81] There were other general accounts which spoke of seeing rockets but did not give their locations.[82]

There are two possible explanations for the rockets observed by Columbians on the night of the fire. The first, that they were a

[74] Affidavit of Goodwyn, Nov. 3, 1866, in *Burning of Columbia, Letter and Report*, p. 7; Goodwyn to Colin Campbell Murchison, June 8, 1866, Goodwyn Letter. The letter simply stated that the rockets "went up" without giving a specific location.

[75] Trezevant, *Burning of Columbia*, p. 22; Anthony Toomer Porter, *Led On! Step by Step: Scenes from Clerical, Military, Educational, and Plantation Life in the South, 1828–1898*, pp. 159–160.

[76] Trezevant, *Burning of Columbia*, p. 17.

[77] Sill, "Who is Responsible," p. 363. Sill mistakenly believed the wind was from the west.

[78] Deposition of O. Z. Bates, April 8, 1872, No. 103, *Mixed Commission*, XIV, 4.

[79] Shand to Mrs. Howard Kennedy, March 9, 1868, Peter J. Shand Papers, South Caroliniana Library, University of South Carolina, Columbia.

[80] Deposition of James G. Gibbes, May 1, 1872, No. 103, *Mixed Commission*, XIV, 25.

[81] Ravenel, "Burning of Columbia," Harriott Horry Ravenel Papers.

[82] The number forewarned who presented affidavits to that effect to the Carroll committee was quite small. Trezevant, "Notes on the Burning of Columbia," Trezevant Papers.

signal to a group of conspirators who were determined to burn the city, is plausible, but extremely difficult to substantiate. That some of the Federal troops expressed hatred for South Carolina and its capital is abundantly clear. How many of these men were engaging in mere rhetoric and how many transferred their feelings into burning and looting is not so lucid. In the final analysis, the entire case of a camp conspiracy to destroy Columbia is based on a meager amount of hearsay. Mayor Goodwyn reported that on the night of the fire he asked soldiers "at different times if they thought it was an accident and they invariably replied. No! that from the first night they left Savannah, Ga. until they arrived in Columbia, it was camp talk what they would do with our City."[83] Catherine P. Ravenel, as noted earlier, had been told by her faithful guard that a regiment had sworn to burn the South Carolina capital.[84]

Talk of a conspiracy also existed in the Union army. George A. Stone, the officer to whom Mayor Goodwyn surrendered, reported in a letter to the *Chicago Tribune* of January 2, 1873, that he believed a plot existed to burn Columbia.[85] O. O. Howard told the Mixed Commission in 1872 that the thought of a plot entered his mind after the fire because of a comment by a young Federal lieutenant who had been a prisoner in Columbia. The lieutenant told Howard that he had seen escaped prisoners "doing mischief." Howard stated that he assumed that their imprisonment had motivated their actions.[86]

---

[83] Affidavit of Goodwyn, Nov. 3, 1866, in *Burning of Columbia, Letter and Report*, p. 7; Goodwyn to Colin Campbell Murchison, June 8, 1866, Goodwyn Letter; Carroll, "Burning of Columbia," p. 209.

[84] Conner et al., eds., *South Carolina Women*, II, 147. She did not identify the regiment.

[85] *Senate, Destruction of Property*, 71st Cong., 2d sess., 1930, Senate Doc. No. 149 (Serial 9220), pp. 99–100.

[86] Deposition of Howard, *Mixed Commission*, XIV, 11. On February 20, 1865, from Rice Creek Springs, S.C., Howard wrote the following letter to General Blair dealing with stealing by foragers: "I desire to call your attention to the fact that some of our soldiers have been committing the most outrageous robberies of watches, jewelry, &c. A case has come to my notice where a watch and several articles of jewelry were stolen by a foraging party under the eye of the commissioned officer in charge. Another, where a brute had violently assaulted a lady by striking her, and had then robbed her of a valuable gold watch. In one instance money was stolen to the amount of $150, and another, where an officer with a foraging party had allowed his men to take rings off

The other explanation of the rockets was that presented by the Union officers who had been in Columbia. For purposes of communication, Sherman and Howard told the Mixed Commission, flags were used by the signal corps during the day and rockets at night. The rockets informed each wing of the army of the other's most advanced position. Henry W. Howgate of Sherman's signal corps put it succinctly: "Our order was to exchange communication by means of rockets at a certain hour every night—eight o'clock—an hour when it was supposed the different columns, marching over different roads, would be in camp."[87] Though the charge that rockets signaled the fire has been extensively articulated by Columbians—the number of general accounts grew steadily as the years passed[88]—it is difficult to believe that the relationship was anything more than coincidental. In compiling information for a pamphlet on the burning of Columbia, Daniel H. Trezevant seemed to reach the same conclusion, as one of his obtusely worded notes indicated: "No one seems to know the hour of the night at which the incident occurred. I have assumed the throwing up of the signal rockets as the time from which I date every thing either as it occurred before or after."[89]

---

the fingers of ladies in his presence. To-day a soldier was found plundering, arrested, placed under guard of one of General Corse's orderlies, and was liberated by some of his comrades who had arms in their hands, and who threatened the life of the guard. These outrages must be stopped at all hazards, and the thieves and robbers who commit them be dealt with severely and summarily. I am inclined to think that there is a regularly organized banditti who commit these outrages and who share the spoils. I call upon you and upon all the officers and soldiers under you, who have one spark of honor or respect for the profession which they follow, to help me put down these infamous proceedings and to arrest the perpetrators. Please furnish to every inspector, provost-marshal, and officer in charge of a foraging party a copy of this letter, and enjoin them to be on the watch to stop these infamous proceedings, and to bring to justice the individuals who commit them" (*OR*, Ser. 1, XLVII, pt. 2: 505–506). See also George S. Bradley, *Star Corps; or, Notes of an Army Chaplain During Sherman's famous March to the Sea*, p. 255.

[87] Deposition of Howard, *Mixed Commission*, XIV, 10; deposition of Sherman, Dec. 11, 1872, *Mixed Commission*, XIV, 64; deposition of H. W. Howgate, Dec. 17, 1872, Nos. 103, 292, *Mixed Commission*, XIV, 275–276.

[88] See No. 228, George Symmers *vs.* United States, *Mixed Commission*, XXIII.

[89] Trezevant, "Notes on the Burning of Columbia," Trezevant Papers.

The sixth criticism of Sherman growing out of the tragedy, and one which never wavered in certainty, was that he was personally responsible for the burning of Columbia. "Tecumseh Sherman was the incendiary," wrote Dr. Trezevant in 1866, "and he, and he alone, is responsible for the terrible destruction that has been occasioned, and the retarding of prosperity for the next fifty years."[90] The Trinity Episcopal Church minister, the Reverend Peter J. Shand, agreed. In a letter to a Northern friend in March, 1868, Shand assigned the blame "*to General Sherman and to him alone,*" though he conceded that the general may not have "*literally ordered*" the fire. The absence of a "*positive order*" not to burn Columbia, coupled with his belief that the Northern general desired the city's destruction, convinced Shand that Sherman "*winked & connived*" with his troops, giving them the impression that they had a free hand to sack the town.[91]

The testimony that Sherman was either directly or indirectly culpable for ordering the burning of Columbia was the result of a sincere "belief" surmised by citizens who had experienced the tragic event. They thought it impossible that Union troops could participate in the sacking of their city without Sherman's having ordered them to do so, and their position was that "any statement made by General Sherman to the contrary was a lie."[92]

Sherman's response to the allegation that he willfully burned the South Carolina capital, a charge which Allan Nevins said "seems incredible," was an absolute denial. The general was sensitive to the criticism that he casually rode through the streets during the fire puffing on a cigar, showing no interest in what transpired, and giving no orders to suppress the flames.[93] Therefore, anxious to clear his reputation and that of his army by presenting his case, he testified on two occasions before the Mixed Commission, and his defense, composed of typically candid statements, had a ring of truth. On March 30, 1872, Sherman stated: "The ulterior and stragetic [*sic*] advantages of the occupation of Columbia are

[90] Trezevant, *Burning of Columbia*, p. 24.

[91] Shand to Mrs. Howard Kennedy, March 9, 1868, Shand Papers.

[92] Deposition of Charles F. Jackson, Aug. 10, 1872, No. 292, *Mixed Commission*, XXVII, 16.

[93] Gibbes, *Who Burnt Columbia?*, p. 9.

seen now clearly by the result; the burning of the private dwellings, though never designed by me, was a trifling matter compared with the manifold results that soon followed. Though I never ordered it, and never wished it, I have never shed many tears over the event, because I believe it hastened what we all fought for, the end of the war."[94] His final testimony was given December 11, 1872, when he stated: "If I had made up my mind to burn Columbia I would have burnt it with no more feeling than I would a common prairie dog village; but I did not do it. . . ."[95] Despite the opinions long held by advocates of the lost cause, the evidence is clear that Sherman cannot be held personally responsible for the burning of Columbia.

The final accusation—the charge involving the greatest amount of testimony—was that the Northern invaders sacked Columbia, firing it in hundreds of places and leaving the entire city in ashes. According to Simms, the Union troops began their pillage and plunder shortly after they entered. Stores were broken into all during the afternoon, and those contents too large to steal were thrown into the streets. Gold, silver, jewels, and liquors were most in demand, but citizens who carried purses, watches, or gold chains or who wore expensive hats, coats, or boots had them stripped from their bodies "in the twinkling of an eye." Simms estimated that perhaps twelve hundred watches were stolen from Columbians during its occupation. The "demonic saturnalia" which began in the business section soon spread to the residential areas. Guards sent to protect private property in "at least" one-half the cases betrayed their helpless victims by looting and burning.[96]

According to Columbians, at the signal of the rockets Union soldiers dispersed throughout the town, starting fires in many dif-

---

[94] Depositions of Sherman, Dec. 11, 1872, *Mixed Commission*, XIV, 91; March 30, 1872, *Mixed Commission*, III, 12; Sherman, *Memoirs*, II, 285–286; Rachel Sherman Thorndike, ed., *The Sherman Letters: Correspondence between General and Senator Sherman from 1837 to 1891*, p. 266.

[95] Deposition of Sherman, Dec. 11, 1872, *Mixed Commission*, XIV, 90.

[96] *Columbia Phoenix*, March 23, 25, 1865; Edwin J. Scott, *Random Recollections of a Long Life, 1806 to 1876*, pp. 177–178; Mary S. Whilden, *Recollections of the War, 1861–1865*, pp. 9–10.

ferent places simultaneously.[97] In residential sections, where the streets were wide and well-kept gardens separated the beautiful old mansions, "thousands of wanton hands" waited to ignite those homes that had escaped the path of the flames. From house to house the soldiers ran with vessels containing such combustibles as phosphorus and turpentine. Cotton balls, saturated with flammable materials, were thrown into room corners and closets, starting new fires.[98] As if possessing clairvoyant powers, the Union troops ran through the streets asking, "Is this the house of Mr. Rhett?" and pointing to the exact location, or "Is that the dwelling of Mr. Middleton?" again identifying it correctly. In each case, the stories go, the house was promptly set on fire.[99]

When the first fire in the cotton developed during the afternoon, James G. Gibbes wrote, the Federal troops began a policy of interfering with the firemen and citizens attempting to extinguish the flames.[100] This harassment continued when the conflagration began that night, Simms maintained, when soldiers hacked and chopped the fire hoses with bayonets and axes, disabled the engines, and by vehement threats forced the firemen to give up their charge.[101]

It was during the night, Columbians would later recall, that the real atrocities, the "reign of terror," began.[102] As citizens ran from their homes to seek safety in the streets, some were attacked, and their watches and jewelry were stolen,[103] while others were taunted by carousing, drunken soldiers who hurled insults at them.

[97] Anonymous letter, March 3, 1865, Anonymous Collection; *Columbia Phoenix*, March 23, 1865.

[98] Swindell, *Burning of Columbia*, pp. 11–12.

[99] Sophie Sosnowski, "Burning of Columbia," manuscript, Sosnowski-Schaller Papers, South Caroliniana Library, University of South Carolina, Columbia.

[100] Gibbes, *Who Burnt Columbia?*, p. 7.

[101] *Columbia Phoenix*, March 23, 1865.

[102] Ibid.

[103] Ibid., March 25, 1865; George Huggins, "Burning of Columbia" [1865?], manuscript copy, George Huggins Papers, South Caroliniana Library, University of South Carolina, Columbia; Chapman J. Milling, "Ilium in Flames," *Confederate Veteran* 36 (May, 1928): 181.

Still others who carried small bundles of clothes and food from their burning homes had them snatched by passing soldiers, some of whom threw the packages into the flames, thus depriving citizens of the few possessions they had managed to claim from the fires.[104] There seemed to be no limit to the despicable acts, the charges of Columbians continued. Soldiers trailed gunpowder down the streets and set it on fire to frighten the women and children, asking them as they screamed in terror how they liked the "beautiful sight."[105] There was no escape. Some citizens fled to the churches, thinking they might find safety there, but "thither the hellish perseverance of the fiends followed them, and the churches of God were set on flame." Those who ran to Sidney Park, located below a cliff in the northwest section of the city, were soon imperiled by torches "thrown from the heights into the deepest hollows of the park. . . ."[106] Ironically, the only haven of relative safety the citizens found was the South Carolina Insane Asylum in the northern part of town. There, a large number of frightened citizens managed to pass the night without injury, though there were threats of violence by drunken soldiers.[107]

The Union troops did not confine their activities to the streets, the local account persists. Indeed, William Gilmore Simms wrote, it was within the homes of citizens that the atrocities were most tragic, "rarely softened by any ludicrous aspects." Brutal villains, including officers as high as colonels, mercilessly thrust their pistols to the bosoms or heads of women, demanding "Your gold, silver, watch, jewels." They allowed no time to answer, and before one could proffer her keys to a trunk or wardrobe, it had been dashed to pieces by an axe or the butt of a gun, with the cry, "We have a shorter way than that!" A plea to spare one's furniture was wasted on barbarians utterly devoid of "human feeling." Sentimental portraits and mementos of departed loved ones were crushed underfoot or dashed to pieces; the "more the trembler pleaded for

---

[104] Carroll, "Burning of Columbia," pp. 207–208; Anonymous, "Burning of Columbia," Anonymous Collection; *Columbia Phoenix*, April 1, 1865.

[105] Deposition of Joseph H. Marks, April 12, 1873, No. 236, David Jacobs *vs.* United States, *Mixed Commission*, XXIII, 67.

[106] *Columbia Phoenix*, April 1, 1865.

[107] Anonymous, "Burning of Columbia," Anonymous Collection.

the object so precious, the more violent the rage which destroyed it."[108] "Ladies had their dresses violently torn open and were searched for their gold," Mary Leverett wrote, and "negro women were carried into Ladies chambers and ordered to flog them (I don't think it was actually done however) & ladies rushed frantically away from these insults."[109] Dr. D. H. Trezevant told of a situation in which a soldier caught a "lady by the throat, and thrust his hand into her bosom to feel for her watch, or purse" and of cases in which a man lifted a woman's dress "because she was not quick enough in freeing her purse from her girdle. . . ."[110]

Before the night was over, citizens would later claim, Columbia had experienced a series of events unknown in history for their barbarity.[111] Cemeteries were searched and graves opened and robbed. Flower gardens were probed with bayonets for buried family valuables.[112] Treasures of art, silver plate, jewels, and valuable papers from all over the Confederacy, sent to Columbia banks because of a presumed immunity from attack, were stolen or destroyed.[113] The sick and infirm were abused by profane language, robbed, and left to die in their flaming houses.[114] What the invaders could not steal or burn, they destroyed. Fine collections of art, such as that of Dr. Robert W. Gibbes, were slashed "zig-zag"; private libraries were sought out and the books "hacked and hewn

---

[108] *Columbia Phoenix*, March 26, 1865. While Simms stated that there was a marked absence of humor in the actions of Union troops during the fire, his newspaper account contained numerous illustrations of comical situations, usually at the expense of the soldiers.

[109] Leverett to Caroline, March 18, 1865, Mary Leverett Letter, South Caroliniana Library, University of South Carolina, Columbia.

[110] Trezevant, *Burning of Columbia*, p. 10.

[111] August Conrad, *The Destruction of Columbia, S.C.: A Translation from the German by William H. Pleasants, of 19th, 20th, 21st, and 22d Chapters of "Lights and Shadows in American Life During the War of Secession," by August Conrad*, p. 3. The material cited here is from the preface written by Pleasants.

[112] Columbia, S.C., Board of Trade, *Columbia, S.C., The Future Manufacturing and Commercial Centre of the South. With Some Account of its Foundation, Destruction and Subsequent Rehabilitation and Growth*, p. 18.

[113] *Columbia Phoenix*, March 21, 1865; Gibbes, *Who Burnt Columbia?*, pp. 4–5.

[114] *Columbia Phoenix*, March 30, 1865.

and trampled."[115] Churches were entered and mockery made of the sacraments.[116]

Though Columbians were unanimous in their criticism of the harshness of the events, they invariably claimed that they refused to be overawed by the Union troops. Indeed, the women of Columbia "almost universally" bore up "nobly" in the face of their adversaries, exhibiting the pluck for which they were famous. William Gilmore Simms told of a "typical" conversation on that fateful night. When a lady refused to admit her fear, a soldier grasped her by the throat and put a gun to her head. "Her eyes never faltered. Her cheek never changed its color," Simms wrote. Her unflinching courage led the soldier to put away his gun, comparing her bravery to that of a "whole regiment."[117] Some cases of brutal assaults upon women were reported, but "usually there was a restraining comrade among the squad of housebreakers" to protect their honor.[118]

When the smoke cleared and Columbians looked around at dawn on the eighteenth, they saw total destruction—an allegation which has continued to this day. The sight was too much for Mayor Goodwyn, who collapsed with a nervous breakdown the day after Sherman's army withdrew.[119] The task of guiding the bewildered citizens fell to the acting mayor, James G. Gibbes, who reported to the Mixed Commission in 1872 that he "ascertained officially" that thirteen hundred houses, making up the entire business section of town, had burned.[120] He reiterated this figure in an article in the

115 Ibid.; Swindell, *Burning of Columbia*, pp. 10–11. Dr. Gibbes made no mention of such acts in his description of the events. He possessed about eighty-three paintings by such well-known American artists as Washington Allston, Thomas Sully, Henry Inman, and James DeVeaux. In addition, he had a large collection of copies of European paintings and engravings. See *Catalogue of Paintings, Marbles and Casts in the Collection of R. W. Gibbes, M.D.* The most complete biography of Gibbes is Arney R. Childs, "Dr. Robert Wilson Gibbes (1809–1866)," master's thesis, University of South Carolina, 1925.

116 Smythe, Poppenheim, and Taylor, *South Carolina Women*, I, 295.

117 *Columbia Phoenix*, March 28, 1865.

118 Milling, "Ilium in Flames," p. 181.

119 Scott, *Random Recollections*, p. 194; R. W. Gibbes to A. G. Magrath, Feb. 28, 1865, Robert Wilson Gibbes Papers, South Caroliniana Library, University of South Carolina, Columbia.

120 Deposition of Gibbes, May 1, 1872, *Mixed Commission*, XIV, 25.

Philadelphia Times in 1880, adding that the fire swept over eighty-four squares containing 366 acres.[121]

Two other citizens made similar estimates of the damage within one month. Dr. Robert W. Gibbes wrote Governor Andrew G. Magrath on February 28, 1865, that "upwards of 1200 houses, on 84 squares" had been burned,[122] and Mrs. S. McCam wrote her daughter on March 5, 1865, that eighty squares containing 1,390 of the finest homes had been devastated.[123] To these reports must be added the estimate of William Gilmore Simms in the *Columbia Phoenix* one month after the fire. Simms stated that the flames had burned eight-four blocks "with scarcely the exception of a single house."[124] Other estimates ranged from "over five hundred"[125] to complete "obliteration."[126]

These charges of incendiarism, atrocities, and total destruction were, of course, the most crucial indictments against the Northern invaders, and an attempt was made in previous chapters to describe and evaluate them. But since Columbians never doubted that what they saw or believed or surmised was the complete story, one last look must be made at several complicating factors which seem to correct some of the most scathing accusations. Several seemingly obvious factors can be pointed out with regard to the statement that "every store in the city was sacked" by Union troops during the afternoon.[127] This account, which was widely articulated and believed, was obviously not observed by all who proclaimed it; it neglects completely the established fact that retreating Confeder-

---

[121] Reprinted in Gibbes, *Who Burnt Columbia?*, p. 9.

[122] R. W. Gibbes to Magrath, Feb. 28, 1865, Gibbes Papers. Two weeks later, in a letter to his son, Gibbes stated that 1,350 houses had burned. See R. W. Gibbes to W. A. Gibbes, March 14, 1865, Gibbes Papers.

[123] Mrs. S. McCam to daughter, March 5 [1865?], in "Burning of Columbia," miscellaneous manuscripts and printed materials, Yates Snowden Collection, South Caroliniana Library, University of South Carolina, Columbia.

[124] *Columbia Phoenix*, March 21, 1865.

[125] Columbia Board of Trade, *Columbia, S.C.*, p. 19. See also *An Historical and Descriptive Review of the State of South Carolina, and the Manufacturing and Mercantile Industries of the Cities of Columbia and Charleston, Including Many Sketches of Leading Public and Private Citizens*, II, 25.

[126] Conrad, *Destruction of Columbia*, p. 3.

[127] Gibbes, *Who Burnt Columbia?*, pp. 7–8; *Columbia Phoenix*, March 23, 1865.

ates and townspeople, both white and black, entered many stores and possibly homes on Richardson Street before the entrance of the Union forces. A safe assumption would be that the Federal troops seized what was left. How much of this activity by all participants was outright looting and how much was a search for food, clothing, or other needed supplies has been impossible to determine. One salient fact remains clear, however, and that is that only four citizens officially informed the Carroll committee that they saw Union soldiers break into stores and private dwellings.[128]

The widespread claim by Columbians that the Union troops interfered with the firemen as they fought the flames is another confusing issue. Fire Chief William B. Stanley presented a general, quite emotional, account of the actions of Union soldiers in Columbia, claiming that they cut hoses and destroyed fire engines as the firemen fought the flames. Unfortunately, Stanley did not describe any of the activities of his fire company during the conflagration. Indeed, the only fire chief who left a record of his fire fighting was John McKenzie, who was assiduously engaged in extinguishing fires during the afternoon and evening. McKenzie reported that he saw no hoses cut or fire engines destroyed. Further, when the Carroll committee began collecting testimony in 1867, only four Columbians reported seeing soldiers destroy the hoses and fire engines, while there are numerous accounts which tell of soldiers helping fight the fires.[129]

The most telling charge involved the actual sacking and burning of Columbia. The criticisms of Federal soldiers and their leaders were vociferous and universal, and though they were often vague, emotional, and general in nature, several facts emerged in the accounts of the event that were previously lost in the torrents of denunciation. One such fact was that many of the guards assigned to protect homes remained faithful throughout the night, and other citizens told of being aided in the streets by Union troops during the fire. Since not all Columbians left a record, and since some extant accounts did not mention guards or whether or not the writers were aided in the streets, it has been impossible to

---

[128] Trezevant, "Notes on the Burning of Columbia," Trezevant Papers.
[129] Ibid.

determine the exact number of Federal troops involved. William Gilmore Simms did estimate, however, that perhaps one-half of the assigned guards were faithful. The Carroll committee was told of only three instances in which guards betrayed their duty by firing the homes they were assigned to protect.[130]

Another phenomenon that can be gleaned from the letters, diaries, and reminiscences of those who experienced the burning of Columbia is that many of the writers, after describing wild tales of atrocities and burning, proceed to indicate a relative lack of violence on the part of the soldiers with whom they had had contacts. Some told of taunts and threats, but they inevitably described the soldiers who personally confronted them as being civil and well-spoken. All too often the stories of rudeness and personal searches were general accounts which did not identify the victims. When the events were over and citizens began collecting testimony against Sherman, only six cases of actual violence—all of which consisted of pushing, shoving, and striking—were reported by citizens.[131] There were no reports of murder of whites, nor were there any cases of rape reported in Columbia, though the Carroll committee report contained six affidavits which testified that soldiers "insulted and outraged women."[132] Rumors of the death of blacks existed, but only one case was ever made public.[133] The Carroll committee report contained one affidavit which claimed that black females were "taken as paramours."[134] The only verified deaths to occur during the night were those of the two Union soldiers who were shot by the troops sent in by General Hazen to suppress the riot.[135]

[130] Ibid.

[131] It should be remembered that two of these cases were "heard of" and a third was not reported in the account written by the man said to have been attacked.

[132] Trezevant, "Notes on the Burning of Columbia," Trezevant Papers.

[133] Simms stated that Goodwyn and Sherman, during their Thursday afternoon walk thrugh Columbia, happened upon a group of soldiers who had just killed a black man. According to Simms, Sherman dismissed the event with the statement: "We have no time now for courts-marshal and things of that sort!" (*Columbia Phoenix*, April 8, 1865). Mayor Goodwyn did not mention the event in his written accounts.

[134] Trezevant, "Notes on the Burning of Columbia," Trezevant Papers.

[135] *OR*, Ser. 1, XLVII, pt. 1: 310.

The deeds that transpired during the fire were, to say the least, terrifying for many. A riot existed, and houses were pillaged and burned by Union troops; these facts have been established. The question remaining, however, is of the extent of these acts. To accept the charge that thousands of soldiers scattered throughout the city igniting homes and businesses ignores a substantial amount of evidence that tends to minimize some of the more all-encompassing charges. One important consideration is the effect of the wind. All accounts are unanimous in proclaiming that once the fire began, it was impossible to control until the wind abated. The testimony is unanimous that the wind carried burning shingles, boards, and sparks in all directions and was responsible for spreading the flames. Further, some important observers who were in the streets that night, including John McKenzie, Francis W. Wing, and the Union generals, reported that they did not see soldiers set buildings on fire. James G. Gibbes, another important witness, saw only one house deliberately fired. The eyewitness accounts of soldiers spreading the flames are also notoriously small in number. The Carroll committee collected fourteen affidavits of citizens who observed soldiers firing buildings, and Dr. Trezevant listed only six.[136] Added evidence that all parts of Columbia were not ignited by Union soldiers is the fact that far more houses remained unburned after the fire than the reports of Columbians admitted. An analysis of Simms's account indicates that 458 buildings were burned. The residential area north of Sidney Park was almost untouched, and the section south of the park was relatively unscathed. The homes east of Richardson Street were hardest hit, but in the final analysis the number of homes and businesses burned total about one-third of the South Carolina capital, far below the claims of the inhabitants.

[136] Trezevant, "Notes on the Burning of Columbia," Trezevant Papers.

7

Conclusions

THE burning of Columbia was a great tragedy for South Carolina and the Union, full of untold misfortune, sorrow, and loss for
the city's inhabitants and the cause of great psychological damage
to the state's relationship with the nation. It was not a single act or
the events of a single day, but the culmination of eight days of
riots, robbery, pillage, confusion, and fires, all of which were the
by-products of war. The event was surrounded by coincidence,
misjudgment, and accident. It was the fault of no one person or
single group of persons, though there were those who were not
blameless in the series of events which transpired.

The failure of Confederate leadership in the defense of South
Carolina and the evacuation of Columbia played a major role in
creating a situation which resulted in the destruction of the city.
Beauregard's defeatism, Hampton's reticence, and the confusion in
Confederate command led to misfortune on the battlefield and pes-
simism on the home front. Local officials were misinformed of the
prospects of success, and no preparations were made by Beauregard, Hampton, or the city fathers for the official surrender of the
town. Resolute decisions at that point could have led to the formal
declaration of Columbia as an open city, with possibly different
results.

The handling of the cotton by the Confederate leaders both at
the central and local levels was another critical blunder. The Confederate government in Richmond continued to order that cotton

be burned to prevent its confiscation long after the policy had lost
its meaning. The order to burn the cotton in Columbia was, therefore, reckless from the beginning. Neither the laborers nor horses
and wagons existed to move the cotton out of the city, yet the order
was given. The eventual placing of the cotton in the city streets,
where it was ordered to be burned, was a poor substitute for removal. The danger to the city was only belatedly recognized by
Hampton, who at the last moment argued vigorously against firing
the cotton. The order to burn the cotton, however, was not counter-
manded by Hampton until the morning of the seventeenth, only
three and one-half hours before Union troops entered Columbia.
Since the evacuation had begun during the previous night, it would
have been impossible to have communicated the new orders to all
troops, possibly even to all officers. Furthermore, Confederate authorities failed to place guards over the cotton during the night, or
even after the decision was made not to burn on the morning of
the seventeenth, thus increasing the chances for error. The confusion in the Southern command about the surrender of the city
was illustrated by the attack on Colonel Stone's men after the
official surrender.

The failure of the Confederate generals and the local officials
to destroy the large supply of liquor in Columbia was another indication of the breakdown in leadership. In the crisis in which
Columbians found themselves in 1865, it was clear what had to
be done. Mayor Goodwyn recognized his duty but was overruled
by Beauregard and Hampton, who believed it imperative to respect
"private property." It was a grievous *faux pas*.

The trend in bad judgment was not diminished with the entrance of the Federal army. Giving whiskey and wine to the occupying army, in seemingly inexhaustible amounts, was certainly
a mistake. Soon many troops of the Third Brigade were drunk, and
as other soldiers passed through town they fell out of the line of
march and indulged excessively. Allowing this drunkenness was,
of course, a failure of the Union officers and men. The upshot,
however, was that in this abysmally confused situation it was the
Northern invaders who ordered the destruction of the liquor in
Columbia, and it is reasonable to assume that it was more difficult
for the Union army to carry out such an order than it would have

been for the Confederate officials to have done so before the evacuation.

While the record is clear that General Howard made a sincere effort to keep order in Columbia, it appears that the major failure of the Union general was his tardiness during the late afternoon and night in ordering fresh troops into the city to patrol the streets. Howard was in charge; he had the authority to act and a sufficient number of troops to enforce his decision. The late afternoon order for a new guard should have stressed speed, thus alleviating the extensive loss of time that occurred. When the relief brigade entered town, it was diverted from its assigned task of clearing the rioters from the streets to fighting the fire, a seemingly normal reaction. The error was that another brigade was not immediately brought into town to end the riot.

Once the fire began, almost all the Union generals, including Sherman, entered the city at one time or another during the night. Five hours of unfortunate delay passed before an order was given for more troops to sweep rioters from the streets. It is understandable that in moments of intense crisis leaders are often found wanting. Nevertheless, their very position of authority demands that they be responsible for the failures as well as the successes. The Union generals—especially Howard—should have acted earlier to end the riot. If properly done, it would have terminated further incendiarism by drunken Federal troops.

There was no one fire which burned Columbia, but a series of fires over the space of forty-eight hours, none of which can be identified positively as the act of a single individual or group of individuals. Not even Columbians claimed to know "the person" responsible for the conflagration. The best analysis, with Columbia a virtual firetrap on February 17, 1865, is that the fire was an accident of war. The most probable explanation was that it began from the burning cotton on Richardson Street. Another plausible solution is that it was started by Federal troops. Unfortunately, it is impossible to determine the fire's origin with certainty. Nevertheless, it is difficult for a fair-minded person who is aware of the events of the evacuation and capture to assign guilt to the leaders of either side except secondarily. It seems impossible to believe that Sherman ordered the town burned and that Howard did not do his best to prevent disorder. It is equally impossible to believe that Beauregard and Hampton, regardless of their intentions, acted wisely in handling the evacuation. Both sides lost control of the situation for a time.

Unfortunately, the ending of the riot by Federal officers would not have terminated the fire or the spread of the flames. As long as the strong wind blew out of the northwest, there was no stopping the fire. On this point the witnesses are unanimous. In the end, when the wind subsided, the fire was controlled. That coincidence convinced Columbians that if some earlier move had been made to control the riot, the fire would have ended.

These, then, were the errors, miscalculations, mistakes, and misapprehensions of the Southerners and Northerners in Columbia. But there were in the midst of all the horrors some redeeming factors which tend to place the entire episode in a new perspective. Many accounts of Columbians told of Union soldiers who acted in a civil manner, of humane treatment in the streets during the fire, of general nonviolent behavior, and of actual aid in saving goods from houses which were on fire. Others told of faithful guards, and the number appears to have been greater than previously has been admitted. It is also clear that a smaller number of bands of intoxicated soldiers roamed the streets than was later claimed. There were few accounts of actual attacks on citizens, no reported rapes, and no confirmed murders of any citizens. The only deaths authenticated were those of the two Union soldiers killed when the riot was suppressed. In short, Sherman did not conduct war against civilians in the sense of killing women, children, or non-combatants in general.

Another important point that can be made is that a smaller number of buildings was burned than Columbians have maintained. While the war was certainly real to Columbians, the claims of destruction were out of proportion to the actual loss of property, with no more than one-third of the town destroyed. Enough buildings remained unburned to house all the citizens who remained in Columbia, and the Union authorities made an effort to provide food for those left in the capital after the fire.

But when the Union army left Columbia on February 20, 1865, it left behind bitter hatred. Many citizens had lost everything they possessed, while others had gone through the catastrophe relatively unscathed. All, however, suffered psychologically. They had promised to give their "all" in the defense of South Carolina and the Confederacy; it was painfully apparent that few had done so. Long before Columbia was captured, Columbians had given up. They simply did not have the will to win, as E. Merton Coulter and Robert L. Kerby have pointed out in their studies of the Confederacy.[1] A proud people who had long talked of honor had been humiliated by the war. They would not forget; indeed, they could not forget.

[1] See E. Merton Coulter, *The Confederate States of America, 1861–1865*, pp. 533–568; Robert L. Kerby, *Kirby Smith's Confederacy: The Trans-Mississippi South, 1863–1865*, pp. 431–434.

Inventory of Ordnance Stores Captured in Columbia, S. C., February 17, 1865

Source: *War of the Rebellion: A Compilation of the Official Records of the Union and Confederate Armies*, Ser. 1, XLVII, pt. 1: 180–182.

Article		Total
Ball cartridges (no caps)		1,200,000
Percussion caps		100,000
Rifle powder (kegs)	pounds	13,600
Cannon powder (kegs and boxes)	pounds	8,750
Meal powder (kegs and boxes)	pounds	3,800
Case-shot, fixed, 12-pounder gun		183
Fuse-shell, fixed, 12-pounder gun		216
Grape, 12-pounder gun		460
Canister, fixed, 12-pounder gun		148
Shot, fixed, 6-pounder gun		1,680
Case, fixed, 6-pounder gun		550
Fuse-shell, fixed, 6-pounder gun		372
Canister, fixed, 6-pounder gun		1,250
Shot, fixed, 24-pounder gun		112
Shell, fixed, 24-pounder gun		120
Canister, fixed, 24-pounder gun		314
Shell, fixed, 8-inch		64
Shot and shell, not fixed, 8-inch		2,280
Shot and shell, not fixed, 10-inch		1,320
Yager muskets		960
Palmetto rifles		500
Remington rifles		100
Mississippi rifles		200

U.S. muskets, caliber .69	3,440
Enfield rifled muskets	1,900
Enfield rifles (short, sword bayonet)	2,000
Austrian rifled muskets (old)	560
Whitney rifles (old)	50
Springfield rifled muskets	100
Morse rifles (South Carolina)	400
Musket barrels and stocks, unfinished	6,000
Pikes	4,000
6-pounder guns (bronze)	10
6-pounder guns (iron)	4
Blakely guns (rifled, iron)	4
James guns (rifled, bronze)	2
12-pounder mountain howitzers	5
3-inch gun (rifled, iron)	1
10-pounder gun (iron)	2
10-pounder gun (rifled, iron)	1
18-pounder gun (rifled, iron)	2
18-pounder gun (re-enforced, iron)	1
4-inch rifled gun (iron)	1
4-inch mortars	2
1 (.10)-inch Coehorn (bronze)	1
Bronze guns (caliber 1½ inch)	2
2-pounder gun (bronze)	1
Repeating battery (caliber 1 inch)	1
Breech-loading gun (caliber 1½ inch)	1
10-pounder Parrotts found and destroyed by General Hazen	2
Gun carriages	9
Gun caissons	14
Mountain howitzer caissons	3
Forges	2
Sponges and rammers	1,125
Blacksmith vises	20
Anvils	11
Artillery harness, sets	38
Naval cutlasses	175
Artillery sabers	220
Cavalry sabers (all kinds)	2,700
Saber knots	700
Cavalry-pistol holsters, pairs	300
Saber belts	800
Bayonet scabbards	4,000

Cartridge-boxes, caliber .54	2,450
Cartridge-boxes, caliber .69	1,400
Cartridge-boxes, caliber .68	300
Cartridge-box plates	3,500
Cartridge-box belts and plates	2,500
Waist-belts	2,900
Waist-belt plates	3,000
Bail screws	2,000
Pistol-cartridge boxes	550
Shot-pouches (gunners)	600
Knapsacks	1,100
Haversacks	900
Slow match, yards	500
Ten-inch fuses	900
Wall tents	8
Wedge tents	50
Cartridge paper, tons	20

APPENDIX B

Soldiers Directory of Public
Officers in Columbia

Source: *Columbia Daily South Carolinian*, Oct. 9, 1864.

Lieutenant J. M. Benson, Enrolling Officer for Richland District. Office in rear of Court House.

Lieutenant Colonel Richard Caldwell, Commissary General of South Carolina. Office on upper part of Main Street.

Brigadier General James Chesnut, Commanding State Reserves. Office in State House.

Surgeon J. J. Chisolm, Medical Purveyor. Office opposite Congaree Hotel (Richardson Street).

Captain Coles, Assistant Quartermaster, Inspector of Field Transportation.

College Hospital No. 1, Surgeon W. H. Horlbeck. South Carolina College.

College Hospital No. 2, Surgeon J. P. Prioleau. South Carolina College.

Captain J. T. Colt, Post Quartermaster, Tax in Kind, 6th Congressional District. Office near *Carolinian* office.

General A. C. Garlington, Adjutant and Inspector General of South Carolina. Office in State House.

Colonel Allen J. Green, Post Commander. Office Richardson Street (northwest corner of Richardson and Plain street, upstairs).

Major Grice, Quartermaster.

Captain Daniel H. Hamilton, Provost Marshal. Office Main Street.

Captain T. S. Jeffries, Assistant Chief of Staff and Commissary for Hospitals, Traveling Troops, etc. Office over Fisher & Agnew's store (southeast corner of Richardson and Plain streets).

General James Jones, Quartermaster General of South Carolina.

Ladies' Hospital, Surgeon Edmonds. Near Charlotte depot.

Professor Joseph LeConte, Chief Niter Bureau. Residence College Campus.

Major C. D. Melton, Commanding Conscripts, State of South Carolina. Office on Richardson Street (near market).

Major John Niernsee, Engineer.

Major T. W. Radcliffe, Quartermaster of Conscripts.

Captain A. M. Rhett, Assistant Quartermaster. Office on Main Street (over Milling's store).

Major Roland Rhett, Post Quartermaster. Office Richardson Street (near market).

Second North Carolina Hospital, Surgeon Thomson. South Carolina College Chapel.

Captain T. R. Sharp, Assistant Quartermaster and Transportation Officer. Office Richardson Street (northwest corner of Richardson and Plain streets).

Major J. B. E. Sloan, Confederate Quartermaster Tax in Kind for State of South Carolina. Office Richardson Street (over Fisher & Agnew's store, southeast corner of Richardson and Plain streets).

Captain J. J. P. Smith, Assistant Quartermaster, Paymaster. Office over Miot's Drug store (196 Richardson Street).

Major Trezevant, Ordnance Officer. Office near Greenville Railroad.

Wayside Hospital. Near South Carolina Railroad depot.

Captain I. D. Witherspoon, Assistant Chief of Staff and Post Commissary. Office over Fisher & Agnew's store (southeast corner of Richardson and Plain streets).

Bibliography

Primary Sources

MANUSCRIPT MATERIALS

Chapel Hill. University of North Carolina. Southern Historical Collection. Edward W. Allen Papers.
———. John Judge Papers.
———. William Porcher Miles Papers.
Charleston. South Carolina Historical Society. St. Julien Ravenel Papers. Mrs. St. Julien Ravenel, "Burning of Columbia," undated manuscript.
Columbia. South Carolina Archives. James L. Orr Papers.
Columbia. University of South Carolina. South Caroliniana Library. Allen Macfarlan Papers.
———. Andrew Gordon Magrath Papers.
———. Anonymous Collection.
———. Daniel Heyward Trezevant Papers. "Notes on the Burning of Columbia," miscellaneous manuscripts and copies of letters.
———. George Huggins Papers. "Burning of Columbia," manuscript.
———. Harriet H. Simons Papers. "Burning of Columbia," manuscript.
———. Harriott Horry Ravenel Papers. "Burning of Columbia," March 12, 1898, manuscript article from letter of March, 1865.
———. Joseph LeConte Collection. "A Journal of Three Months Personal Experience During the Last Days of the Confederacy," manuscript.
———. Mary Leverett Letter, March 18, 1865.
———. Peter J. Shand Papers.
———. Robert Wilson Gibbes Papers.
———. Robert Woodward Barnwell Papers.
———. Sosnowski-Schaller Papers. "Burning of Columbia," manuscript.

———. Thomas Jefferson Goodwyn Letter, June 8, 1866.

———. W. K. Bachman Papers.

———. William James Rivers Papers.

———. Williams-Chesnut-Manning Papers.

———. Yates Snowden Collection. "Burning of Columbia," miscellaneous manuscripts and printed materials.

Des Moines. Iowa Archives. H. C. McArthur Collection.

Durham, N.C. Duke University Library. Manuscript Division. Rachel Susan Cheves Papers.

Washington, D.C. Library of Congress. Manuscript Division. W. T. Sherman Papers.

PUBLIC DOCUMENTS

Atlas to Accompany the Official Records of the Union and Confederate Armies. 2 vols. Washington, 1891–1895.

Great Britain. *Parliamentary Papers.* "Foreign Office Report by Her Majesty's Agent of the Proceedings and Awards of the Mixed Commission on British and American Claims Established Under the XII Article of the Treaty between Great Britain and the United States of America Concluded at Washington, May 8, 1871," 1874 (no. 2), 75: 54.

Mixed Commission on British and American Claims. Appendix: Testimony. 55 vols. Washington, 1873.

South Carolina. *The Governor of the State, to the People of South Carolina.* Undated printed proclamation in miscellaneous manuscript and printed materials folder entitled "Legislative System, Messages, 1860–1865." South Carolina Archives, Columbia.

———. *Report of the Special Joint Committee, in Regard to Certain Public Property on Hand at the Evacuation of Columbia, and the Surrender of Gen. Johnston's Army.* Columbia, 1866.

U.S., Congress, House. *Report of Robert S. Hale, Esq., Agent and Counsel of the United States before the Commission on Claims of Citizens of the United States Against Great Britain, and of Subjects of Her Britannic Majesty Against the United States, Under the Twelfth Article of the Treaty of 8th May, 1871, Between the United States and Great Britain.* 43d Cong., 1st sess., 1873–1874, House Exec. Doc. No. 1 (Serial 1596).

U.S., Congress, Senate. *Congressional Globe.* 39th Cong., 1st sess., May 1, 1866, 36, pt. 3: 2301.

———. *Destruction of Property in Columbia, S.C., by Sherman's Army. Speech of Hon. Cole. L. Blease, a Senator from the State of South Carolina, Delivered in the Senate May 15, 1930.* 71st Cong., 2d sess., 1930, Senate Doc. No. 149 (Serial 9220).

———. *Supplemental Report of the Joint Committee on the Conduct of the War.* 39th Cong., 1st sess., 1866, Senate Reports (Serial 1241).

U.S., Department of Commerce, Bureau of the Census. *Ninth Census of the United States: 1870. Population.* 3 vols. Washington, 1872.

War of the Rebellion: A Compilation of the Official Records of the Union and Confederate Armies. 128 vols. Washington, 1880–1901.

NEWSPAPERS

Charleston Daily Courier. Jan., 1865.
Columbia Daily South Carolinian. 1864–1865.
Columbia Daily Southern Guardian. Dec., 1864.
Columbia Phoenix. Mar. 21–May 13, 1865.
Columbia Tri-Weekly South Carolinian. 1864–1865.
New York Herald. Feb.–Mar., 1865.
New York Times. Feb.–Mar., 1865.
Richmond Dispatch. Feb. 23, 1865.
Richmond Whig. Mar., 1865.
The State (Columbia). Mar., 1893; Feb., 1932.
Yorkville Enquirer. Mar., 1865.

BOOKS

Angle, Paul M., ed. *Three Years in the Army of the Cumberland: The Letters and Diary of Major James A. Connolly.* Bloomington, Ind., 1959.

Aten, Henry J. *History of the Eighty-Fifth Regiment, Illinois Volunteer Infantry.* Hiawatha, Ill., 1901.

Bradley, George S. *The Star Corps; or, Notes of an Army Chaplain During Sherman's Famous March to the Sea.* Milwaukee, 1865.

Bryce, Campbell. *The Personal Experiences of Mrs. Campbell Bryce During the Burning of Columbia, South Carolina, by General W. T. Sherman's Army, February 17, 1865.* Philadelphia, 1899.

The Burning of Columbia. I. A Letter of Gen. Wade Hampton, June 24, 1873, With Appendix. II. Report of Committee of Citizens, Ex-Chancellor J. P. Carroll, Chairman, May 1866. Charleston, 1888.

Burton, Elijah P. *Diary of E. P. Burton, Surgeon, Seventh Regiment Illinois, Third Brigade, Second Division, Sixteenth Army Corps.* 2 vols. Des Moines, Iowa, 1939.

Carroll, James Parsons. *Report of the Committee Appointed to Collect Testimony in Relation to the Destruction of Columbia, S.C., on the 17th of February, 1865.* Columbia, 1893.

Catalogue of Paintings, Marbles and Casts in the Collection of R. W. Gibbes, M.D. Columbia [n.d.].

Columbia, S.C., Board of Trade. *Columbia, S.C., The Future Manufac-*

*turing and Commercial Centre of the South, with Some Account
of Its Foundation, Destruction and Subsequent Rehabilitation and
Growth.* Columbia, 1871.

*The Columbia Directory, Containing the Names, Business and Resi-
dence of the Inhabitants.* Columbia, 1860.

Conner, James; Thomas Taylor; A. T. Smythe; August Kohn; M. B.
Poppenheim; and Martha B. Washington, eds. *South Carolina
Women in the Confederacy.* Vol. II. (Collected by A. T. Smythe,
M. B. Poppenheim, and Thomas Taylor.) Columbia, 1907.

Conrad, August. *The Destruction of Columbia, S.C.: A Translation
from the German by William H. Pleasants, of 19th, 20th, 21st,
and 22d Chapters of "Lights and Shadows in American Life During the War of Secession," by August Conrad.* Roanoke, Va., 1902.

Conyngham, David P. *Sherman's March Through the South, with
Sketches and Incidents of the Campaign.* New York, 1865.

Dodge, Grenville M. *Personal Recollections of President Abraham Lincoln, General Ulysses S. Grant and General William T. Sherman.*
Council Bluffs, Iowa, 1914.

Fletcher, William Andrew. *Rebel Private, Front and Rear.* Austin,
Texas, 1954.

Gibbes, James Guignard. *Who Burnt Columbia?* Newberry, S.C., 1902.

Hazen, W. B. *A Narrative of Military Service.* Boston, 1885.

Hinkley, Julian Wisner. *A Narrative of Service with the Third Wisconsin Infantry.* Madison, 1912.

*An Historical and Descriptive Review of the State of South Carolina,
and the Manufacturing and Mercantile Industries of the Cities of
Columbia and Charleston, Including Many Sketches of Leading
Public and Private Citizens.* 2 vols. Columbia, 1884.

Howard, Oliver Otis. *Autobiography of Oliver Otis Howard, Major
General, United States Army.* 2 vols. New York, 1907.

Howe, M. A. DeWolfe, ed. *Home Letters of General Sherman.* New
York, 1909.

Jackson, Oscar Lawrence. *The Colonel's Diary: Journals Kept Before
and During the Civil War by the Late Colonel Oscar L. Jackson,
sometime Commander of the Sixty-Third Regiment Ohio Volunteer Infantry.* Sherron, Ohio, 1922.

Johnson, Robert Underwood, and Clarence Clough Buel, eds. *Battles
and Leaders of the Civil War.* 4 vols. 1887. Reprint. New York,
1956.

LeConte, Joseph. *The Autobiography of Joseph LeConte.* Ed. William
Dallam Armes. New York, 1903.

——. *'Ware Sherman: A Journal of Three Months' Personal Experience in the Last Days of the Confederacy.* Berkeley, 1937.

Martin, Isabella D., and Myrta Lockett Avery, eds. *A Diary from
Dixie as Written by Mary Boykin Chesnut.* New York, 1929.

McArthur, Henry Clay. *Capture and Destruction of Columbia, South Carolina, February 17, 1865*. Washington, 1911.

Miers, Earl Schenck, ed. *When the World Ended: The Diary of Emma LeConte*. New York, 1957.

Nichols, George Ward. *The Story of the Great March: From the Diary of a Staff Officer*. New York, 1865.

Nicholson, William Alexander. *The Burning of Columbia*. Columbia, 1895.

O'Connell, J. J. *Catholicity in the Carolinas and Georgia: Leaves of Its History*. 1879. Reprint. Westminster, Md., 1964.

Oliphant, Mary C.; Alfred Taylor Odell; and T. C. Duncan Eaves, eds. *The Letters of William Gilmore Simms*. 5 vols. Columbia, 1955.

Porter, Anthony Toomer. *The History of a Work of Faith and Love in Charleston, South Carolina, Which Grew Out of the Calamities of the Late Civil War, and a Record of God's Wonderful Providence*. New York, 1882.

———. *Led On! Step by Step: Scenes from Clerical, Military, Educational, and Plantation Life in the South, 1828–1898*. New York, 1898.

Sabre, Gilbert E. *Nineteen Months a Prisoner of War*. New York, 1865.

Salley, A. S., ed. *Sack and Destruction of the City of Columbia, S.C., by William Gilmore Simms*, 2d ed. Atlanta, 1937.

Scott, Edwin J. *Random Recollections of a Long Life, 1806 to 1876*. Columbia, 1884.

Sherlock, E. J. *Memorabilia of the Marches and Battles in which the One Hundredth Regiment of Indiana Infantry Volunteers Took an Active Part: War of the Rebellion, 1861–5*. Kansas City, 1896.

Sherman, William Tecumseh. *Memoirs of General William T. Sherman*. 2 vols. New York, 1875.

Smith, Daniel E. Huger; Alice R. Huger Smith; and Arney R. Childs, eds. *Mason Smith Family Letters 1860–1865*. Columbia, 1950.

Smythe, A. T.; M. B. Poppenheim; and Thomas Taylor, eds. *South Carolina Women in the Confederacy*. Vol. I. Columbia, 1903.

Story of the Fifty-Fifth Regiment Illinois Volunteer Infantry in the Civil War, 1861–1865. Clinton, Ill., 1887.

Thomas, John Peyre. *The History of the South Carolina Military Academy, with Appendixes*. Charleston, 1893.

Thorndike, Rachel Sherman, ed. *The Sherman Letters: Correspondence between General and Senator Sherman from 1837 to 1891*. New York, 1894.

Trezevant, Daniel Heyward. *The Burning of Columbia, S.C.: A Review of Northern Assertions and Southern Facts*. Columbia, 1866.

Trowbridge, John T. *The Desolate South, 1865–1866: A Picture of the*

Battlefields and the Devastated Confederacy. 1866. Reprint. New York, 1956.

Whilden, Mary S. *Recollections of the War, 1861–1865*. 1887. Reprint. Columbia, 1911.

Williams, Ben Ames, ed. *A Diary from Dixie by Mary Boykin Chesnut*. Boston, 1949.

Williams, J. F. *Old and New Columbia*. Columbia, 1929.

ARTICLES

"The Burning of Columbia—Affidavit of Agnes Law." *Southern Historical Society Papers* 12 (May, 1884): 233.

Byers, Samuel Hawkins Marshall. "The Burning of Columbia." *Lippincott's Magazine* 29 (March, 1882): 255–261.

Carroll, J. P. "Burning of Columbia." *Southern Historical Society Papers* 8 (May, 1880): 202–214.

Chisolm, A. R. "Beauregard's and Hampton's Orders on Evacuating Columbia—Letter from Colonel A. R. Chisolm." *Southern Historical Society Papers* 7 (May, 1879): 249–250.

Davidson, James Wood. "Who Burned Columbia? A Review of General Sherman's Version of the Affair." *Southern Historical Society Papers* 7 (April, 1879): 185–192.

Disbrow, Donald W., ed. "Vett Noble of Ypsilanti: A Clerk for General Sherman." *Civil War History* 14 (March, 1968): 15–39.

Eaton, Clement, ed. "Diary of an Officer in Sherman's Army Marching Through the Carolinas." *Journal of Southern History* 9 (May, 1943): 238–254.

McCarter, James. "The Burning of Columbia Again." *Harper's Magazine* 33 (Oct., 1866): 642–647.

Nichols, George Ward. "The Burning of Columbia." *Harper's Magazine* 33 (Aug., 1866): 363–366.

Sill, Edward. "Who is Responsible for the Destruction of the City of Columbia, S.C., on the Night of 17 February, 1865." *Land We Love* 4 (March, 1868): 361–369.

Wood, A. E. "Burning of Columbia, S.C." *North American Review* 146 (April, 1888): 400–404.

Secondary Sources

Barrett, John G. *Sherman's March through the Carolinas*. Chapel Hill, 1956.

Boatner, Mark Mayo, III. *The Civil War Dictionary*. New York, 1959.

Cauthen, Charles Edward. *South Carolina Goes to War 1861–1865*. Chapel Hill, 1950.

Childs, Arney R. "Dr. Robert Wilson Gibbes (1809–1866)." Master's thesis, University of South Carolina, 1925.

Coddington, Edwin B. *The Gettysburg Campaign: A Study in Command.* New York, 1968.

Connelly, Thomas Lawrence. *Autumn of Glory: The Army of Tennessee, 1862–1865.* Baton Rouge, 1971.

Coulter, E. Merton. *The Confederate States of America, 1861–1865.* Baton Rouge, 1950.

———. "Sherman and the South." *North Carolina Historical Review* 8 (Jan., 1931): 41–54.

Cunningham, H. H. *Doctors in Gray: The Confederate Medical Service.* Baton Rouge, 1958.

Dowdey, Clifford. *The Land They Fought For: The Story of the South as the Confederacy, 1832–1865.* Garden City, N.J., 1955.

Dyer, John P. *"Fightin' Joe" Wheeler.* Baton Rouge, 1941.

Eaton, Clement. *A History of the Southern Confederacy.* New York, 1954.

Evans, Clement A., ed. *Confederate Military History.* 12 vols. 1899. Reprint. New York, 1962.

Falk, Richard A., ed. *The International Law of Civil War.* Baltimore, 1971.

Fenwick, Charles G. *International Law.* New York, 1924.

Freehling, William W. *Prelude to Civil War: The Nullification Controversy in South Carolina, 1816–1836.* New York, 1965.

Freidel, Frank. *Francis Lieber, Nineteenth-Century Liberal.* Baton Rouge, 1947.

Green, Constance McLaughlin. *Washington: Village and Capital, 1800–1878.* Princeton, N.J., 1962.

Green, Edwin L. *A History of the University of South Carolina.* Columbia, 1916.

Hennig, Helen Kohn, ed. *Columbia, Capital City of South Carolina, 1786–1936.* Columbia, 1936.

Hollis, Daniel Walker. *University of South Carolina: South Carolina College.* Columbia, 1951.

Hughes, Nathaniel Cheairs, Jr. *General William J. Hardee: Old Reliable.* Baton Rouge, 1965.

Hyde, Charles Cheney. *International Law Chiefly as Interpreted and Applied by the United States.* 2 vols. Boston, 1922.

Kerby, Robert L. *Kirby Smith's Confederacy: The Trans-Mississippi South, 1863–1865.* New York, 1972.

Kibler, Lillian Adele. *Benjamin F. Perry, South Carolina Unionist.* Durham, N.C., 1946.

Lewis, Lloyd. *Sherman, Fighting Prophet.* New York, 1932.

Liddell Hart, B. H. *Sherman: Soldier, Realist, American.* New York, 1929.

———. *Strategy, the Indirect Approach.* New York, 1954.

Merrill, James M. *William Tecumseh Sherman.* Chicago, 1971.

Miers, Earl Schenck. *The General Who Marched to Hell: William Tecumseh Sherman and His March to Fame and Infamy*. New York, 1951.

Milling, Chapman J. "Ilium in Flames." *Confederate Veteran* 36 (May, 1928): 179–183.

Operations on the Atlantic Coast 1861–1865; Virginia 1862, 1864; Vicksburg. 9 vols. Boston, 1912.

Randall, J. G., and David Donald. *The Civil War and Reconstruction.* 2d ed., rev. Boston, 1961.

Rhodes, James Ford. *History of the United States from the Compromise of 1850 to the Final Restoration of Home Rule at the South in 1877.* 9 vols. New York, 1893–1919.

Simons, Jane Kealhofer, and Margaret Babcock Meriwether. *A Guide to Columbia, South Carolina's Capital City.* Columbia, 1939.

Snowden, Yates. *Marching with Sherman: A Review by Yates Snowden of the Letters and Campaign Diaries of Henry Hitchcock.* Columbia, 1929.

Swindell, Anna Tillman. *The Burning of Columbia: Prize Essay of Wade Hampton Chapter, U.D.C.* [N.p.], 1924.

Taylor, Rosser H. *Ante-Bellum South Carolina: A Social and Cultural History.* Chapel Hill, 1942.

Vandiver, Frank E. *Jubal's Raid: General Early's Famous Attack on Washington in 1864.* New York, 1960.

———. *Ploughshares into Swords: Josiah Gorgas and Confederate Ordnance.* Austin, Texas, 1952.

———. *Their Tattered Flags: The Epic of the Confederacy.* New York, 1970.

Williams, T. Harry. *McClellan, Sherman and Grant.* New Brunswick, N.J., 1962.

———. *P. G. T. Beauregard, Napoleon in Gray.* Baton Rouge, 1954.

Winks, Robin W. *Canada and the United States: The Civil War Years.* Baltimore, 1960.

Index

Adams, J. U., 92
alcohol, 67–68, 88–89
Alexander, John, 131n
Alexander's foundry, 123
Allen, Edward W., 107
Alston, S.C., 84
Anderson, Albert R., Maj., 75
Army of Georgia, 31
Army of Northern Virginia, 30, 137–138
Army of the Tennessee, 31
Arsenal Academy, 24, 46, 126n
Arsenal Hill, 27
Arthur, E. J., 130
Athenaeum Hall, 96
Atlanta, Ga., 30
Audenried, Joseph C., Capt., 120
Augusta, Ga., 31, 41–45, 138

Bachman, Kate, 115
Bachman, W. K., Mrs., 115–117, 142
Baptist Church, 23
Barhamville Female School, 113–114
Barnwell, Robert W., Rev., 25, 37
Barry, William F., Bvt. Maj. Gen., 97–98
Bateman, Charles D., 105–106, 110
Bates, Orlando Z., 92, 109, 150
Baylor, T. G., Col., 124
bayonet factory, 28
Beauregard, P. G. T., Gen.: and handling of alcohol, 68, 164–165; and

handling of cotton, 64, 66–67, 163–164; defeatism of, 45n, 45–47, 163; defense of South Carolina by, 41n, 41–44, 46; and evacuation of Columbia, 56–57, 61, 64, 69–70
Belknap, W. W., Brig. Gen., 77
Berry, Milo H., 109
Blair, Francis P., Jr., Maj. Gen., 31, 82, 121, 125
Blease, Coleman L., Sen., 134
bombardment. *See* Columbia, bombardment of
Bonham, M. L., Gov., 56, 56n
Branchville, S.C., 36, 40, 42
Broad River, 19, 74, 78, 82
Broad River bridge, 73
Brown, Joseph E., Gov., 37
Browne, William M., Brig. Gen., 42
Bryce, Campbell, Mrs., 113
Burton, Elijah P., Dr., 106, 119
Butler, M. C., Maj. Gen., 38, 41n, 70–71
button factory, 28
Byers, S. H. M., Capt., 86, 99, 104

Caldwell, Richard, Lt. Col., 61, 62, 62n, 63
Calhoun, John C., 23
Campbell, James A., 45n
Camp Sorghum, 56. *See also* Columbia: Union prisoners evacuated from; military prison

Carolina Blues, 24

Carroll, A. F., 114

Carroll committee, 130–131, 131n; affidavits of, 131n, 136n, 136–137, 148–149, 150n, 160–161

Carroll, J. P., 130

Catholic Church, 120

Cedar Creek, 124

Central Association for the Relief of Soldiers of South Carolina, 25

Chambliss, N. R., Maj., 59, 60n, 60–61, 61n

Charleston, S.C., 31, 36, 37, 42–47, 136

Charlotte and South Carolina Railroad, 22, 63, 81; destroyed, 70, 71, 126n; in evacuation, 52, 58

Charlotte, N.C., 46, 62, 63

Chattanooga, Tenn., 30

Cheatham, B. F., Maj. Gen., 42

Chesnut, Mary Boykin, 33

Chester, S.C., 43, 43n

Cheves, Rachel Susan, 34, 136n

Childs, L. D., Col., 130

Chisolm, J. Julian, Dr., 26–27

Chrietzberg, J. R., Capt., 62

Civil, John A., 109

Cochran, R., 109

Cohen, Melvin M., 112

Columbia Artillery, 24

Columbia, Battle of, 47, 49

Columbia Canal, 27

Columbia Directory, 125, 127

Columbia Phoenix, 125, 130

Columbia, S.C.: alcohol in, 67–68, 75, 76; antebellum fires in, 21, 22, 22n; apprehension in, 33–36, 40–41, 78; bombardment of, 49, 58–59, 59n, 141–144; burned-out citizens of, 120–122; Confederate assurances to citizens of, 39, 40; confusion in evacuation of, 40, 41n, 51–64, 66, 70; cotton burning in, 68–69, 76, 79–80; cotton in streets of, 65–66, 78–79; cotton stored in, 21, 64–67, 163–164; cotton unburned in, 124; defense of, 22n, 35, 36, 39–49; description of, 19–23, 34–35, 72n; destruction in, 119–120, 126n, 126–

128, 158–159; final assault on, 72–74; first Union troops in, 75, 76, 77–80; panic of citizens in, 51–53, 60; pillage during evacuation of, 53–54, 55, 68–69; refugees in, 34–35; residential areas in, 127–128; responsibility for events in, 134, 160–162, 165; sacking and burning of, 102–117, 154–161; strategic value of, 24, 29–30, 137–141; surrender of, 69–70, 78, 143; Union camps in, 81–82; Union discipline in, 88–90, 93; Union prisoners evacuated from, 55–57, 57n; Union provost guard in, 76–77, 83–86, 94–95, 117

Confederate armory, 27, 123

Confederate offices, 29, 173–174

Congaree Cavalry, 24

Congaree River, 19, 47, 72, 77

Congaree River bridge, 49, 72

Conyngham, David P., 94n

Cooper, Samuel, Gen., 65n

Corse, John M., Bvt. Maj. Gen., 81, 124

Corti, Louis, Count, 132

cotton card factory, 29

cotton mill, 28

Cotton Town, 21, 65, 75, 78, 126–127, 150

Coulter, E. Merton, 140–141, 167

Daily South Carolinian, 36

Davis, Jefferson, Pres., 35n, 139

Davis, Jefferson C., Maj. Gen., 31

Davis, Mr., 53n

Davis, Pvt., 116

DeGress, Francis, Capt., 49

DeSaussure, Henry W., 19

DeSaussure, William F., 130

Devine, Lt., 104

DuBose, F. F. C. H., 62

Duncan, Blanton, 81, 104

Early, Jubal, Maj. Gen., 140n

Eason, W. G., 63

Eaton, Clement, 135

Elmore, F. H., 114

Emmett Guard, 24

Evans, B. F., Capt., 63

Evans and Cogswell Company, 122–123, 126n
Ewing, Charles, Col., 78, 120

fairgrounds, 24, 26, 123
fire departments, 21
fires, 21–22, 22n; during afternoon of Feb. 17, 92–93; as Union troops entered Columbia, 91; as night of Feb. 17 approached, 93; before Union troops entered Columbia, 90–91; during night of Feb. 17, 93; responsibility for, 102–103, 153–154, 165; stragglers attracted to, 95, 102; Union generals at scene of, 95–98
First Illinois Light Artillery, 143
First Missouri Light Artillery, 143
Fisher, John, Dr., 130
Force, Manning F., Brig. Gen., 82
Fort Moultrie, 86–87
Fort Sumter, 23
Frazer, James S., 132

gasworks, 123
Gibbes, James G.: on bombardment, 142; on burning cotton, 92; on conduct of soldiers, 90, 155; on devastation, 158–159; on effect of the wind, 101; on incendiarism, 108, 109–110, 162; on rockets, 150
Gibbes, Robert W., Dr., 103–104, 108, 157–158, 158n, 159
Gilbreth, Frederick W., Capt., 95
Gist, Malvina S., 111
Goodrell, William H., Lt., 77
Goodwyn, Thomas Jefferson, Mayor: and alcohol, 68; anxiety of, 80, 87; on conduct of soldiers, 114, 151, 161n; and defense of Columbia, 36; and handling of cotton, 69n; on rockets, 149–150; and surrender, 69–70, 75, 143, 147
Gorgas, Josiah, Gen., 58, 59, 61
Governor's Guards, 24
Granby, S.C., 70
Grant, U. S., Lt. Gen., 37–38
Great Bazaar, 26
Green, Allen J., Maj., 53, 65, 67

Greenville and Columbia Railroad, 22, 52
guards: faithful, 111–114; unfaithful, 114–115
gunpowder mill, 27, 27n, 126n
Gurney, Russell, 132

Hale, Robert S., 133
Halleck, Henry W., Maj. Gen., 135n, 135–136, 139
Hampton Roads Peace Conference, 45n
Hampton, Wade, Maj. Gen., 35, 46, 92; charge against Sherman by, 129; and command situation, 38, 38n, 41n, 45n, 66; in evacuation, 54, 54n, 58, 70, 70n; and handling of alcohol, 68, 164–165; and handling of cotton, 64, 66, 67, 163–164; and responsibility for failures during evacuation, 64, 163
Hampton, Wade, Mrs., 52n
Hanckel, Annie, 110
Hardee, William J., Lt. Gen., 42, 43, 43n
Hazen, William B., Maj. Gen., 47n, 73, 81, 117, 124; on conduct of troops, 88–89, 90; on effect of the wind, 99, 101
Heyward, Mary, 110
Hill, D. H., Maj. Gen., 41
Hood, John Bell, Gen., 30
Hospital Aid Association, 25
Howard, O. O., Maj. Gen., 31, 136n, 152; and aid to citizens after fire, 120, 121–122; and failure to act decisively, 93, 94–95, 117–118, 165; headquarters of, 86, 95; and security in Columbia, 78, 81, 84, 85, 85n, 121; on troop misconduct, 81, 85, 106, 151, 151n
Howgate, Henry W., 152
Huger, Alfred, 112
Hunter, R. M. T., 45n

incendiarism, 108–110
Independent Fire Company, 92, 96
"Indian" (Union soldier), 116
Invalid Corps, 56

Jacobs, David, 67
Janney, James C., 114
Janney, Mary, 111
Jenkins, Jeremiah W., Lt. Col., 77, 83
John Judge and Company, 28
Johnson, William, Col., 52
Johnston, Joseph E., Gen., 63
Joyner, L. Catherine, 136

Kerby, Robert L., 167
Kilpatrick, Hugh J., Brig. Gen., 31, 137
Kinard, J. H., 92
Kraft, Goldsmith, Kraft and Company, 28

LaBorde, Maximilian, Dr., 25, 100–101
Ladies' Hospital, 24
Law, Agnes, 108–109, 114
LeConte, Emma, 33–34, 100, 114; on pillage, 53, 69, 90; on XV Corps, 145, 148
LeConte, John, 53
LeConte, Johnny, 53
LeConte, Joseph, 19, 111, 130; Confederate service of, 26, 27, 40, 51; doubts of, about holding Columbia, 40, 41, 52; and flight from Columbia, 53, 53n
Lee, Robert E., Gen., 33, 37, 46; on South Carolina troop strength, 35n, 38
Lee, Stephen D., Lt. Gen., 42
Leverett, Mary, 110, 157
Lexington, S.C., 136–137
Lieber and Agnew's store, 96
Lieber, Francis, 19, 139n
Liddell Hart, B. H., 44–45, 138
Lincoln, Abraham, Pres., 23, 30, 45n
Logan, John A., Maj. Gen., 31, 78, 107, 125, 144; actions of, during fire, 90, 95, 97, 99; and first order for fresh troops, 93, 94n; headquarters of, 82, 94; and second order for fresh troops, 117
Lynch, John, Dr., 114

McArthur, Henry C., Lt., 77, 77n

McCam, S., Mrs., 159
McCarter, James, 98
McCord, L. S., Mrs., 149
McCullough, Robert, 104
McDougal, Robert, 114
McKenzie, John, 70, 131n; and activities during fires, 91, 92, 93, 96, 160; on effect of the wind, 99, 101; as witness of fire, 109, 162
McPhail, C. C., Capt., 57, 58
McQueen, John A., Lt., 104–105, 105n
Magrath, Andrew Gordon, Gov., 36, 37, 37n, 39, 63–64, 138
Marks, Elias, Dr., 113
Means, R. Stark, Col., 56
medical purveyor's office, 67, 111
Meetze, Rosa J., 136–137
Meister, W. D., 110–111
Memminger, Christopher G., 29
Methodist Female College, 66, 66n, 115, 120, 142
Miles, William Porcher, 38n, 138
militia organizations, 24
military prison, 55–56
military storehouse, 27
Mills, Robert, 107–108, 108n
Mixed Commission on British and American Claims, 151; claims and arguments before, 132–133, 145; Sherman's testimony before, 144, 148, 152, 153–154
Mower, Joseph A., Maj. Gen., 82

Nashville, Tenn., Battle of, 30
National Archives, 108
Nevins, Allan, 153
Nichols, George W., Maj., 96, 99, 106
Niter and Mining Bureau, 27, 40, 53n
Noble, Vett, 106
Northrop, L. B., Gen., 138

O'Connell, J. J., Rev., 99n, 108, 146n
Oliver, John M., Brig. Gen., 117
O'Neale, Richard, 92
open city, 143
Orchard, William H., 149
Ordinance of Secession, 23
Osborn, T. W., Maj., 92–93
Otey, John M., Col., 59, 60n

Palmetto Iron Works, 27
Perry, Benjamin F., 19
Philadelphia Times, 159
Phillips's Warehouse, 96
Poe, Orlando M., Bvt. Brig. Gen., 108n, 136n
Porter, A. Toomer, Rev., 104–105n, 108, 109, 114, 150
Portlock, E. E., Col., 54
Pratt, William B., Capt., 75
Preston, John S., Brig. Gen., 82, 120
prisoners of war, 56–57
provost guard: first, 77, 83–84; second, 93–95; clears rioters, 117
psychological warfare. *See* total war, concept of

railroads, destruction of, 122, 124
Ravenel, Catherine P., 112–113, 149n
Ravenel, E. V., 112
Ravenel, Harriott Horry, 90n, 111
Ravenel, St. Julien, Dr., 40
Ravenel, St. Julien, Mrs., 114
Reese, C. B., Capt., 73
Reynolds, J. L., 100
Reynolds, William, Dr., 104–105, 130
Rhett, Roland, Maj., 59, 60n
Rice Creek Springs, S. C., 151n
Richland Rifles, 24
Richmond, Va., 36
Richmond Whig, 54
rifle factory, 28
Rivers, W. J., 100, 130
rockets, 148–149, 150–152

"Sack and Destruction of the City of Columbia, S.C.," 125, 130
Saint Albans, Vt., 140n
St. Mary's College, 99n
Saluda Factory, 29, 73, 73n, 74
Saluda River, 19, 72, 73
Saluda River bridge, 73
Savannah, Ga., 30, 34, 137
Scott, E. J., 70n, 114
secession, 23
Seddon, James A., 35, 35n
Seibels, John T., 98, 112
Senate Committee on Claims, 134

Seward, William H., 45n
Shand, Peter J., Rev., 89n, 107, 108, 150, 153
Sharp, Thomas R., Capt., 57–58, 60n
Shelton, Malcolm A., 109
Sherman, William T., Maj. Gen., 22, 30, 106, 120, 152, 161n; and bombardment of Columbia, 141–144; and bombardment of Union troops, 47, 49–50, 144; charges against, 135–162; and Columbia fire, 96–97; on effect of the wind, 99–100, 101; and failure to suppress riot, 118, 165; and invasion of South Carolina, 30–31, 33, 47, 49, 137–141; and Mayor Goodwyn, 80, 81, 87–88; and protection of convent, 78, 120; and protection of private property, 80, 81, 87–88, 147–148; rhetoric of, 84, 135n, 135–141, 145, 153–154; and right wing of army, 31, 31n, 72–73; surrender to and occupation by, 49, 75, 78, 79–81; and visit with old friend, 86–87; on XV Corps, 144–147
"Sherman's March to the Sea" (poem), 86
Shields Foundry, 28, 126n
shoe factory, 28
Sidney Park, 120, 127–128
Sill, Edward, 98–99, 108, 150
Simms, William Gilmore, 90, 108, 130, 145, 161, 161n; on bombardment, 141–142; on conduct of retreating Confederates, 54n; on effect of the wind, 99, 101; on extent of devastation, 125, 126, 130n, 159; on sacking and burning, 125, 154, 155, 157n, 158
Simons, Harriet, 98
Sloan, John T., Col., 62, 63, 130
Slocum, Henry W., Maj. Gen., 31, 72
Smith, Giles A., Bvt. Maj. Gen., 82
Smith, G. W., Maj. Gen., 42
Smith, J. J. Pringle, Mrs., 99
Smith, John E., Bvt. Maj. Gen., 82, 89
Smith, Mason, 114
sock factory, 28
Sosnowski, Sophie, 113–114

South Carolina College, 19, 23, 120n; and Confederate government, 24, 27; threat of fire to, 100–101

South Carolina, Confederate defense of, 31, 36, 41–47, 82

South Carolina General Assembly, 23, 26, 33

South Carolina Insane Asylum, 56, 119, 156

South Carolina Railroad, 22, 68, 80; during evacuation, 52, 58; explosion at, 69, 91

Special Field Order No. 26, 49, 78

Squire, Emeline, 109

Stanley, William B., 91, 109, 131n, 160

State Arsenal, 24, 123, 126n

State House, 20, 26, 29, 126–127, 150

Stenhouse and Macaulay, 62

Stephens, Alexander H., 45n

Stevenson, Carter L., Maj. Gen., 70, 74

Stewart, A. P., Maj. Gen., 42

Stone, George A., Col., 94n, 151; in capture of Columbia, 73–77, 147, 164

Stratton, Mrs., 114

Stuart, J. E. B., Maj. Gen., 38, 140n

Swindell, Anna T., 142

sword factory, 28, 28n

Talley, A. N., Dr., 130

tarpaulin and oilcloth factory, 28

Thompson, John, Mrs., 149

total war, concept of, 134n, 139–140, 140n, 143n, 163–167

Tourtelotte, John E., Col., 92

town hall–market, 20–21, 76, 79

Treasury Department, Confederate, 60

Treasury Note Bureau, Confederate, 29

Treaty of Washington, 132

Trenholm, George A., 92

Trezevant, Daniel H., Dr., 33, 130, 152–153, 157; affidavits of, 109, 131, 131n, 149, 162

Trezevant, John T., Maj., 59–60

Tri-Weekly South Carolinian, 22, 35

Tweeddale, William, Col., 74

Twelfth Wisconsin Battery, 143

uniform factory, 28

Union army, 30, 47, 72; departure of, 125; encampment of, 81–82; organization of, 31; XV Corp of, 144–147, 146n

Ursuline Convent, 78, 99, 120, 134

Vandiver, Frank, 135

Wallace, John, Dr., 92

war matériel, destruction of, 122–124, 169–171

war mobilization camp, 24

Washington Street Methodist Church, 134

Wateree River bridge, 124

waterworks, 21

Wayside Homes, 24–25

Wayside Hospital, 24, 25n

Wells, J. H., 70

Wheeler, Joseph, Maj. Gen., 38, 41n; and his cavalry, 42, 47, 54, 54n, 70, 77

Whilden, Mary S., 79

Williams, Alpheus S., Brig. Gen., 31

Williams, T. Harry, 139, 146

Wilson, Robert, Rev., 90

wind, effect of, 79, 98–102, 117–118, 166

Winder, John H., Brig. Gen., 56

Wing, Francis W., 109, 109n, 162

Winnsboro, S.C., 72, 84

Wood, A. E., Capt., 77, 93

Woodhull, Maxwell, Maj., 94

Woodlands (plantation), 130

Woods, Charles R., Maj. Gen., 47, 81, 85, 124, 125, 144; on effect of the wind, 99, 101; and entrance into Columbia, 74, 76, 78, 81; and the fire, 95, 97; and orders to suppress the riot, 94n, 94–95

Woods, William B., Bvt. Brig. Gen., 94–95, 121

Yates, William, 150

Yorke, L. E., Lt. Col., 27n

Yorkville Enquirer, 110–111

Young, P. M. B., Maj. Gen., 41n

Zion Church, 72